The True Dynamics of Relationships

The True Dynamics of Relationships

Mike Robinson

SOL Promotions 2004

The True Dynamics of Relationships

Edited and typeset by Synthesis of Life Promotions
Cover by SR Print, North Walsham

Printed by:
Leiston Press, Unit 1 Masterlord Industrial Estate, Leiston, Suffolk IP16 4XS

1st Edition 2002
Revised Edition 2004

Copyright: SOL Promotions, 2002

All rights reserved. No part of this publication may be reproduced, stored on a retrieval system, or transmitted, in any form or by any means, without the prior consent of Mike Robinson.

ISBN 0-9544478-2-4

Dedication

*How beautiful upon the mountain
are the feet of the messenger,
who announces peace,
who brings good news,
who announces salvation,
who says to Zion,
'Your Divine being reigns.'*

Isa.52:7 (The voice of the inner Master)

I dedicate this book to those who seek wholeness and to know themselves.
With thanks to the light and love that has truly touched my heart and Soul in this life.

May you know Love,
Surrender to Love,
And serve Love.

Contents

Acknowledgements	1
Introduction	3
My Journey	7

PART 1 The Levels of Your Being
Chapter 1 The Earth is a Planet of Emotions	15
Chapter 2 Love is the only True Emotion	57

PART 2 Looking into the Mirror
Chapter 3 The Conditioning Years	73
Chapter 4 The Rebellion Years	115
Chapter 5 Relationships	157

PART 3 The Journey Home
Chapter 6 The Wisdom Years	259
Chapter 7 Your Personal Relationship to God	289

References	351
About the Author	357

Acknowledgements

Every person who I have met since being upon the earth has taught me something about myself. Each person is a unique Soul who carries a special gift to enhance the beauty of life.

Thank you….
Jo Le-Rose, whose light, love, understanding and patience has made this book possible.
My family, Mandy, Cheyanne, Gabrielle, Joanne and Ian, for giving me the beautiful gifts of fatherhood & love.
My brother Stephen, who has enriched my life.
Elisabeth, who has given her time, patience and expertise.
Jenny, whose input has made a valuable difference!
Marillyn, John, Gwen, Pam, Sara, Angela, Heather, Marion, Julie & Vanessa, Sue, Hassan in Egypt, Aya and Connie in Israel, Lisbeth in Denmark and to all those in Australia, for organising my talks, workshops, seminars and courses.

Kim, for your love and support.
Louiza & Tara…for your endless patience…
Lucy & Vince at S.R. Print…for your creativity…

Many thanks to those who have attended the courses throughout the world, who have given their dedication and commitment to God.
To those who have allowed me to observe their aura whilst seeking my counsel.
To those who have shared their truth with me and stood by me through the difficult times.
To J.S Bach and authors of inspirational books, for teaching us about the love of God.

Finally, but the most important of all, thank you to Our Lord and Our Lady, the light of this world. Your love and guidance has brought me back to life.

Introduction

After many years of offering counsel and advice to people, I have finally completed a book that reveals the depths of the Soul. The information contained in the book is not designed to feed the intellect, but is a living teaching to be incorporated into daily life. It is a tool for looking within to find the answers to our life issues. The inner journey has a magnitude that makes our solar system pale before it. The key to self-knowledge and self-healing lies in this inner journey, which leads you to being the master of your own world, where truth and love become one.

We are told to live in the now, yet the practice of now exposes issues that need to be understood. Hopefully this book will help you understand that you hold your world within you. Observation without judgment brings you into the moment. It allows your past to come into the present so that it can be worked on. Your mind created all that you are now by building your life upon the fears of the past. If you can understand this, it is possible to go back and draw your past into the present where it can be observed and healed. For example, maybe as a child, because you were too small and weak to defend yourself, an elder overpowered you and abused you. Now, as an adult you are strong enough mentally and emotionally to be able to call back the experience, observe it and deal with it.

Everyone is either consciously or subconsciously yearning to know themselves and God. We are here to love and to be loved. The blocks that inhibit the expression and reception of love bring about the suffering of humanity. These blocks consist of stored negative emotions and judgments held by the mind. You have a right to be yourself, you have a right to be free, and freedom is truth. It is time to evict the squatters of illusion.

This book is designed to be a workbook, therefore you may need to take time to assimilate the information. It is a book that can also be read over and over, each time revealing another depth to your being as you grow in understanding. Its purpose is to look first at the different levels of our being so that we may understand, not only are we physical, but we also have a Soul which resides on the spiritual plane, a mental body which resides on the mental plane, and an emotional body which resides on the astral plane. Each plane is a different vibrating world of its own. The Soul is our inner voice, the mental plane is our thoughts, and the astral plane is our emotions. The one thing that pollutes these worlds is fear, because from fear all other negative emotions arise. This book therefore looks at all the different aspects of negative emotions. The point of life is to bring the planes into balance with each other by mastering them, which in turn masters fear. The individual then becomes God-conscious whilst living on the earth.

The second aspect of the book is to look at our childhood, for it is our upbringing that conditions our way of thinking and feeling. The traps we have created for ourselves by thinking that the external world is our only reality have led us into illusion. We are taught not to think or accept anything beyond what we can see, and we have lost our conscious contact with the invisible worlds. From here we move into the adult years, which reveal our way of relating to the world and how we have allowed fear to govern our lives. We also discover that everyone we meet is a mirror to our subconscious self.

The last part of the book shows us what we need to do in each moment to become aware of our hidden agendas. It also describes our relationship with God and what prevents us from being God-conscious. The exercises help us to master our inner worlds.

The journey to wholeness takes dedication and courage. It is not something that can be picked up and put down. It is a moment-to-moment process of awareness. The fact is, that only you can make the effort and become yourself. Nobody else can reach wholeness for you. What is wholeness? It is a space of love, joy and peace. Is there a better place to be?

My Journey

There are those who know and those who do not know. Those who know, no longer search.

If I ever had to write a book on my life story, I would probably call it 'The luckiest man alive'. The love and rewards this life has given me have made me feel truly blessed. The opportunities that have graced my life and flavoured it with a true beauty have brought me a joy that I could not have imagined.

Some may call me an optimist, but I would rather be an optimist than a pessimist. This world of ours is going through dramatic changes. Never before has change been forced upon us at such a fast rate and what is happening externally is reflected within. The Soul is parched and it is crying out for sustenance. Why am I here? Where am I going? Who am I? To find out, we have to begin an inner journey.

I have had various clairvoyant gifts since I was very young. I have been able to see things beyond what is known as 'normal sight'. I could see mists, colours and lines of energy around people. I also knew a person's inner nature upon meeting them. I learnt to expand these gifts by silently observing what was happening around me. I would often watch people I knew energetically change their appearance as if they were living in times past. For example, when I was young one friend would appear as a confederate soldier during the American Civil War. I later realised that we have lived lives before our present one and I must have been observing my friend as he was in a past life.

In the last thirty years of my life I have used aspects of my gifts to offer advice and counsel to all those that I have met. Looking back over my life I can see the stages I went through to know myself. There was the first stage, which was the struggle. I was placed in a children's home at three months old and right up into my twenties I struggled with trying to live within society and all its rules. The carers in the home were not allowed to hug the children, so I received very little loving human contact. By the time I was a teenager, I had been given no foundation or preparation for the world. There were many things I did not understand. One of the most prominent was the employment system. It came as a shock to realise I did not have parents who went out to work, but carers who came to the home, because we were their work. This awakening made me aware that I had been a job to someone for most of my young life, and it left me with very little confidence in myself. I therefore left the home with very few options. I fell into low-paid labouring jobs, into production and shop work. There came a turn around when I was employed as a manager of a run-down housing estate. Here I learnt to deal with people, understand their suffering, and try to clean the area to provide a better standard of living for some of society's forgotten Souls. I also trained in Tai Chi, Chi Gong and Kung Fu and became a teacher of these practices.

The second stage came when I realised I could let go of society and the need to prove myself as someone worthy. I began to search for the meaning of my life; I searched for God. I moved from London to Norwich. At the time I had no money or prospects, but I still had my God-given clairvoyant ability that had been with me since I was a child. I started to travel throughout the country doing readings and lectures. I also spent a lot of time in nature and by the sea healing myself. In time, I was beginning to understand and know the different facets of my being.

The third stage came when I stopped searching. At this point I had finally accepted myself. I knew myself. I was no longer unworthy, trying to prove to the world that, even though my parents rejected me, I was still lovable. I was no longer superior to other people because I had mysterious abilities which made me different. I knew myself to be none of these, for I recognised this was my ego defending myself from possible pain. My unworthiness was the female side of myself, the lost and rejected parts which were too weak to stand up for me and say no to those who took advantage. The superior part of myself was my male side, which wanted to be powerful, be above being loved and therefore avoid being hurt and disappointed. My truth came when I faced these false parts of myself and they became one. The female within me rose, became strong, supportive and began to communicate my needs to me. My male side relaxed, let in love and dynamically acted in the outside world on the promptings of my inner female. I became whole.

We are all searching for God, whether we are consciously aware of it or not. You may disagree with this statement, but that reaction shows you are trying to stop love from coming into your life. God is love, he is male and female combined, there is nothing he is not, as nothing can exist without His presence. To take the time to look at yourself is one of the greatest gifts you can give to your Soul. So ask yourself, are you still struggling to prove yourself and be accepted within society? Do you still want to get to the top of the social/business ladder? Why? Will it bring you peace, truth, inner knowing and happiness? Have you started a search to find the hidden meaning of your life? Do you know who you are? Do you know your creator? Do you know what will happen to you when your body dies? Do you know the deeper purpose of your relationships? Do you know your inner male and female? Do you know how to heal your pains, memories and emotions? This book is about looking at the different facets of yourself. It will look at your struggles, help you on your search and it will show you the real you, so that you may know yourself.

The saying 'Know thyself and then you will know the Universe and the Gods' gives us a direction. The more you get to know the inner you, the more of the universe is revealed and you begin to recognise that you are a reflection of the universe. Your inner sight opens as you see aspects of yourself reflected in other human beings. Through this realisation you become aware of the hidden dynamics of your Soul and you begin to understand those around you. The more you accept others as they are without any conflict, the more you accept yourself and the universe. More of God is then revealed to you.

We have tried to intellectualise and understand who God is, what God is and the workings of the universe. Until we look within and recognise that the universe is within us, then God will always seem far off, or up in the sky somewhere and the universe will always be a puzzle to solve. When we finally know we are God and we created the universe, then all the answers of life will be found within as we come to realise our oneness and connectedness to all life. It is the forces we create with the mind, which give us the illusion of separation, and we need to go inside ourselves and throw out all those forces that are not the true self. It is a process of evicting the squatters from within us. Each time we do not express our thoughts and emotions truthfully in each and every moment we store this unexpressed energy in our being, which creates blockages. These blockages begin to take form and they become autonomous. These are the squatters and in order to evict them we have to release the energy of old patterns, beliefs, emotions, memories etc, that are held within the cells. It is these energies that keep the squatters fed.

Once we face and release our issues, the squatters will move out of our energy bodies and we will feel lighter, more liberated and more loving towards ourselves. We then begin to see the world as it really is, through a clear non-judgmental way of being. This is true knowing of the self.

During the readings, talks and courses I have given, people would often ask me if I had written a book. I always answered 'no,' as I never wanted to write a book which would intellectually fill people's minds with more spiritual knowledge. I have always felt it is important for a person to find the answers to their life questions from within themselves, because by going within, they are not relying on any external source. I came to realise that it was possible to write a book that spoke directly to the Soul, which would help people to find their own answers within. In this book the topics of auras, energy bodies, karma, love, reincarnation etc, will be mentioned, but what I write about is not a belief system, it is my own knowing. All Souls come here to love and to be loved. This need within us to express and receive love is the cause of all our frustrations with our self and others. What we are saying is 'love me for who I am,' but we are not being the real us, just as we are not loving others for who they are. Judgment has entered in, and we have to go back to a state of non-judgment, because to observe without judgment is the only way forward.

As this book nears completion, a new chapter in my life is about to begin. There is only love or fear and it is the voice of love that beckons me on.

Part one

The Levels of Your Being

1

The Earth is the Planet of Emotion

Honesty is love and it comes from the heart.
It is very pure, yet very strong.
What we need to heal our world,
Is honesty.
That's why the words 'be true to yourself'
Are so important,
Because if you are true to yourself
You will automatically be true to
All others that you meet.

The Creation of the Soul

If a drop of water is taken from the ocean, it still has within it the ocean. This is how the Soul came into being. It started its journey as a particle of light within the Godhead. When the particle started to move out from the Godhead it became a ray of Divine Essence, which is known as the Soul. By travelling outwards it entered into different vibrations, these vibrations cloaked the Soul and became what is known as the aura. It is the aura that enables the Soul to consciously experience, understand and learn of its God-Self.

By the time the Divine Essence had neared the earth's atmosphere, it had lowered its vibration into the mental planes and shaped a mind. It then moved down into the astral planes and shaped an emotional body. Finally, it travelled down into the etheric plane, took energy from the earth and created a physical body. It was now ready to enter into the school of the earth to consciously realise its true self and travel back up through the planes whilst in a physical body. Therefore the Soul's purpose is to manifest its God-Self whilst cloaked in dense matter on the earth. Here our journey begins as we heal the illusion of being far away from home.

The personality is created through the mental, astral and etheric planes coming together. Therefore what we think, feel and do determines what we daily create as our reality. This is why what we did yesterday shaped our today and what we do today will shape our tomorrow. The Soul is the mediator between the personality and God. Its purpose is to purify the personality so that God can fully enter in on every level and experience Himself through human physical existence.

Why Me? Why Here? Why Now?

Every morning we wake up from our sleep and begin another day. We usually follow a routine that surrounds itself with thinking and doing. It is very rare that we stop to contemplate the purpose of our life and the deeper meaning of our being. When a child is born we may stop and question the magical wonder of life. When we lose a loved one the pain we feel may cause us to begin the search for the haven of an after-life. We all go through this cycle of birth and death. If you look at the earth, you will recognise that everything which lives within and upon her goes through this same cycle. We also see that everything changes and evolves through time. The earth is therefore a planet of growth and constant change, but there are also two elements that either help or hinder us through our growth and changes. These are the emotions and the mind.

Emotion is energy. It is not something we can see with the physical eyes, but we know it exists because we feel it. This energy has a natural flow as it either expands outwards or contracts inwards. We can observe this motion in action by observing the course of our breathing: we inhale and then exhale. Through this understanding we know that all energy has an opposite force which works to balance itself. Life on the earth teaches us about the aspects of these opposite forces, which are often known as duality. The light and the shadow, the truth and the illusion, the good and the bad are examples of these forces. Through observing the workings of duality we can see that emotional energy will also have both positive and negative poles. In order for us to receive and express this emotional energy, we have to let it flow through the aura. It is the aura that contains the interpenetrating spiritual, mental, astral and etheric energy bodies that we collected on our way to earth. The level that is responsible for feeling, understanding and processing the earth's emotional energy is called the astral or emotional body.

The earth is so unique that nowhere else in the universe does a planet like ours exist. As Souls we have been allowed to occupy a physical body within the race of humanity, and we have been given the earth as a place to exercise our free will in order to feel and understand the consequences of this free will. It is the emotional body within us that allows this learning to take place, until eventually, through experience, we align our free will with the greater Universal Will. By doing this we master our emotional body. We then begin to feel and understand in a clearer and more harmonious way. Humanity is presently at the stage where it is still experiencing the range of positive and negative emotions. In a sense we are stuck, because we have got caught up in the drama that these emotions bring through our experiences. We have forgotten that the purpose is to master the emotions and not be subservient to them.

In the East certain teachings describe a system that helps us become aware of our emotions and reactions to situations. The system uses tools that resemble wheels and are known as the chakras. There are seven major governing chakras along the spinal column and chakras over the spleen and liver plus minor chakras throughout the body. Each one corresponds to and governs certain emotions. The chakras also store information that is related to experiences and beliefs from this and past lives, a process known as karma. Our energy system is therefore a reflection of every thought we have thought, every word we have spoken, and every action we have performed since the beginning of our first incarnation on the earth. Our chakra system can be likened to a diary, as it keeps a note of everything that has occurred, from a single thought to actions implemented out of love or fear. There is no hiding place because this information is stored within us until we face and clear it. We can do this by letting go of the fears that cause us to feel negative emotions. Once we have cleared our past karma we are then responsible for constant observation of our thoughts, words and actions, so as to maintain a clear and harmonic balance of karma for this life and for future lives if we need to come back here.

As humans we are expressive and receptive beings. Our true purpose is to give out and receive love, but when our system becomes polluted by negative emotions, this no longer occurs. We need to understand the fear that has caused us to stop expressing love. It is the Soul who sees, hears and breathes life into the physical body. If the words are not pure when we speak and our limbs cause chaos in their actions, then something other than the Soul is working through us.

Fear

The energy of fear is unique to this planet and its atmosphere. On its own it is neither positive nor negative. It has come into being because humanity brought the mental plane to the earth. Over the eons of time we have deviated from our lofty thoughts of God, which reached high into the cosmos, into low vibrating earthly thoughts. We did this by forgetting our true heritage as we began to focus our energy on using and changing the earthly elements around us. We became centred on external power and survival and we lost the ability to master our minds. This created lower vibrating thought energy that could only stay in the earth's atmosphere. This then began feeding on and polluting the living energy around us, creating the force called fear.

The artificial emotion of fear has now become a living entity. When the Soul comes onto the earth and encounters this fear through its energy bodies, there is a slowing down of its responsiveness. This hinders the soul in its progression, growth and learning. Fear pollutes all other emotions and the majority of humanity is addicted to its essence. It has become autonomous, it has its own intelligence and it is able to get into the body through the aura, into the sacral chakra below the navel and into the kidneys. It then weakens the whole body and affects our will by opening us up to the influence of others and the energy around us. If we follow the advice of those around us who have fear in their systems, who or what is governing our life?

We forget that the earth is a free will zone. As Souls we have the right to evict fear from our systems and we can do this by becoming detached. This comes from looking at our habits and addictions within our everyday life and breaking them so that we no longer feed the entity and egregores of fear. An egregore is a collection of similar thought energy that becomes an autonomous being. I have often seen them hovering above cities or groups of people who hold the same beliefs.

If our situations in life do not bring us joy and freedom, then they have their roots in fear. Fear is a pulling energy, so it actually draws towards us the experiences that we fear facing. The saying, 'feel the fear and do it anyway,' literally means allow the fear energy to move through your system, feel it and take action. To fully experience fear is to be free of it. When you let go of it, the entity cannot hold you anymore.

We do not consciously recognise that we live in fear. Only when it becomes apparent through a challenging experience are we able to see it. Fear is subtle in nature and it is this that leads us into illusion. Our everyday fears reveal themselves through our likes and dislikes of people and situations. If we are in judgment of other people, situations or ourselves, then there is a hidden fear.

When we fear the negativity of the earth, we fear acknowledging the shadow within ourselves. When we gossip about other people, we are making them appear small in fear of them being different and not like us. When we fear not being good enough, we no longer try or we say, 'I can't' or 'I shouldn't'. When we fear not being accepted by our work colleagues, our friends or our family, we adapt to what fits. We are constantly in fear of self-judgment and external judgment. All this comes back to our tribal beliefs, which reflect the society we were born into. To become free of fear we have to observe our day-to-day preferences and question whether they have their roots in a hidden fear. If we find our preferences hold no judgment, only observation, then we are seeing the truth, which is love.

The Warning System

When the Soul comes onto the earth, it needs emotions so that it can experience life in order to grow through the physical body. If the emotions are received, experienced and immediately let go of, then the earthly experience will be a positive one. However, if they become polluted by fear, then we also pollute our warning system, which is sometimes known as the 'fight or flight instinct'. People often mistake this for fear, but it is actually a natural system that has been polluted by fear so that we no longer know what is right or wrong, what is safe or what is dangerous. What we must learn to do is master the emotions and bring our warning system back into function. We shall then once again be able to clearly feel what is right or wrong for us.

I first became aware of this system within me on my first visit to Australia. While growing up in England, I had heard so many stories about the Australian spiders and snakes, I had been told they were to be found under plant pots, in your shoes, under toilet seats. This created a block within me, as I strongly believed they were something to be feared. Whilst visiting Queensland I became agitated and concerned because my warning system could not help me. It had been polluted by the fear that was now instilled in me from the stories. I asked local Australians about the snakes and spiders, but they shrugged them off and told me not to worry. Nobody was helping me to understand so that I could overcome my fear. Eventually, I was lucky to meet someone who was able to show me a red backed-spider. He taught me about their hiding habits and roughly how many there were in the region. He was also able to teach me about snakes as he had grown up with them. He could sense a snake by the taste of it in his mouth! He gave me the trigger I needed to let go of the belief system I was holding onto and allow my own warning system to speak to me. On my next visit to Australia, as I was walking down the road, I was able to pick up and sense nearby snakes. In the process of trusting my senses, I knew that my system would alert me to any immediate danger. The more I relied upon my inner system, the more of what was around me became revealed. My warning system was my natural state of being, its message was to be aware, which is the key to freeing yourself from the negative aspects of emotions.

Fear and the Emotions

Emotion is a free-flowing energy that we receive and allow into our energy bodies. We then feel it and let it go. However, if our thoughts are focused on low earthly pursuits, then we open the door for the fear energy to enter in. This pollutes the aura, chakras and physical body, eventually ending in illness. The emotional energy can now no longer pass through and it becomes stuck. It then builds up and changes from free-flowing to stagnant and this is what is known as negative emotion. Imagine fear as a tree whose main root is the fear of not being loved and all the other roots have grown from this one fear. Let us look in more detail at these roots of negative emotions.

Anger

In the physical body each organ holds different emotions, and it is the liver that holds our assertive energy. This energy allows us to speak our truth with love in each and every moment. If at any time we hold back from asserting our truth, this energy becomes polluted and may later show itself as anger. This polluted energy can cause an imbalance in the liver, which may create issues of depression and blood disorders. People often feel better after expressing their truth in an argument, as they have cleared the air and emptied their liver of toxic build-up. What can sometimes happen though, is that a person will express their truth to another, then apologise later, taking it all back in again so it re-manifests in the next argument. What we need to recognise is the difference between expressing our truth in the moment and the build-up from years of keeping our truth suppressed, thus storing it as anger.

Irritation and annoyance are the feelings we get when we are holding our anger in. Effectively we are putting the lid on a steaming pan, hoping to control the pressure. Outbursts of anger and violence then occur when we can no longer hold the lid on and the steam bursts forth, burning everything in its path. For example, you are in a shop and the assistant is rude to you; rather than speak out, you hold in your feelings. In the next shop the same thing occurs. On the way out someone accidentally bumps into you and suddenly you turn on them and release all your built-up feelings. If you had been assertive and expressed your emotions in the moment to the rude assistants, you would have reacted differently to the person who bumped into you. We often take our pent-up annoyance and irritations out on weaker people whom we feel will not reject us or cause us difficulty, hence our closest loved ones are usually the outlets for our pent-up anger.

Anger has its roots in fear. We fear not being loved and accepted, therefore we hold back our feelings so that we will not be rejected and hurt, but this is at a price. At work, how many times has the boss irritated or annoyed you? Yet you let it go, smile and cope with it through fear of losing your job, but before long you find yourself having angry outbursts at the smallest of things. You need to ask yourself, 'If I cannot be firm and express myself assertively in the moment, then I am reacting through fear. What internally and externally needs to change?' Then make those changes so that all your emotions are justified. I know this is easier said than done! So how do we reach this point of inner tranquillity? We have to recognise that our external experiences bring us what we need in order for our hidden parts to be revealed. If you feel worthless when you are with your boss, then closely watch your reactions to him/her? What are your thoughts when you are around him/her. Can you bring your awareness to your breath and breathe through your emotions? Can you see why you have placed yourself in this situation? Is it possible to do things at work that prove your worth to yourself?

If you have years of built-up emotions then another good way of diffusing anger is to write two letters, one which has all the negative thoughts and feelings expressed and the other which is the positive side of the situation. When you can write no more, burn both of the letters and imagine your anger is burning with it. From that moment on, start being assertive with the small things. As you gain confidence then you will find outside scenarios affect you less and less. In the last section of this book there are also other exercises that can help you get to the root of your emotions and master your inner responses to outside situations.

Justified anger is when you recognise, either through your own actions or those of someone else, that you stand strong within your inner truth and you will not betray this truth no matter what. It is at this point that you will neither hold in your true feelings nor will you have an out-of-control outburst, but you will be firm in your dealings with yourself and others. This is the balanced middle way, as the anger is not being expressed through irritation or annoyance, nor is out of control. It is a point of assertiveness, honesty and self-love.

Desire

Desire is one of the most dominant emotions within humanity. As Souls, we desire to come into incarnation and experience life within a physical body. We can have whatever it is we desire. We can be kings and queens, have wealth and power. In fact we can have anything at all. The problem is that we are not aware of the full power of our thoughts and we do not appreciate that we can create our own lives as we desire them to be. If we set forth our thoughts and desires, then we will eventually achieve them. Some people achieve their desires straight away, for others it takes longer. The point is that our thoughts always materialise, and if they do not manifest in this lifetime then they will in the next, or the next, or the next...

At times we all desire wealth and power. However, it is important to understand that many people in power do not have complete happiness. This is the allusion of the saying, 'The grass is always greener on the other side.' If we desire peace and joy then we have set in motion an everlasting force which is more obtainable, as power and wealth are materialistic and short-lived. True happiness can manifest itself in all situations even in that of extreme poverty. It is easier for someone who has not known wealth to be happy and at peace in a simple situation living his or her life with joy and pleasure. Those with wealth often find they have to work continually, toiling for many hours in order to maintain their standard of living. For example, you may have a big house, expensive car and like exotic holidays. In order to afford these things, you work long hours and get home late. You hardly see your family and have no time to eat your food properly. You are under constant stress and have no time to relax and enjoy yourself. Desire is the cause of all that suffering.

Often desire and fear together create situations in our lives from which it is difficult to extract ourselves. Our desire for wealth may put us into a job where we are abused. There may be strict rules which control us, but we do not have the courage to walk away. Perhaps we feel we would not survive if we walked away as we need the financial security. We have to realise that we have placed ourselves in a trap, and to free ourselves from negative desires, we need to create positive desires. These include being of service, helping others, creating a homely environment that is not based on fear but true creativity, where desire is being expressed for the love of our work and not for the sake of the wage packet. True desire is fulfilling the Soul's requirements, which are to love and to be loved. When we are fulfilling this, the desire for material gains fades away. It is also true that when we are in alignment with our Soul's desires, all our material gains appear when they are needed and we no longer have to struggle for them.

Buddha said, 'Desire is the cause of all suffering,' so when a desire arises, try to think of the purity of your thoughts, words and deeds. Think about the purity of the self, as it is only through purity that you can achieve true joy, truth and happiness. Trying to obtain your desires often means you will go against the grain of the self and then you struggle. You need to ask yourself, 'Is this what I really want? If I achieve my desire will it bring me joy and happiness? Is the journey to receiving this desire pleasant?' Remember that you can have anything you wish for upon the earth. So what is it that you really wish for?

Jealousy

Jealousy is often known as 'the green-eyed monster'. We sometimes say that people are green with envy, and jealousy actually appears in a person's aura as the colour green. The positive aspect of this emotion is pure inspiration, and inspiration is what moves us forward in life, to become like God. The same inspirational energy, when polluted by aspiring to be like someone else or yearning for what someone else has, becomes its negative counterpart which is jealousy. We have all felt this emotion in our lives at some point. It is especially noticeable in children who desire something that another child has. It is a yearning and it is in all of us. In most people it can be worked out whilst they are still children, but sometimes children have their jealousy suppressed by their parents and teachers. What tends to happen in these cases is that the jealousy sits in the aura and chakras. Because it still needs to be experienced, it will manifest itself in later life. It is therefore very important not to suppress any emotions, but allow them to come to the surface so that they can be experienced and cleared. As a parent it is beneficial to observe this as a natural process within our children and not to stifle its expression.

It is important that we recognise and accept jealousy as part of a driving force within human desire. Once this is accepted, then it is important to understand why we have these tendencies. Whatever anybody has in this life, it is their karma to have it, so why desire something that is another person's karma? Why not work towards your own karma and free yourself of these negative desires?

Jealousy and desire often go hand in hand. In the astral body they also sit closely together, both residing in and around the heart and lung areas. They are so closely linked that they could almost be the same emotion.

Jealousy occurs because we are focused on the external self rather than the internal self. We need to accept that the people we are jealous of are revealing our desires. It may be that they have more material gains than us and this brings up our issues around self-worth, financial abundance or love. By acknowledging our deeper feelings and focusing upon our internal needs, we can step out of our jealous tendencies and into our inspiration. This sets in motion a powerful force, which will show us an inner way to express and physically bring forth our own unique abilities.

If you desire to be anything, desire to be like God, desire to love God, desire to love others. Having this desire actually controls the whole energy known as jealousy and envy.

Possessiveness

When we want to possess something it means we want to control it. What is it we really want to possess? It is love. Love cannot be possessed, yet we demand it from others consciously and unconsciously through our desire to love and to be loved. Even when we think we have grasped love, we realise that in the moment of possessing it we have lost it. We then try to control the object of our desires in order to possess more love.

There are three types of possessiveness. The first is the person who collects and stores material things that they will never use. These people fear a shortage of love. By holding onto possessions they are trying to draw love into their life, but because objects soak up events from the atmosphere, what they are actually collecting is stored stagnant energy. Unconsciously they fear that if they let go of the possessions there will be a shortage of love in their life. They may even hide their treasures in spare rooms, in the bank, in the cellar, in the cupboards, in storage warehouses, etc. They have a 'what if' view and are prepared for their worst fears being realised. If only they could see that by living this way they are actually living the fear.

Another form of possessiveness is emotional. Instead of collecting and taking the energy out of material things, they collect and take other people's emotional energy. They demand the attention of others. The possessor may want to know every move another person makes or insists that they have no other friends than them. These kinds of people are very good at manipulating. It is as though they only give of their energy when they want to control the outcome of a situation. They often try to hem in those they love, making them feel trapped. The hugs and the closeness become suffocating for the receiver who often breaks away from the relationship in order to maintain breathing-space. These possessive people fear not being the first priority on other people's lists. We can see this as an example in children who have a fear of their mother loving them less than others, so they cling to her and try to make life emotionally difficult.

Mental possessiveness is where people try to possess the knowledge of something. They dislike sharing their knowing with others so they give out small pieces, talk in riddles or waffle. They try to retain their knowing, as it is a way of seeming special and therefore they are deemed worthy. Their fear is that if they shared everything then they would be left with nothing. They would no longer be special. This is the fear of not being enough. Many intellectual people and so-called spiritual teachers fall into this trap. If the person could only realise that when they let go and give, there is a natural spiritual process of being filled up with the new. We need to give constantly in order to make space to receive. Otherwise we stagnate and only regurgitate the old.

We have to be open to receive, just as we have to be open to give. Love cannot flow freely through us until the blockages have been cleared. Fear is what stops the reception of love, for if we fear not being loved, then we will not draw love towards us, we will only draw what we fear. Possessive people do not trust that love is given freely. They try and trap the love that comes their way and then hold onto it. The solution is to let go of control and trust that what we give will come back to us. When we give we become worthy of abundance and our generous giving will always be repaid through the abundance that will be ours. Every form of possession is a conscious or unconscious call for love.

Pride

Pride is often known as the 'stuck ego'. Ego means self-expression. When it becomes stuck, you no longer express the 'self', but present an illusion to the world. This illusion is like a shield that you use to defend yourself.

If you were to sit in heaven and look upon the earth, you would instantly recognise that it is a place of 'conditioned love' so the God part within you, your 'unconditional love', goes unrecognised. By entering into the earth's plane, you immediately enter into a zone of rejection. It is a rejection of the parts that do not fit within the society you have been born into. This rejection of 'self' allows the force of pride to enter in. It allows you to defend yourself against hurt and rejection by masking over the true loving you and moulding it into what fits with others. Pride then does one of two things. You either become submissive, expecting not to be loved and therefore open to abuse, or you become superior. You retreat so far into yourself that love cannot get near you and so it protects you from being rejected.

If we go back to our childhood, we can see that the first time we were rejected or not shown unconditional love we allowed fear in. If we have since become defensive and hidden our true self behind a façade, then we have pride in our systems. With pride it is important to be conscious of the judgments we have made about our parents and our upbringing. These are the reasons why we have created our defensive wall. It is quite probable that you, the Soul, chose your upbringing as an experience, so that you could work on pride in this lifetime. Your parents may have helped you by creating situations, so that pride would surface from within and give you an opportunity to work on your karma. It is therefore important to remove all judgments and accusations, but accept that there may have been abusive tendencies and look deeper at the issues within yourself.

By recognising your reactions to people and situations, you can ask yourself probing questions: 'Do I defend myself?' 'Do I always know better?' 'Do I have a lot of weak people around me who rely on me for support?' 'Do I dominate people, situations or conversations?' 'Do I allow people to dominate me?' 'Do I constantly judge others on their clothes, skin, occupation, etc?' 'Do I have abusive relationships?' 'Do I reject others before they reject me?' 'Am I always being rejected?' 'Do I have low self-worth?' Once you recognise what you do, whether it is through feeling small and unworthy compared to others or through feeling superior to others, then acknowledge your fear of not being loved, feel it and let it go.

When the emotion of pride is free-flowing, a person recognises their achievements and knows they have given to the best of their ability. This is sometimes known as justified pride. Life then becomes an adventure of self-discovery. By focusing within to find our strengths and weaknesses, we no longer compare or worry about what everyone else is doing!

When the Soul achieves a goal, it praises itself for its own discovery. It uses the experience to gain insight about itself and its growth towards the conscious merging of its God-Self. It then feels its worth, lets go of the experience and moves to the next phase of development. The 'stuck ego,' however, takes the achievement and claims it for itself. It continually praises itself and lets everyone know how wonderful it is and how much better it is than those who did not make the standard. The 'stuck ego' forgets that it is the Soul who sets up the experience, gives the mind its nourishment and uses the available tools. It is the Soul who experiences justified pride, and it is the 'stuck ego' that experiences the achievement as either lack of self-worth or superiority.

Grief

Grief is a very devastating emotion. It usually comes up through the lungs and is expressed through the heart. If grief is suppressed, over time it can cause damage to the energy bodies. The intensity of this damaging energy often pulls a person down and prevents them from living an active life. Usually people who are seriously depressed have suppressed grief.

Grief can stem from loss, fear of change or rejection and often gets suppressed by pride. We hide behind a false façade trying to cope and we avoid asking for help. Many people believe it is wrong to grieve for the loss of a loved one. How many of us are guilty of thinking that someone we know should have got over a death or the break-up of a relationship by now? With grief we also feel sadness. We remember the times past and we feel they will not be repeated in the future. We compare issues now with issues then, we become judgmental, seeing all the things we could or should have done.

We often blame ourselves, yet it is important to remember the bad times as well as the good and to ask ourselves honestly if everything was really perfect in that relationship? In our grief are we covering up what our true feelings really were and making everything seem rosy and perfect?

When we judge ourselves from an emotional viewpoint we can often get caught up in constantly recycling the same issue. If we observe ourselves from a point of detachment, without any emotion or self-judgment, then the observation can release the learning and the lesson. This frees us of the guilt that often comes with judgment, so ask yourself if you can you look at your life with an open heart. There is no judgment, just acceptance, as you have not made a mistake. It is a learning experience on the journey to wholeness (holiness).

To heal grief we have to be honest with ourselves. We have to see everything as it is and allow our emotions to be expressed. This cleansing process can help prepare us for a new future without the wounds of the past. Grief is the Soul's way of preparing a new beginning. When the old is gone the new can enter in. If we can accept that grief is the Soul's way of releasing energy, then letting it go is the only way forward. The karma, which was held by you and the person or situation you grieve over, is finished. This energy that has involved both of you has to be cleared in order to free you for the next stage of your life. Listing both the positive and negative aspects of the situation can be a start towards that liberation.

If we can accept that some aspects of the relationship were less than perfect, then we can let go to achieve perfection in a new situation. This will call for acceptance and forgiveness for yourself and your partner because when you drop judgment in this way, you see the truth of the situation. This is the lesson that you needed to learn which will free you for your next stage of the journey.

In some countries, it is traditional to wear black whilst grieving and to mourn for long periods. Some people even mourn for the rest of their lives, especially after a death of a partner. I wonder if the sadness that you see upon their faces is because the loved one has gone or is it due to living by tradition and a belief system which says that they will never love again?

Sadness

Sadness is a similar emotion to grief, yet it has something that is uniquely different. Grief is more related to loss and rejection, whereas sadness is linked to lack of self-love and to the need to find comfort.

When we watch a sad movie, read a sad book or hear a sad love song, we immediately tune our emotions into the sadness of the situation. We find the common ground with the actors, the words and the melody. In a sense, we go into ourselves and give comfort to our past pains and memories. If used to its full advantage, sadness can be an amazing healing tool.

Most of the other emotions, anger, pride, jealousy, etc, have more of a projecting force, whereas sadness covers a person, almost like a ball of cotton wool. It becomes a false protection, in that it does not let anything in and it does not let anything out. We are then in another world. To give us comfort in this world, we do many things. We may eat comfort foods, drink excessive amounts of alcohol, become non-communicative and become lethargic. Through any of these means, we are substituting our need to feel the emotion and speak out with a false friend.

There are two types of sadness. One is where there is a need for personal space to feel the emotion and release it. The other is where the mind controls the sadness. When the mind has control, powerful past memories and future scenarios are acted out in the thoughts. Instead of feeling the deep emotion, the energy is thrown up into the mind. At this point the mind is avoiding the pain through fear of what it might bring up and we are no longer using sadness as a healing tool, but we are allowing it to feed the negative vibration of the planet.

To heal sadness you have to become aware of your moment-to-moment thoughts and emotions. The second your mind uses a past memory or creates a future scenario, then you have moved away from your sadness. The key is to bring your awareness back to the abdomen and your breathing and begin to feel the sadness rather than think it. Each time your mind begins to wander to the past or future then bring it back to the present moment.

This process of transmuting the emotion takes very little time and is very powerful. Another way of realising sadness is to look at your habits. Do you comfort eat? Do you become removed from life? Can't be bothered? Or reach for a drink? Before you reach for anything, stop and ask yourself why you feel the need to give comfort to yourself through a false friend. Then allow your awareness to enter into the craving. You will find that behind the craving lies an emotion. Allow yourself to feel that emotion.

With sadness we can also enter into a state of actually liking the feeling, especially if we live in an environment where there is very little love and comfort, because the protection of the cotton wool energy keeps us separate from the outside world. Here is where honesty and courage come in, because sadness is not a natural state for the Soul to be in for long periods of time, so you need to accept, feel and release the emotion then make changes to your life. Sadness is an, 'in the moment' emotion. If it lasts for longer than this, then you are in the mind and if you use false friends for comfort, then you are suppressing the sadness.

Loneliness

One day I was walking in the garden reflecting upon the problems that were present in my life at the time. Suddenly a small voice within me said, 'Do you feel lonely?' I looked around the garden and saw the life growing. Even in the air I could sense and see a pulsating life, all of nature was conversing with me telling me about the unseen worlds and our oneness with them. 'No,' I answered my inner voice, 'I do not feel lonely.' I then realised that the mind strives for other minds to converse with in order to receive confirmation of its existence, yet if the mind conversed with the heart, it would never experience the illusion of loneliness again.

Loneliness is a state of mind, it is an illusion and what we need to acknowledge within ourselves is the desire to be understood. For loneliness is the mind's belief that we are on our own and no other person can understand our needs. It is also a feeling of being somehow disconnected from something greater than our self. For instance, if you woke up tomorrow and God was sitting at your breakfast table and you could happily converse with Him, you might tell Him of your problems and He could answer you with solutions. Would this kind of communication make you happier because you could see and hear Him? Spiritually, this encounter would only please the mind, for the heart sees and hears God everywhere. Know that you can communicate with Him in every moment and the still inner voice of the heart will always answer you. If God then left your house later that morning, would you go back into your loneliness and illusions?

I have often heard people say they 'feel lonely in a crowd'. These are people who feel misunderstood in life. We hold back from speaking our truth in the moment, and more importantly we do not ask for help in getting our needs met. Some of us feel lonely due to a lack of human company. Here we can do several things: we can either stop living on the fringes of life and participate, or we can see our solitude as an opportunity to observe our thoughts and emotions and get out into nature, so that she may teach us the truth of our being.

To be alone is to be ***all one***. Therefore we could say that when we have feelings of loneliness, it is an inner message to remind ourselves to meet our needs by self-expression through honesty.

Observing our thoughts and emotions will reveal our expectations of others, which we require to fill this emptiness within us. The illusion is that we have grasped the outside world as the only reality and when it does not provide us with our needs, we feel empty and misunderstood. We cannot fill ourselves up with life from the outside world, as it is our inner being that gives us life and love. Observation of nature can reveal this to us.

Guilt

Guilt is an emotional reaction of the mind. It happens when we think we have affected someone in a negative way; we can negatively affect another person by our thoughts, by our words and by our physical actions. Often we feel guilty if we do not please them and provide them with their desires. We then judge ourselves and feel that we are not a good person because we have let them down. The criminal system is a form of judgment as to whether a person is guilty of committing a sin against society or not. Even if a person steals to feed his family it is a crime, yet we forget it is society who helped to categorise and place him in his situation. We only have to look at how easy it is to get into debt, but how difficult it is to get out again. We often try to acquire material comforts because of our desires or by our need to be accepted within society. We then feel guilty if we cannot provide our family with the latest fad or gadget. This guilt eats into our system as we begin to feel we are not good enough. We feel that somehow we have caused our family to suffer because of it.

After having an argument with our loved ones we may feel guilty for the things we said or did in the moment. We then punish ourselves and try to make up for it. We often do this by reverting back to being a child who sheepishly tries to please the other in order to receive forgiveness. We sometimes even relinquish our will and end up bending to the other person's will in order to release the guilt. Because we are not being true to ourselves, resentment builds up over time, which will be vented in the next argument and so the guilt goes on.

When we desire to please another, what are we really saying? It is as though we want to support them so that they do not feel any of the pain that comes through living in a tough society. We then feel guilty or experience pain if they complain or make more demands. Often people who have been abused feel guilty about what has happened to them, they find it difficult to express their feelings to others as they feel somehow they were responsible for the abuse that took place. You are not responsible for other people's actions; they are responsible for their own.

It is time to realise that the only true support comes from our own Soul, from our God-Self. If you are supporting another, then to truly love them is to let them experience and rely on their own Soul for support. You did not come to the earth to carry others on your back, but fairly share your journey as you walk alongside others. If you are being supported, whether emotionally, financially, mentally etc; then you need to stop relying on other humans and rely on yourself. You need to become Soul-reliant, you need to become God-reliant. This reliance will reveal that God has been quietly supporting you all of your life and if you let go, you will only fall into His arms.

Fear is guilt's crutch, because we fear speaking our truth, we fear letting those around us down, we fear not being accepted, we fear not being worthy and we fear not being loved. All these things keep us striving for some imaginary security that will end our suffering and take away the guilt. Well, there is no such place. To live a guiltless life is to be free to express, free to experience, free to follow your heart and free to hold the hand of another and walk this journey of life, not because you need them or they need you to survive, but because you joyfully want to.

Apathy

Apathy can be described as a state of inactivity. It is possible to describe sufferers of M.E. (chronic fatigue) and similar illnesses as extreme cases of apathy. With apathy we often feel that we do not have the energy to be active. In a sense our strength and fire for life has disappeared. It may be that we have created the belief system that the universe will provide us with our needs and so there is a lack of the urge to do anything.

Apathy is a real emotion; it is the fear of not being accepted within society, so we tend to look on the negative side of life. If I go for the new job, I could be turned down, if I go for a lovely walk in the sunshine, I could be mugged etc. We can get into such an extreme state that we become stuck. Our energy bodies then begin to contract and lose their vitality.

Quite often apathy will show as a weakness within the spleen. It is the spleen that receives energy from the sun and distributes this energy into the physical body. People who suffer from apathy find that they do not want to go outside and so they do not absorb the sunlight into their spleens. This then weakens their energy and they no longer receive fresh new energy to keep the body strong and healthy. Apathy requires action, as it is an emotion that can only be healed and changed through action. Many people who suffer from this emotion tend to worry excessively about what people say and do. They also complain of memory problems and are not able to retain thoughts.

The best way to heal apathy is to go outside and be in the fresh air and sunshine. In effect, become active. If we are inspired to apply for a new job but are unable to put pen to paper, then we are perhaps missing a chance to be of service. By being active, we achieve. By being inactive, we become stuck. If you have been putting things off, get up and do them. If you have left the cobweb in the corner of the ceiling because you are unable to reach it, then get the stool and stretch. We can do anything in our lives if we really want to, we can be assertive and strong, we do not need to rely on others for we can rely on ourselves and we can feed ourselves light rather than expect others to bring it to us.

In life five per cent of people make things happen. Fifteen per cent of people watch things happen and eighty per cent of people wonder what has happened! Those people suffering from apathy are in the eighty per cent range. In the first place, the important thing is to strive to become a part of the fifteen per cent and once there, then aim for the five per cent. We could say if there is a God, he would come and save us right now. Well, he has. He is saying, 'Come out with me now into the sunlight, deeply inhale the air and take a walk in nature'.

False Security

What is security? Is it the securing of a relationship? The security of a job, home, finances? Who do we look towards to provide us with our security? Is it our parents? Our partner? Society? Ourselves? And whose lives do we try to make secure? Our children's? Our partner? Our parents? Ourselves?

There is no security on the earth, but we have spent endless lives trying to root ourselves in this idea of security. How many of us have felt that the next promotion will bring the security we need, yet when we get there, it becomes the next promotion and so on. How many of us, in the first rush of love, feel secure in the relationship, only for it to evaporate as the relationship progresses? We then become insecure about our partner's feelings for us. Security is not real. Everything has been created through a belief or a desire, therefore it can be destroyed. It is this fear of everything around us collapsing, which drives us to make life as safe as possible, yet by focusing on an illusory safety, we miss the only true security there is.

If you came home from work tomorrow to find that your house had been burnt down, then externally you would have lost the security of your home, but from within a will of strength would grow as you dealt with the crisis. A learning takes place as you realise that although you lost your material security, inwardly your Soul gained. The idea of security then takes on a different form, as you understand that there is something deathless within you and that outside events cannot shatter your inner foundations. This is the only true security that there is.

So many insurance companies make profit out of our need for security. They sell us life insurance, pensions, accident protection, redundancy cover, etc. Some of these we pay for but will never use, so we are always living in a 'what if' state. I am not saying that you should not have insurance, what I am asking you is, do you need it? Instead of entering into insurance deals through fear, let your inner guidance direct you to what you need. This fear of the unknown future keeps us from freely experiencing the newness each moment brings.

There are many people who stay in loveless relationships because of the home, the children, or financial commitments. They lack the courage to step out of the security zone, fearing the unknown, and they worry about others around them losing their security while they take a step to freedom. You cannot provide someone with security. To do so only leads them into illusion and away from the roots of their true self. To be truly honest with yourself and take action is loving yourself and those closest to you. If you take a step towards change, then, yes, those around you will enter into their fears as you uproot them from their illusions, but they will also be shown their own inner strength, courage and potential as they face their own lack of external security. They in turn, will be able to move on.

You may be in a job that brings you the security of a good pay packet, but very little joy. If you were to give up this joyless act, what fears would you have to face to gain your freedom? Only the love of your daily work overrides the security aspect, as the joy from acting out of love extends into everything. Even if you live in poverty, you can find joy in the simplest of things and miracles will happen every day because the love you give out will attract all that you need back to you. Life then becomes a discovery, an adventure, as love radiates out of you into your work, into your partner, into your children, into your family pets and out into the world. Fear no longer keeps you searching for security as you begin to live life with innocence and joy.

The only true security is the security in God. This is the act of trusting that everything that is presented to you is God asking you to have faith and place your roots firmly in Him.

Reaching out to God to have all your needs met is relying on your inner world and becoming detached from the outside world. If you lost all your money, your house, your car, your family, your job and your friends, what would be left? Only you and what is within you would be left. And what is it that resides within you? It is your pulsating heartbeat, which is life and life is love, and love is God. You were born with nothing, yet in accordance with your karma God provided for you. You will die with nothing, yet in accordance with your karma, God will provide for you in the inner realm. What is karma? It is the effect of all your thoughts, words and actions. If you choose to look for security in the external world, then it is your karma that you are building for the future moment, for everything in the outside world is subject to change, and everything in the inside world is subject to eventual perfection. Therefore you cannot become secure in an ever-changing world, yet you can become secure in your inner love of God and His love for you.

Beliefs

When you watch a young baby in its surroundings, you realise that everything it touches, hears, sees, smells and tastes is an experience. Within this short duration of baby time, because it cannot understand the spoken language, it does not know how to judge or label anything. It is simply discovering things for itself. As the baby moves into understanding the spoken language, then beliefs become a part of the picture and it no longer discovers for itself, but starts to believe what another tells it. The strength of its will determines whether, as an adult, it will follow the beliefs of others, or it will retain its innocence and find out for itself.

If you find yourself following the will of society and what other people want for you, then somewhere within you there are patterns of childhood beliefs. You can see what beliefs you hold by looking at your habits. For example, if you are obsessed with keeping your house tidy and you get upset with family members for being less tidy than you, then there is a controlling element and a belief of not being accepted by others. If someone should call when your house is in a mess, then a panic arises within you as to how they will judge you for not being perfect.

Every habit we have is suppressing an emotion due to a belief we have about ourselves. Beliefs are like imprinted memories, because at the time they were formed, a strong emotion formed along with them, creating a distortion in the energy bodies. For instance, as a child you are hungry, so you take something from the fridge, but you are scolded for your actions and reduced to tears. Your mind then tells you it is not acceptable to reach out for food when you are hungry. Your emotions tell you that to reach out for food when you are hungry brings pain. A child will then hold onto this belief and may even build on it from similar incidents it experiences, until in its teens this trapped energy may come forth as an eating disorder or, as an adult, the person resorts to comfort eating.

Later in the book there is a section on emotional healing. This is a way of healing that allows us to enter into the emotions that we have stored in this life and previous lives in order to release the built-up hurt, sadness etc. We can even go into our memories of situations and, whilst observing, allow the emotions to rise. What we need to do first is look at the mind so that we can understand how we store our memories, beliefs and judgments about ourselves and others.

The Mind

The mind was created on the mental plane as a tool for the Soul to form its desires on the earth and to master its astral body. There is a hierarchical system, in that first there is Spirit, then Soul, then mind, then emotions and finally the physical. What we need to understand is the Soul interprets the mind, the mind interprets the emotions and the emotions interpret the body. Basically, each time we feel an emotion it sends a signal to the mind, which should send it on to the Soul in order for us to receive direction on how to react in each moment. What humanity has actually done is created mind as a separate entity, so that the message no longer reaches the Soul, and therefore the Soul cannot pass the message on through the heart for us to act in the right way. This separation was caused by humanity projecting low, earthly thoughts that attracted the energy of fear. This fear entered into the emotional body and polluted it. This also affected the mind, which in turn shut down its communication with the Soul. The fight and flight instinct, which is the conversation and awareness of the Soul, now no longer worked because of this separation.

The mind has since created this illusion of separation as a defence system to protect the human body. By using the emotions as its ally, it gives us distorted messages. It will tell us we are no longer loved or worthy, then it will throw up a defence system of rejecting others to avoid being hurt. This prevents our hearts from being open to others and remaining loving even in difficult situations. The mind is always protecting itself. It will do this to such an extent that when the inner being confronts it in search of the Soul, the mind will try to fob it off. It has become so separate that it believes there is nothing beyond itself. When a Soul chooses to take control of its life, it is trying to get the mind out of the way in order to seek and understand itself.

Not only does the mind create defence systems, but it also creates systems of attack. Attack is a form of defence. After an argument with someone, you will continue the argument in your thoughts by still defending and attacking. Because mind energy travels to where it is directed, if you think negative thoughts about somebody, then it is an attack on their energy body. Observe your mind. Become aware of when you are defending yourself and when you are attacking. Your mind can be your greatest tool to freedom or it can be your gaoler.

The mind has cut itself off from its spirituality, from its God-Self. Through its low vibrating thoughts, it has manipulated the energy in the atmosphere and created fear, which is the root cause of all the pollution and problems on the earth. We only have to look at some of our so-called amazing inventions to see what our creations have caused. These creations stem not from the lofty intent of the Soul, but from a separated mind whose only intent is to have power and wealth, as it thinks this is what will bring it eternal life. Only reuniting with the Soul can bring it true life, because it is the Soul that understands the universe, the cosmos and God. What greater power can there be?

By remaining detached from experiences and emotions, we begin to master the mind. Observation of our thoughts slows down the flow of the mind. The Soul then starts to get control again. We have allowed the mind to be influenced by people and society. It is these influences which have created rules. By becoming attached to these rules, the mind has been tricked into 'protecting' us. We need to quieten the mind so that it knows it does not have to protect us in this way. This is why it is important to understand the psychology of the self and to understand the influences that the Soul has taken on through its experiences.

The mind is responsible for the storage of energy within the body. If we release and free the mind, we will free the energy from within the body. A good way of quietening the mind is by bringing our awareness to the breath in the abdomen, and each time the mind struggles to get our attention, we come back to the breath. This concentration changes the flow of energy in the body. If we focus our awareness on the abdomen, the energy shifts from being directed into the top half of the body to becoming more grounded. Peace then enters in.

It is true that whatever we think, we are. Energy follows thought. This is because thought is the first step towards creating form. This thought energy enters into our emotional bodies and if we put feeling into the thought energy, then it is one step away from being physically created. For example, if you think yourself to be fat, then this sends a thought picture into your emotional body. Your emotions react by sending a signal to the etheric body, which alters your cells to accommodate your thoughts and feelings. This is why purification of your thoughts is important to your well being. If before you think yourself fat, you enter into yourself and consult with your Soul, then your Soul will filter the correct thought to your mind. This gives the correct picture to the emotions, and the etheric body then creates correctly at a cellular level.

If our thoughts are constantly tuned to God, then our emotions can only be love and our actions will be perfectly at peace. When we then put our trust in God and not in the mind, something else happens.

Worksheet

I have travelled to Israel many times and there is a mountain there called 'the pink mountain', which turns pink in the sun. Now I know this because I have experienced it, and the breathtaking energy of being on the mountain alone with nature and the sun filled my heart. Now you know about this scene in your mind, because I have just told you, but you have not filled your heart with it unless you experience it.

You can read this book in two ways. The information can either pass into you and become a section stored in your mind's library, or it can pass into you and you can take the information, experience it, and then know for yourself. So all the worksheets and questions in the book are designed to help you look at your relationship to yourself and gain valuable insights. You will need pen and paper to record your findings.

1. Ask yourself right now, 'Who am I? What created me?' then question within, 'Am I just this body or is there more to life than what I see with my eyes?'

2. Ask yourself, 'What are my beliefs?' Write down a list of your beliefs. For example, do you believe yourself to be in control, organised, good-looking, moody, a chocoholic, untidy, financially broke, a workaholic, fat, too thin, a failure, ugly, beautiful etc.? List as many as you can.

3. Make a list of what you feel are your mother's beliefs and then your father's beliefs. Look at their financial beliefs, their environment beliefs, their career beliefs, their relationship beliefs etc, then compare them to what you have written as your beliefs.

4. You may find that from your childhood you have taken on a lot of what they believe or believed in. Now look at the fear behind these beliefs and look into the emotions that you may be suppressing that keep these beliefs in place. Take one belief at a time. For example, if your mother believes money is hard to come by and she is financially poor, look at the underlying issue, 'I am not worthy enough to have money.' This lack of self-worth has its roots in pride. If you have taken this belief as your own, then look back at your life. Where have you been rejected and hurt? Where have you been taught that life is a struggle? Why do you have so little faith in your abilities?

5. Each time you really look at a belief, you begin to see the fear that holds you. When you feel and let go of the emotion that was suppressed at the time of creating the belief, then you free more of your true self and life becomes a journey of self-discovery.

6. On an emotional level what are your triggers? Would you say you were a person that easily becomes angry? Or jealous? Would you say you were apathetic with not much energy to do anything? Do you comfort eat? Or drink excessively? Then look for the fear behind the emotion. Whose love do you fear losing? Why can't you have a wonderful job, loving relationships, etc.? What is it that stops you from taking action and being assertive and meeting your inner needs?

7. From moment-to-moment what are your thoughts doing? Are they attuned to the highest vibration there is, or are they like a running train at full throttle, never stopping? Bring your awareness to your breathing and observe your thoughts.

Behind each belief lies the original emotion and the memory of the event that triggered it. Whilst you are doing the worksheet it is important to be aware of emotions as they come up. Give yourself time and space to experience them in a gentle and loving way. Do not allow judgment to creep in. Try to observe your experience so that you are not overwhelmed by the feeling, but still allow the emotion to rise. Staying with the feeling enables it to change. Eventually it loses its intensity and dissolves, leaving a feeling of peace, as the energy that was bound by the emotion is once more free to flow.

2
Love is the Only True Emotion

Life leads us to life
And love leads us to love.
The mystical union of a Soul with his God
Is love with its lover.
Let that jewel within your heart
Light a thousand flames,
For love is unlimited.
It knows naught but itself.

What is Love?

Poets write about love, philosophers reason about love, musicians play melodies of love, and singers voice the words of love, yet very few can say what love is. The Soul is the vehicle of love, it moves this energy through the different levels of its being and allows it to be expressed through the heart chakra. Love is pure, it knows no limits or conditions and it flows on its own course. It wants to replace your fears, desires, anger, pride, thoughts, words and deeds, but for some reason we pile up rocks of hatred to dam the river of love. We use our intellectual minds to define love and, through our beliefs, we judge what love is and what it is not.

Mind is responsible for all on this earth, good or bad, as it governs our reactions to emotional energy. It is the Soul slayer. It stops the Soul from being itself. The mind constantly wants to know this or that, yet it does not want to know itself. Therefore when we master the mind, the Soul becomes free to express its love on the earth.

We can still the mind by learning to listen. We can focus our listening on nature, other humans and ourself. It is true that while we are listening we are not thinking. Therefore what hears and what thinks? Are they the same thing, or separate? The only constant in this world is love. Everything else is impermanent and it is love that causes its impermanence. Love changes everything, so we have to yield to love and its ways. To do this demands honesty to yourself and others. This means doing what is right for you, and not doing what causes you pain in order to please others.

We often expect others to fulfil a certain role or do a certain task to prove that they love us. If they do not act out our needed scenarios, we feel rejected and unloved. This is conditional love, which stems only from the mind's illusion of love. It is this that brings so much confusion to humanity. Unconditional love carries within it joy, peace, happiness and self-love. It can be passive and powerful, so allow it in and allow it out! Let it come into every aspect of your life. Invite it into your relationships, your job, your finances and let it show you the weaknesses and the solutions. Have the courage to face your fears and problems. Love shows no mercy to the negativity in your life, but exposes it for healing. We are Divine Spirits who have allowed the mind to control the flow of love into our hearts, so that only trickles are expressed in our lives. We have followed the same path life after life, stumbling in the darkness. However, love never left us. It is we who closed the door on love. Are you willing to realise that you are worthy of the abundance of love flowing into your life right now? Can you allow it in?

We, as Souls, came here so that we could learn to embrace love completely within our lives. This is the path home, so what are our obstacles to realising this? We have placed too much value on society and its acceptance of us, instead of turning within, using courage as our guide, and expressing love no matter what assails us in each moment. To stand up and be yourself no matter what it means, is loving the Soul. Each time you speak your truth, you face, collect and re-integrate a lost piece of yourself. So be honest and ask within, 'What changes can I make that reflect the love that I have for myself?' Then start the process.

Self-Love

Self-love is self-forgiveness, self-acceptance.

Every time you forgive and accept the cause and effect of all that has happened to you throughout your life, you arrive at a deeper state of self-love. Until you love and accept yourself, it is not possible to love and accept others. It is easy to say, 'If I knew then what I know now, things would be different.' You were not meant to know *then* what you know *now*, because you had karma to fulfil which needed you as you were. Realising this, you can release the guilt. You have not failed at anything, only learnt. This removes self-judgment.

In the past, because you did not listen to your inner self, you may have done things in anger, pride or jealousy. This is acting through fear. By forgiving and accepting the self, a new life calls to you and it is saying, 'Be true to yourself, grow from the lessons of the past, accept you are worthy and that you have a purpose for being.' Look back at what you gained from past experiences. You have a right to love and to be loved and a right to be yourself in all that you do. The past is another country and you do not live there any more. A prayer for those you feel you have wronged will open the door for change.

Ask if you really love and accept yourself. We spend so much time comparing ourselves to other people: 'I'm too fat/thin, my sexual parts are too small/big, I'm too small/tall'. The list is endless. Who are we really comparing ourselves to? If you look at a beautiful model who has a so-called perfect body, you can go into envy. What if the perfect model stepped out of her physical world and looked at you, she might become envious of your joy, your family, and your home. She would face her own emotional and mental world, and that makes you her mirror, her teacher. The whole of life is based on comparison, judgment of self and judgment of others. You are perfect right now, and at the end of your life there will be only you judging you and, if you end self-judgment now, then you will not have to face it in the inner realms after death. It is your thoughts that are important, not your looks.

In death, will you say 'I did not know I was perfect, that I had it all, I was waiting for someone to tell me?' Do you go on diets because you believe you do not make others happy if you are fat? Do you drive a sports car to prove to others your worth? In order for us to receive love we spend large amounts of time making other people happy. Some people even mask their true feelings by saying, 'I am happy to be fat/thin etc.' As long as this is true, then you have accepted yourself. However, if you are covering up your feelings, you are in denial. Only acceptance of the self is liberating. We should have written on our mirrors, 'Stop telling yourself lies, you are beautiful.'

Exercise

See a vision of you standing in front of yourself. Are you happy? With what you see can you embrace yourself and allow love's healing balm to permeate your being? If you see yourself as fat, ugly, unkempt, old, etc., then you need to continue your inner quest to self-acceptance.

I once heard someone say, 'It takes a man to say sorry and a fool to walk away.' Stand and accept yourself as you are, you have come here to work on your weaknesses, not to become a slave to them. You only have to please yourself. If you need to please anyone, then please God. Dress for Him and act for Him. Live in Him, through Him and with Him, only then does true joy reign supreme in your life.

True Joy

If you are not happy with your life, then start to observe what it is you have done, or are doing, which is bringing about the suffering to destroy your joy. If you cannot find happiness now, when will you find it? If you cannot find joy from within yourself, where will you find it? We can demand it from others, but expecting others to behave in a certain way is conditional and impermanent. True joy can be found even in the most difficult of circumstances. I have met many people who have disabilities, yet joy shines out from within them. They have accepted their position and are giving their all to enjoy life. There are people who live in a state of sheer poverty, yet still their hearts are open and joy pours from them. What is it that these people have that joyless people do not? They understand that in the struggle of life, there is always something wonderful and good to be found. They are seeing the beauty of life.

Even in our moments of unhappiness we can go out into nature and see the joy in flowers, plants and trees. We may hear the joy in children's laughter, words from a loved one or the song of birds. We can receive joy in music, art and beautiful objects made by humanity. All these things will open the door to our Soul and trigger the joy from within.

Ultimately, in order to have joy we have to give it, and this starts with appreciating all the good and beautiful that is present in our life today. If we cannot find joy, then we need to challenge ourselves and look at what needs changing. No one is ever trapped. It is desire, that keeps us in our life situations. If we let go of the desire we receive freedom and abundant joy.

Desire and pride distort the energy of joy. For example, a person may feel joyful after winning a fight. Is this true joy? Another person may feel joy at seeing his competitors fail in business. Is this true joy? This is pride revelling in joy at the failing or destruction of others. It is the creation of a mind that has become separated from the Soul. This false joy is self-destructive, because in order to heal it, we will have to face the effects of what we have created through our way of being.

There is no better school than this material world. It is through our failings and gains that we learn how the Divine manifests in our physical life. Being true to your inner self brings about a change. It allows you to live life, to be life, to be alive. The journey of a Soul brings many adventures. Too many rules and rigidity block the Soul and stop joy from finding expression. Make sure you have fun and enjoy life. Share with others for the pure joy of sharing and not for the acknowledgement of worth. You do not need an external gauge to measure your success or your failure. You are already the eternal God. The journey is finding this out. Smile, we created this world.

True Peace

Peace is a word that is bandied about freely, but do we know what it really means to have peace? We call out for peace in the neighbourhood, in the country and in the world. We forget that true peace starts with ourself. If we have peace within our thoughts, peace within our words and peace within our actions, then our external experiences will follow in this same peaceful state. Even if chaos is happening out in the street, peace will still reside in our being.

Our sun has divided itself into planets and moons, the universe into stars and galaxies, yet there is a oneness, a wholeness that pervades all. It is the mind that separates and divides. It has taken the wholeness and fragmented it because it cannot accept the eternal One. Until we let go of mind, let go of division and stop being one of the fragments, we cannot become whole. We give our fragments names just as we do to races, tribes, football teams, or political parties, and we take the wholeness apart and re-blend it according to the acceptance of the mind. We fight, cheer, protest, die and live in support of our fragmentation. We fight wars, some we even call holy wars and some are tribal. We hope that our fragment will dominate and rule all other fragments, and we try to bring this about. Do we want peace or just a piece?

There is not just external division there is also an inner division. We split emotions and store these within our bodies, yet it is the mind that creates these divisions. The deeper part of us, that which is our Soul, knows only the One. So what is the solution to this dilemma of ours? We need to become aware of our actions and look for the source of each act. Do we do things through fear or love? By acting through fear we allow our Souls to be dragged down into spiralling depths. Over thousands of years we have permitted fear to pervade our being and steal the essence of love that we truly are.

We cannot expect external peace until we have found internal peace. The true peacemaker is the one who has found it within himself and then helps others to find it inside themselves. Only by each individual finding it within, will it become projected outwards into the world. We can start this process by observing our moment-to-moment way of being. Look at where your thoughts are, acknowledge your emotions, and be aware of the actions that you take in your daily life. These observations will reveal where you lack peace and where you have it. Let go of trying to change things according to how you believe they should be. If you can accept each moment as it is without trying to manipulate it, peace will reside. It is the conflict between how things are and how you want them to be that creates the disturbance. Acceptance is love, and love changes everything. True peace is when conflict ends and love reigns supreme.

True Wisdom

In a faraway kingdom lived a king who received word that the neighbouring kingdom was going to attack in four days. He quickly called for his two wisest men. The first man told the king to enter into his heart and pray to his Soul for three days. The king threw him into the dungeons for his stupidity. The second man relayed to the king a plan of attack. He quoted facts, figures and strategy. The king followed the wise man's advice. Two days later he sent out his troops, but whilst they were marching, the nearby kingdom sent out a hidden set of troops to take the king and his city with a surprise attack. The king and his city were defenceless, and fell. The king was thrown into the dungeons with the first wise man. The king asked the wise man what would have happened if he had prayed to his Soul for three days. The wise man told him that his Soul would have advised him to stay put, as the other kingdom's plan was to lure the troops out and leave the city defenceless and open to invasion. The king had listened to his mind rather than to his Soul. It is the Soul who knows the bigger picture. The mind is limited in its knowing.

True wisdom comes from the Soul. It is inspiration and truth. The mind's wisdom comes from intellectual study. It can quote amazing knowledge from memory, impressing those around it, but

it does not have an unshakable knowing. A wise man is someone who has full contact with his Soul. He no longer searches and gathers facts to fill his intellect, on the contrary, he seeks to empty it in order to receive the impressions of the Soul. How many times have we looked at people and thought them to be wise? The true question is, are they speaking and acting from the Soul, or from the mind?

In society we often depict aged people as being wise, and experience certainly does bring wisdom. Problems can occur though if the wisdom is tainted by beliefs. This is not from the Soul. True wisdom is not limited, and we can easily find it being imparted through the words of a child, the shape of a cloud, or the wonder of a seed. Nature is a pure giver of wisdom. We only have to observe her way of being and the whole workings of man and the universe is reflected.

In silence, stillness, and by listening we will feel, hear and know the Soul. We cannot obtain wisdom if our minds, home and work are cluttered. If this is the case, then we will search outside ourselves for the wisdom of others. If we receive another's mind wisdom, then we can lose our way. If we are stuck and need guidance, we must go within and ask our own Soul. True wisdom will then be given.

True Compassion

When a loved one is going through a difficult time, do you sympathise or empathise? In other words, do you sit in the gutter with your loved one, or do you offer him/her a hand out? True compassion is from the heart. It is a total understanding of another person's pain. Through this understanding, you can reach out and touch another very deeply.

There are two types of compassion, there is human compassion and there is Soul compassion. Both types are able to step into the shoes of another, but human compassion can easily slide into sympathy or pity. At this point you begin to resonate your own pain through another's experience and you get caught up in the drama rather than observing it. Soul compassion is more accurate and powerful as you are able to see the picture from all the levels of your being. Your soul is able to observe the unfolding drama, but it does not get caught up in the emotional energy of it. For example, your best friend's partner has cheated on him/her. Instead of agreeing that their partner is a rotten person, you guide your friend into looking at what may have caused the situation. You help your friend to explore his/her feelings and look at his/her part in the relationship. This will reveal valuable insights as to their way of being. This is true compassion.

We could also describe true compassion as observation without judgment and total listening. How many of us, when we listen to another, are thinking about our own agenda or what we are going to say next? If we are, then we are not acting in a true compassionate way. When you fully observe and listen, it creates space for a person to enter into. In this space they can hear, feel and know themselves. This is a moment of inner silence where they are experiencing a close liaison with their soul. If you find yourself agreeing, relating or talking about your past experience whilst consoling another, then you have moved out of the heart and become centred on yourself and not on the other person.

There are some very compassionate Souls who choose to incarnate into difficult circumstances. This may include abusive relationships, poverty, starvation, etc. Their presence radiates love, which they use to help and heal people on many different levels, bringing people to an understanding of the path of love. This level of compassion is a form of teaching and can bring about lasting change to those who are struggling with earthly lives.

If you are in a relationship or situation that requires positive changes to be made which may hurt another, then acknowledge the human compassion within you that does not want to cause pain and centre yourself from within. To follow the promptings of your heart and change your situation, is to teach those around you. This is an act of true compassion. Sometimes true compassion can initially hurt others, as compassion is the gateway to honesty. By expressing your truth and taking action, compassion will tear down any illusions and make people face what they may have been avoiding for lifetimes.

Being compassionate will mean you have to speak your truth and say what is in your heart. If your heartfelt truth hurts another, then it is their pride that is hurt and not the Soul, as the Soul only recognises love and not pain.

Jesus, Buddha, Mohamed, Krishnamurti, etc, taught, "Be true to yourself", as this way you will listen intently and become observant, non-judgmental, loving and compassionate. You will think, speak and act in perfect harmony and see through the illusions of pain, hurt, sadness and separation in order to know the truth.

Part two

Looking into the Mirror

3

The Conditioning Years

*W*hen I look at the world,
I see suffering and anguish.
It seems fine to say it is karma and cross over
To the other side of the road,
But that leaves an empty feeling in my heart.
Did I come onto the earth and go through all I
Have been through to simply cross over the road?
I do not think so!

The Conditioning

We are energy. In fact everything that exists is energy, and the level at which energy vibrates is what determines its density. When we first travelled out from the Godhead we were pure vibration; this means we held within us the one light and the one sound. As we moved further out, the light broke down into many colours, and the one sound into many notes. When we entered the earth and mixed with its vibration, we again altered the vibration of our auric coat of many colours. Over countless generations, as fear took a hold, our colours became dirtier and more polluted, until we no longer resembled the original outpouring of God.

This next chapter explains what happens to us energetically as children growing up on the earth in its present state of evolution. On many occasions I have heard it suggested that to look back on our life is meaningless, as the present moment is all that exists. Although I agree that the concept of time is an illusion and the past and the future are created by the mind, we also have to understand that, in order to live fully in the present moment, we have to undo suppressed energy that we have stored within us. Clearing that suppressed energy will clear the colours in our aura, so that they once again shine in their pure state. Only then can we live truly in the moment. For example, if within your aura you mix a muddy blue with a muddy yellow, you create a muddy green. If you then try to live in the moment, this muddy green will keep tapping you on the shoulder, reminding you that it still exists. The key to freedom is to observe the muddy green, allow it to reveal how it came into existence and then deal with the cause of what made the blue and yellow muddy in the first place.

To master our energy bodies, is to return to the one light. We can only do this by reclaiming ourselves through a process of understanding, accepting our truth and releasing the distortion. From a Soul's perspective, our parents are not to blame for whatever we experienced during our upbringing, rather we need to recognise that we chose the situation where our greatest potential for healing could take place. This true way of looking at our life removes guilt and judgment, for everything that occurred has been perfect for our growth. This does not give us licence to do whatever we like now, for example, to abuse another and say it is all part of their growth. Our Soul demands that we always act with integrity.

Pregnancy

When does the Soul enter into the physical body? I have been asked this question many times and I have observed that the Soul often makes links to its parents a few years before the actual birth. At this point it is sending a pattern down onto the earth to draw in certain energies that it will need for its incarnation. As it reviews its previous life, the Soul looks at its karma and decides what it wants to work on in its next lifetime. It then searches for other Souls that are presently incarnated who can help it to do this. Having determined who its parents will be, it ascertains what genes it requires from each one to bring out the desired personality. The incoming Soul now communicates with the Souls of its new parents, so that all three make the agreement to work together in order to help each other clear any karma. When this is finalised, the Soul can begin to live within the energy field of one or both of its parents.

When it gets nearer to conception, the Soul moves closer in. At the point of conception, the Soul sends down a beam of energy which goes into the womb of the mother. It then starts to draw the genetic pattern it requires for its DNA from the sperm of the father and from the egg of the mother. This process anchors the Soul to the parents. The mother not only experiences an internal physical change, but also an energetic change, as her karmic pattern alters. She is now preparing herself for a new stage of karma with the incoming Soul, which brings with it a complex world. This include all its past experiences, its learning from other lives, its traumas and its conditioning.

Often, as the Soul comes closer to the mother, she can go through a very traumatic change, which may include sickness, tiredness, disruptive emotions and fears, as she accepts the new karmic pattern. This world that the Soul brings with it can be huge, and sometimes the blending with the worlds of the mother and father can create major conflicts within their relationship. The new life that is growing inside the mother could have once been a judge, a monk, a nurse, or a soldier, so the added memories, energies and emotions that are now pouring into the system of the mother can seem like a struggle to cope with. She may become vulnerable, prone to outbursts of anger, sadness and tears, as she loses some of her auric protection in order to let the Soul's world move closer in. Often the mother goes through cravings and addictions to certain foods, caused by the incoming soul's needs for essential minerals to build its energy bodies. She may also use these foods as a comfort to quieten down the incoming Soul and to nurture herself.

If the karmic link between the incoming Soul and the parents is positive, then the mother usually has a trouble-free pregnancy. Often the incoming Soul may have been her mother, brother, or even her lover in a previous life. The familiarity of the energy is so compatible, that the mother finds she can cope with the process. If the incoming Soul was an enemy in a past life, when the Soul comes in, a great dislike can build up between the mother and the child. We can often see this where a mother has two children. She may like one of the Souls, but not get on well with the other one. This may be due to a complicated karma that needs to be worked out with the child. It may also be that the karma is with the father, so the mother will have no karmic bond with the Soul. This can often confuse the mother, as she does not feel she knows or understands the Soul, and because it seems a stranger to her, she may have difficulty in connecting with it. This can also be the case with the father. If the mother has the karmic bond, the father may feel distant from the child.

Karma works out in many ways. For example, the person who murdered you in your last life may become your child, so you can teach them that love and caring is the only way, and not violence. The person you may have harmed in another life could come back as a member of your family, so that you can care for them and love them. Ultimately, there is no wrong and no guilt, for the Soul always chooses to come back to help another to love or to be helped to express love. This way karma is a teaching, for if we do not know how to express love properly, we are sent teachers to show us. What better teacher is there than a parent to its child and a child to its parent?

If the parents' relationship breaks up during pregnancy, then the Soul has chosen this experience and it will experience all the emotions around the separation. If the mother or father does not want the child, this too was chosen by the Soul. This experience of rejection will help it to balance and heal an aspect of its karma. The effects of the rejection may, later in life, be revealed as pride or anger. Because the parents acted according to their feelings, they have helped the Soul to bring forth its imperfections.

If a mother chooses to have a termination, then the Soul is fully aware of the choice beforehand and has chosen to enter into the mother's energy field to heal the karma between them. I have also observed that in terminations and miscarriages the Soul stays within the mother's aura for up to twenty-one years, still growing as a child on the astral plane. Usually there has been an agreement for the Soul to anchor in the astral plane and clear its issues there, instead of fully coming into the physical world. The mother is aware of this subconsciously and this is sometimes why she still feels a connection to her aborted or lost child and cannot let go. This is where guilt is often an uninvited guest. There should be no guilt in termination or miscarriage, for it was already set up beforehand and all the Souls involved were clear about the future outcome. A Soul chooses its parents, chooses its environment, chooses what emotions to feel, and it also chooses its own karmic pattern to work on.

Before the Soul incarnates it already has a basic imprint of the first fourteen years of its life. It has prepared itself to adapt easily and accept any new scenarios fairly quickly, so it is already waiting for certain events to happen. It is society which categorises events and tells us whether something is a hardship or easy. I remember, when I was living in the children's home, there was a boy there who felt sorry for me because I had no parents, and I felt sorry for the boy because his parents regularly beat him. The Soul is so intricately woven into the energy fields of its parents, that if abuse takes place, the child would rather hold on in there for the little bit of love that they receive. Many children in the home who had been taken from their parents still yearned to be with them. The loss of the aura that was built in the parents' energy fields is what causes most of the distress. It can take up to two years for the Soul to re-adjust its energy bodies. This is not to say that children should be left in abusive situations. Rather it is a point of becoming aware that we are not just physical beings, but also spiritual beings. Not only do we need to protect the child, we need to take into consideration the lessons the Soul has chosen to learn. This could lead us into healing and educating the family as a whole unit. The solution does not always lie in completely severing the child from its parents, as this is a subtle form of rejection that does not heal it as a whole.

Birth

At the moment of birth, the Soul completes the final stage of its energy bodies. The physical body represents the Soul's entry into physical life. Whilst the child is growing up, the Soul never loses its true identity, and it is always working behind the scenes. By forming a physical body it creates a vehicle for the personality, which has the freedom to choose to express love or not. If the personality forms a two-way connection with the Soul throughout its life, then the personality will be able to heal its non-loving aspects and eventually merge with the Soul. This is a gradual process that allows the Soul to slowly reveal more of itself.

Birth is a very special time. The Soul may have spent years preparing for the right timing according to the planetary status and its karmic pattern. If the birth is induced, it causes the Soul problems in aligning with the body and its karma. I once observed this in a baby as I was waiting for my second daughter to be born. I saw how the Soul was waiting outside the body and could not align with the baby. Because the mother was distressed, the baby was distressed and the Soul was trying to sort out and re-define all its careful planning of the last few years. I have also observed the energetic effects that painkilling drugs have on the auras of both the mother and the baby. I have seen that the energy does not heal for years. I am not saying these drugs should not be used, only that we are ignorant of the long-term effects these have on the systems of both the mother and the child.

The immediate bonding with the baby at birth is so important. Often before the baby is given to the parents, it is weighed, checked, cleaned and wrapped. At this time the baby has just been born into a very alien world and only recognises the auras of its parents. To be parted from them can be very distressing. I once spoke to a woman who told me that it was not until weeks after the birth that she experienced skin-to-skin contact with her child. From the moment it was born it was wrapped, and she felt pressured to follow the hospital's many rules. The medical profession certainly does have its place within the world, but it has become so impersonal that convenience is considered more important than the beauty of new life born as naturally as possible. There is no awareness of the Soul's involvement and the hard work that has gone into its preparation. The Soul needs to bond with both parents immediately. This crucial moment can affect them all for life.

When my second child was born, the midwife was very clinical and lacked warmth and compassion. Throughout the birth we were handled roughly and in a matter-of-fact fashion. As the baby emerged, the doctor quickly rushed it from the room. After several minutes he re-entered with the baby wrapped in a blanket and I called him over and asked him if anyone knew the sex of the baby. The room went quiet. The realisation sunk in that no-one knew the sex of my child. They had been so caught up in the procedure that no one had really looked at our baby.

The birthing process has become so impersonal now that we use drugs, monitors, and operational methods to speed up the natural flow of life. At conception, we allow the body and its intelligence to fertilise the egg and create a human body with every detail in place and with perfect timing. What marvellous miracles we can perform when we allow nature to take its course. Then at birth we override the intelligence of the body, which knows exactly at what point to break its waters, to push, to stretch the skin for crowning and to finally give birth. The mother's intuition tells her what is the best position, who to have with her, and how the process is going. Female energy unfolds new life from within, but at the point of birth it is the male dominating world that forces it out unnaturally. This is a reflection of how we treat most of the female energy here upon the earth.

We have become so reliant on the doctor's verdict that we forget our own knowing. At one point in my wife's pregnancy, she was taken to hospital because she was overdue. After several days the doctor approached the bed and ordered the medical staff around us to prepare her to be induced. My wife began to panic, as inwardly she knew it was not right. We decided to sign ourselves out of the hospital, but we were made to feel that we had taken the wrong decision by going against the doctor's orders. Three days later our daughter was born effortlessly. My wife felt better for having listened to her inner knowing and not rushing the body, which had already set the day and time in harmony with the Soul.

In many cases the medical profession has saved lives by inducing births and performing caesarean sections. These procedures were part of the Soul's plan and have not interfered with its timing or preparation. There are also many cases where these were unnecessary and have caused great disruption to the incoming Soul and distress to the energy fields of the parents.

Many people forget about the role of the father at birth. As a father myself, it was upsetting to watch my wife in pain, to stand by while she was intimately handled by different people, and to receive my baby wrapped without the acknowledgement of its sex. The presence of the father at birth is very important to the Soul, as throughout the pregnancy the Soul has grown energy cords connected to the father's energy field and it needs to define these cords in its first few moments after birth.

As the baby is defenceless, and the Soul does not have full control of the body, it relies on the mother and father for its nourishment and protection until the body is big enough for the Soul to take full control. The aura and chakras of the baby are still developing, therefore it relies on the mother's aura and chakras to filter and feed it spiritual light. During the baby's time within the womb and its first few years of life, the Soul experiences all the mother's emotions, thoughts and events.

The mother's energy field is very vulnerable after giving birth. Some enter into what is medically called 'post-natal depression'. This is due to the mother trying to adapt to the new world that the Soul has brought with it. The more the Soul's world is full of emotions, past traumas, and strong character influences, the deeper the mother will be inclined to fall into depression. Energetically, depression in the aura is suppressed energy. The mother may feel heavy, weepy and lethargic, as her legs and abdomen areas have become full of stagnated energy. The energy to support her daily life, which enters into her base chakra through the feet, can no longer be received. The energy from the cosmos can no longer enter into her spine through the crown and vitalise her, as it cannot push through the mass energy of the incoming Soul. The new Soul's world has in fact filled the mother's world and stemmed the flow of light through her being.

The way to heal this is to first accept that you have taken on a Soul who needs your love, and by being its parent you have agreed to teach it about unconditional love to the best of your ability. The next step is to become strong in the physical body. You can take a course of vitamins and minerals. You could take up walking or yoga, and eat healthily as this will also clear and energise the etheric body. The astral body needs you to feel your emotions, then let go of them, and honour your needs by meeting them. Your Soul requires you to love yourself, to be patient and honest with yourself. Most important of all, you need to follow your inner advice and not that of those around you who may not understand your inner pain.

The father may also go through a difficult period after the birth as he re-defines his life. I have met many fathers who have felt trapped. Their childhood dreams of travelling the world and being responsible for only themselves become shattered. Many relationships break up either just before or just after birth, as the man decides he cannot commit and surrender his energy to the new family situation. Most early break-ups are karmic, as the child needed the genes from the father, but the karma may solely be with the mother. The father may have future karma with other Souls coming through a different relationship.

Sometimes, due to circumstances, children are given up for adoption at birth. This complex changing of energy could be a book in itself, but basically adoption is karmic. The child needed the DNA from its biological parents, but the life karma is with its adoptive parents. The Soul has probably experienced many lives with the adoptive parents. Sometimes it may take on difficult DNA in order to heal it in a different environment, changing the ensuing generations of its biological parents. The Soul, throughout its life, stays energetically connected to its biological parents. Their thoughts, emotions and actions affect the Soul through the DNA patterning. Later in life they may meet up again and see that when major shifts and changes occurred in their life, they were all affected at the same time.

So much guilt occurs through adoption. The mother never forgets her child and feels deeply affected. If the adoption was forced upon her, then bitterness and deep-rooted anger may shape her life. The child, when it knows its circumstances, may accept its situation or reject its adoptive parents and feel a longing for its natural parents. Adoption is a decision the Soul makes for its learning, and if people were to understand the bigger picture, they would not feel guilty for giving up their child. A mother bears her child, and as a true act of love, she hands it over to its Soul for the best possible growth in its lifetime. Therefore she should forgive herself and let go of the false judgments she has placed upon herself and others.

If you are a person who has been adopted, then enter into your heart where your Soul resides and know you made a decision which would lead you to know more of yourself. Become aware that you have incarnated with the inner tools to specifically deal with this learning. With this knowledge, ask yourself, if it is time to forgive yourself and let go of the false judgments that you have placed upon yourself and others. Know that if you look at yourself and heal this situation, then you do it for all the others who have also lived through the adoption process.

Disability and Illness

For parents it is emotionally painful giving birth to a child who suffers from a disability or illness. Many emotions surface: we may feel guilt, anger, failure, shame, grief. Each case will be unique, but one thing we need to understand is that all disability and illness is a learning. There are several reasons why a Soul chooses to be restricted. It may decide to bring forth a physical imperfection in order to clear a lot of built-up energy from its thoughts, words and actions from previous lives. A Soul may also choose to heal a genetic condition within the family, so as an act of service, it takes on all the negativity from the past generations and clears it through the physical body. The Soul who has the disability or illness may be enabling parents or carers to work out their karma. In this way it helps to bring out the emotions to be healed, as all karma is emotion.

Society has often been wary of disability and illness, simply because subconsciously we fear being imperfect. We believe imperfections are not fully lovable. We therefore put a distance between ourselves and those who have physical limitations. We only have to look at how we treat those who suffer from the AIDS virus, leprosy, cancer, disfigurement, etc., to know how we avoid the unloved parts of ourselves. Disease and disability are an external effect of an internal cause, the result of the negative thoughts, words and actions that humanity has churned forth. We are all responsible for the illnesses and diseases that plague this planet, so when we look at another who is physically limited or suffers in pain, then we should know that because of our fears, we have played a part in allowing this to take form on the earth. In the Wisdom Years chapter of the book, we will look in greater detail at how illness in the aged is an effect from an internal cause.

I would also like to mention a very dynamic process that I was told about by a herbalist friend. He found that when a mother brought a child in for treatment, instead of giving the remedy to the child to take, he gave it to the mother. He found that any changes in the mother's aura affected the child, so when the mother took healing remedies, the child got better. When a mother decides to develop herself and change her way of being, then the child also develops with her. If every mother on the earth purified her thoughts, words and actions, then all the children would become purified. What service this would be to humanity and the whole of this planet!

Childhood

For the first seven years of life, we are trying on emotions for size. What we are really doing is shaping and building our emotional body, ready for the teenage years when the Soul fully takes control of the physical and energy bodies. We do this by expressing our self in the moment, so we may suddenly become angry. If we are allowed to express this anger, then we know within us how this energy feels, how we can process it and let it go. Problems can occur when the parent, teacher, sibling or whoever stops us from expressing the emotion. We then hold this energy within our bodies and it becomes suppressed. Over time it joins with other suppressed emotions and it begins to affect our life force, eventually resulting in illness. During the teenage years, the Soul pushes us to rebel and break out of our suppressed energy and become free from negative conditioning.

These first important childhood years also shape us according to the society we were born into, so rather than be our all-encompassing self, we are taught to make judgments, separating things into acceptance and non-acceptance. We have become part of a tribe and its tribal laws. We are expected to follow doctrines thousands of years old, which have proved time and time again that they do not work. Yet, because we seek acceptance from something outside of ourselves, we as a society are reluctant to change. So as soon as the child can walk and talk, he is taught to shut down his inner world and accept only the outer world as his reality.

Between the ages of seven and fourteen we build the emotional body with even greater intent. We start to express our independence more by moving away from our parents, playing on our own and going to school. At this point the Soul is moving closer to the physical body and it is directing different colours and vibrations into the energy bodies. This is when we start to create our own aura. It no longer consists of many sparks of colour as it did in early childhood, it becomes distinctly coloured, oval in shape, and more defined. This allows us to draw astral energy towards us, and we no longer feel the need to rely on our mother and father to give us their auric energy.

It is at this point that the beliefs instilled in us in infancy by our parents according to the tribe they belong to (religion, status, environment, social etiquette etc.) become ingrained within our system. These tribal laws also create tribal fears: this may be a fear of other religions, tribes, animals, spiders, snakes, other languages etc. All of these fears start to build up within our energy system. Even if we are not affected by animals, or do not worry, these fears still go into our system because they are a part of the social energy. It is something that we have to deal with and process later. As the Soul chose its parents and environment, so it also chose the beliefs it wanted to receive and work on in this lifetime. If, as an adult, it faces these illusory beliefs and heals them then this healing also affects the whole tribe that it belonged to.

If a Soul has not worked out its conflict with certain energies on the earth by the time it is an adult, then it will keep choosing partners to help it resolve the conflict. For example, if a child is beaten regularly by one of its parents, it will often choose a partner who also beats it. This is due to the way the Soul needs to learn and grow. It has to eventually stand up, say 'No more' and take control of its own life, rather than repeating its internalised pattern. A child can become so restricted through the beliefs of its parents, that it does as it is told and becomes the 'good boy or girl', rather than experiencing for itself. For example, the parent tells the child not to put its hand in the fire, the child is obedient but does not understand why. If the parent takes the child's hand and puts it close to the fire and says 'hot, fire, burn', the child will begin to understand that heat is hot and it has experienced and understood the elements, rather than just hearing words. If you restrict a Soul's experience, then it will eventually have to find a way of experiencing all that from which it has been held back. If the restrictions cause it to live a shut-down life resulting in unfulfilled desires, then these will need to be fulfilled in other lifetimes. It is important that children are allowed to fully experience life so that they let the energy pass through their system and become free of it.

So always after a 'Don't do that' or 'You shouldn't do this', there should follow an explanation as to what would occur to help the child to understand it. For example, if a child keeps pulling another's hair and we just say 'No', then it does not understand the effect, but if you gently pull the child's hair, then it understands the effect of its actions and this way it learns. This is the law of karma: if I do this, then it will come back to me. If we are not living life by a perfect example, then how can we expect it from others? Life is all about expression and reception. We express emotion and we feel emotion. We express love and we receive love. Our sole purpose for living is to love and to be loved. If we are not allowed to do this, blockages are created and these blockages affect us later in life.

It is interesting for those of us who were brought up in a happy environment and were not afflicted by any emotional, physical or mental pain, to observe whether we are free from the binds of the earth. Are we living with no fear? Do we have perfect harmonious relationships? Is each thought pure? Is each word pure? Is each action born from peace? If this is your way of being then your Soul has mastered its energy and earthly life. If, however, you are not living the above life, then somewhere within you is your childhood conditioning, childhood beliefs, and your Soul working with its karma. Whilst reading the next few pages you may see aspects of yourself in the rejected child or the emotionally moulded child. To acknowledge this within you reveals that on some level you have stored this energy, in which case it needs to be observed and released.

Abuse

Abuse occurs when we cause fear rather than love to enter into another's energy field. In essence we are misusing our energies and manipulating another's. Sometimes we do this subconsciously and we even believe that we are being loving. This is the great illusion. Abuse comes on many levels and can be very subtle or very apparent. For instance, if you tell someone not to befriend a thief because they are not a 'good' person, then you are basing your decision on a judgment from the mind and you fear what this friendship will bring. What we do not realise is that when the heart is open it sees the act of stealing as only one aspect of the thief. It might also see the thief's struggle. It might acknowledge the thief's artistic ability, the fact that the thief is a father, mother or someone's child. The heart sees the whole picture and not just the small piece that fear would have you see.

I have always felt the word 'abuse' vibrates quite deeply in my energy bodies. I feel this is because abuse carries a sad, fearful, and angry energy, therefore whenever people think of the term 'abuse' they tune into a negative vibration. Society has not helped by making abuse a taboo subject. I have used the term abuse in the following descriptions, to show that it is the misuse of energy. Although you may not have experienced it in its extreme state, on some level you have been affected by the misuse of energy from other people and you have also misused other people's energy as well as your own.

When we abuse someone we actually energetically damage his or her energy bodies. This allows forces or entities to enter into the chakras and affect the system until the person reaches a point of healing themselves. A child's aura is interwoven with the parent's aura until around the age of fourteen. This means that if the parent mentally, emotionally or physically abuses a child, then the parent also suffers the energetic effect of the abuse. When the child becomes an adult, it will still have energetic cords attached to its parent's chakras. Any thoughts, words or actions that occur because of the distorted beliefs it was taught as a child, will energetically feed down these cords and into the energy fields of the parents. The grown-up child also sets up cords with those it has relationships with. Depending on how it affects these people, they also pass this energy through their aura and down the cords to others and so forth, until the whole of humanity has been affected by one thought, one word and one action. Therefore to abuse is to be abused. Energetically there is no exception to this, as the laws of receiving and expressing bind everything. Even if as a child you were hit or severely reprimanded only once, you will carry this experience within your energy bodies. Its imprint will have negatively affected you mentally and emotionally and so this unnatural energetic state will have to be healed and released at some point.

Unless you have lived a life of receiving and expressing unconditional love, within you is a karmic package to heal. As a Soul you have chosen your parents and life situation in order to know and to learn to love and heal yourself of your pains. To understand abuse let us look at some of its forms.

The Emotionally Moulded Child

Emotional abuse is probably the subtlest of all the abuses because it is something that gives a foundation to all other kinds of abuse. If you have been mentally, sexually or physically abused, then you have been emotionally affected as well. When I have observed the astral body of a child who has been emotionally abused, it is always full of unexpressed energy. The child's aura can become so stagnated that it stops functioning and it no longer receives life-sustaining energy. Yet on the outside it goes through the functions of life, seemingly emotionally detached and cool. Often, as adults, emotionally abused people can become very critical, opinionated and ruthless. Children who have experienced an upbringing of strictness, where the expression of emotion was not normal, can sometimes become deceitful or unable to share their ideas. They often become isolated in their own world and this can create a wall of defence, which is actually pride.

To bend a child's will to the will of the parents without taking into consideration the feelings of the child, sets the child's programming as an adult. Sometimes the adult does not realise the extent of its emotional moulding until it enters into intimate relationships or has children of its own. A lot of our childhood beliefs are created by stopping the flow of emotion. For example, take the saying 'Boys don't cry'. Telling a boy this disconnects a piece of him from his Soul, whose main purpose is to experience emotion. Each time we tell a child not to experience its feelings, it then holds them back and stores this energy in its aura, its internal organs, muscles, chakras and the meridian system. Over a period of time this suppressed energy can result in physical illness. It also creates a false reality for the mind to work from and disconnects the Soul from its life path.

One day whilst I was laughing and sharing a joke with four other boys in the children's home, a woman falsely reported us for laughing at her. That night we were beaten by two of the carers. The next day we were taken to church and I had to sit next to one of the abusers while he sang hymns and prayed. In that moment I believed there could not possibly be a God, for if there was, then how could he allow this suffering to happen. Such was my emotional state as I sat next to a man who showed me no love, only anger, yet he loved and praised God and received his forgiveness. If it had not been for the understanding that we create our own reality and as a Soul I had chosen this path, then I would probably still be emotionally scarred by this experience. I would have missed my opportunity to let go and forgive the abusers and ultimately myself for believing I was unworthy of love.

We talk about being emotionally scarred and this is exactly how the astral energy body looks. At first it is cut open as the distorted emotional energy enters and then it seals itself, trapping this energy within. It is only when we are ready to open our old emotional wounds that we can finally release this trapped energy. The scar is then fully healed.

An emotionally abused child can often become depressed, as its sacral chakra, which sits in the lower abdomen area, is usually damaged due to distorted and false beliefs it has had to take on as its own. Around the world are many different religious beliefs, and Souls are emotionally moulded into accepting that the beliefs of their religion are the right way to God. What do we do in order to keep our beliefs protected and in place? We kill each other. We take each other's land and homes. We accuse each other. We pollute the earth and destroy the peace. We have become so separated from our Souls that we allow the mind and emotions to deal with our problems on the earth. We need to understand that to raise a gun and shoot another through the heart in defence of our country or religion is only following the will of society and not God's will. So what is society? It is a collection of individual human beings energetically joining together with their minds and emotions, to create a mass energetic field that influences us in the way we live our life.

God's will is love and we cannot be at war and be one with God at the same time. For if a supposed holy man prays before killing another, then he did not wait to hear God's reply to the prayer. Which may have been, 'Look at your enemy and see me within him.' If he had listened to this inner voice, he would not have raised his gun to another who is an aspect of God.

Love is the only true emotion and if we love another, then we allow that person the freedom to experience life. We do not try to change them or mould them into our way of thinking. I once observed a man who was a skinhead with Doc Martin boots and many earrings pierced in his ear. At his side stood a four-year-old boy who was also a skinhead with Doc Martin boots and many earrings. The man boasted to me how proud he was that his son was a replica of himself. When I looked at the boy's Soul, I saw how its individuality had been taken away. The father had moulded his energy so tightly around the boy that the Soul could no longer enter in. The Soul was waiting for the boy to reach his teens, as it needed an opportunity to push him into a rebellious stage and hopefully regain control.

What we do in each moment reflects our emotional state. If we are following the beliefs of others, then we have closed the door to our own uniqueness. There is no other person like you. It is not written anywhere that you have to belong to, or be accepted by, anything external. You are your own creator, your own other half, your own teacher, your own friend, your own brother/sister your own mother/father and your own inner child. Love yourself, let your own fears reveal themselves and more importantly find the truth out for yourself.

The Mentally Moulded Child

As with emotional abuse, if a child is mentally abused, then this has a domino affect on all the energy bodies. It also eventually ends up as stuck energy in the organs of the physical body and this can lead to illness in later life. It really does not matter what form of abuse is being given, all our energy bodies are so interrelated that each energy body relies on the one before it for its reality. The physical body relies on the etheric body, the etheric body on the emotional body, the emotional body on the mind and the mind relies on the Soul. If as a child you become distorted on any of these levels, then it will affect your whole being. Mental abuse can therefore be very destructive, as it immediately shuts down the connection with the Soul and its Divine reality. It is this disconnection which is the issue of humanity.

Mental moulding is like a disease. It corrodes the inspiration and innocence of a child's way of being. To tell a child 'they are this' and 'they are that' gives them a false identity. I once heard my friend remark to her daughter that she did not do something because she was lazy. I watched as this energy went into the child's emotional body, expanded, pushed into her mental body and became a belief within her. She reacted to the belief by doing things at a slower pace. My friend later told me she overheard her daughter tell a friend in a matter of fact way, 'Oh it's just because I'm lazy.' All three of us had to work energetically to remove this belief from the child's system by tuning into her emotions and letting her feel them and speak her truth. It amazed me how one passing comment from the parent began to shape the child's life. The child later told me she believed the comment because it came from her mother and she trusted her to know the truth. As children how many times did we take on the energy of a passing comment and try to become it or believe it to be true? Later in the book there is a technique called the 11x22s, which will reveal to us how we have taken and stored these beliefs within ourselves.

When a child is born it looks to its parents for guidance in how to deal with the environment of the era in which it lives. The child shapes its world according to the response it receives. If the response is non-loving or judgmental, then it builds walls around its innocent self to keep it protected and unpolluted. For instance, when a child first meets someone, they have an instant awareness of their energy. They understand that essentially the Soul is pure, but they also have an intuitive knowing of the distorted mental and emotional world the person carries with them, which covers up the Soul. We may try to re-programme the child by overriding its knowing, by telling them that they must like this person, for as an adult we may only see their social face. They might be a priest, a family member or an aged pensioner. What we are doing is mentally programming the child with what it can and cannot fear, and more importantly, what it can and cannot love. This leads the child into conflict, because rather than lose the adults' love, it cuts off its own inner knowing and trusts the external judgments.

    As a child I was very aware of the people that came into the children's home looking for a child to adopt. Most of them had the desire to adopt a baby rather than an older child. I soon realised that a baby is like a book waiting for an imprint. It is a blank piece of paper for parents to programme their energy into and create beliefs and moulded patterns. An older child on the other hand is a book half written. To undo what society has already imprinted is too much of a challenge for some. Therefore, the early years of a child's life determine whether or not it stays linked to the Soul. If it loses its link, then later in life it will rebel to try and regain it.

    Without contact with the Soul, the mind can only decide if something is right or wrong according to what has been programmed into it. The parents are the child's role models and it believes that what they think, say and do is the right way. In the child's innocence they trust the parents and if the parents are not in touch with their Souls and are not acting from a space of love, then the child loses its identity. When it reaches adulthood it becomes a product of it parents and society's beliefs. Mental abuse is filling a child's mind with a false and fearful reality, based on what is acceptable to society and not on what is acceptable universally.

The Neglected Child

A neglected child has not only had love withheld from it, but also its physical care. When such children become adults, this neglect often displays itself as either an inability to care for themselves and meet their daily needs or they become obsessive about cleanliness and feel life has somehow contaminated them. Children can often be neglected because one or both of the parents were also neglected as children, and as they have no guidelines or understanding, they cannot give basic care. Energetically, the child has virtually no life force. They become very weak mentally and emotionally, which opens the door for astral forces and entities to enter in. These children can often try to take over the role of the parents for themselves and they become survivors. They quickly learn to physically fend for themselves, as their life so far has taught them that the earth is a painful place to be.

If you were to take a cutting off a plant, embed it in soil indoors and, when it starts to shoot, stop watering it, then what have you done? The difference between the plant and a child is that the child will not physically disappear, but they will shrivel up and die within, for it is love that sustains everything. A child whose life is built on a foundation of love will have an easier road to the Soul than the one who has not experienced care and nourishment. What is it that makes a human being withhold love and care from another who is physically young and limited? We could call it ignorance. We could say it is karmic therefore the child deserves its situation, but are we forgetting one thing? Society is also karmic. We shove troubled Souls into our dark corners and ghettos hoping they will go away. In every moment we are neglecting the cries of those in pain. When a child is found to be neglected, the neighbours say, 'Oh I knew it was going on,' or the family says, 'Well what do you expect from my sister/brother. He/she has always been like that!' All children who have been treated badly need to be healed through love, but so do the perpetrators, because they need to be healed to prevent a recurrence. All abuse reflects itself within society, for it shows us what we do to others whom we believe are less worthy of love than ourselves.

The Rejected Child

To reject a child is to withhold love. Children who have been rejected by one or both of their parents lack self-worth and they defend their vulnerability by becoming defensive, which often appears as pride. From a very early age they decide that if their parents did not love them, then they must be bad or not worthy of being loved. They either set out to prove to the world that they are lovable or they shrink inside themselves and accept their 'punishment' for being bad, which may come forth through letting others push them around. They often feel that nothing they do is good enough for their parents and they are given very little attention and encouragement.

I once observed a child, who had been emotionally rejected by her mother. She tried to attract her mother's attention by smiling and trying to make her mother laugh. When she got a response from her mother, it became an understanding that in order to receive love, she had to be good and act happy. I have also observed the opposite of this where a child only received attention when he misbehaved. This is known as 'negative attention'. Rejected children often spend a lot of their life trying to please others and make those around them happy, even if it means being unhappy themselves. They crave love and security and often have a vision of how family life should be.

Some children become so protective of themselves that they are quick to reject others before they themselves are rejected. They may become angry and frustrated very quickly and can become disruptive at school. Their behaviour is an attempt to tell the world how angry they are at not being shown love and how they want to reject the world in retaliation. Often these children can seem fiercely independent, distant and street-wise, preferring to rely only on themselves. Energetically, the cords to their parents are very weak and they are struggling with the earth energy that flows into their legs. In a sense they are trying to think like adults in order to protect themselves, but with under-developed energy bodies. If they do not make contact with loving people, aunts, uncles, teachers etc., then they may drift aimlessly as adults, believing the earth to be a negative place to live.

Parents who reject their children are often caught up in problems within their own worlds. The child may have been an 'accident' or unwelcome, although karmically everything is perfect. Usually the parent feels that he/she cannot find the time to devote to the child as he/she tries to cope with everyday life. Often parents take on a Soul and its world and when it is born, they may regret or struggle with the responsibility. When a mother has a child within a very abusive relationship, she may reject the child, passing on her belief of unworthiness. If a parent did not bond with the child throughout the pregnancy or birth, then the connection to the child will be under stress. If the parent suffers from depression or lives in fear, then rejection of the Soul on some levels is likely. Sometimes the rejection is very subtle and although the parents cater for the child's needs perfectly well, the child experiences an unspoken communication of pulling away. The Soul would have been aware of this whilst choosing its parents and it may need this rejection to bring forth the karma that it needs to deal with.

As a child I was rejected by both parents. I felt that if my mother and father could give me up, then I was not lovable. I spent a lot of years yearning to be accepted and loved. As a result of this yearning, I got into a crowd of other rejected children and we did disruptive things in order to feel accepted by each other. We had very little faith in adults. The carers in the home increased our sense of rejection by not showing us warmth and comfort. I did not know how to ask for love or show love, as I only understood how to receive rejection and express rejection. I started to build false walls around myself that would prove to others I was strong and able to cope with anything, whilst inside I was crying out to be accepted.

To reject someone who asks to be loved is to fear that if you open your heart and love him or her, they may hurt you or let you down. To be on the receiving end of rejection is to feel you are not worthy of love or that you are 'bad'. Both are an illusion and the way out of rejection is to keep your heart open, speak your truth, and please no one else to get love and acceptance. Only love and accept yourself and this will bring you the healing that you need.

The Sexually Abused Child

When someone says the words 'sexual abuse' to you, what is your first immediate thought or picture within your mind? Sexual abuse is such a judged topic, that within society it is still taboo to talk about it. I have met married couples that did not reveal their childhood abuse to each other until many years into their marriage. They consciously hid it well, but subconsciously they attracted to themselves someone with the same issue to heal. I have met children who have been sexually abused from birth right up to their teen years. For some it never ends, as they move into sexually abusive relationships within their adult life. I have observed the aura of sexually abused children. It is very small, almost pulled tight to the body for protection. The earth energy, which should come up through the legs and into the genital area, is non-existent. It is as if their earthly experience up to date has been so difficult that they are not grounded here and they are ready to leave if the moment allowed it.

I have seen the inner realisation of young children when they become aware that what has happened to them is not right and that their playmates do not have the same experience. At this point shame and blame takes root in the child and they either become unreachable by retreating into themselves or they exert themselves by becoming angry and abusive when they are away from the abuser. Many children experience being detached from their physical bodies whilst they are being abused. Often they report observing the scene from several rooms in the building all at the same time. This splitting of their energy is caused by the Soul parting its energy bodies and trying to prevent itself from being fully present in the physical situation. Due to this energetic removal, the memory of the abuse can become blocked out or it may seem faraway and muffled. As the imprint becomes deeply stored within the emotional body, the effect of the abuse often plays itself out in dreams or nightmares. This is because in the sleep state we enter into the astral world and face what we have emotionally stored there.

The sexual abuser's energy field is always deeply blocked and dysfunctional. Their beliefs and conditional upbringing have given them no guidance on how to love, and what usually attracts them to the child is the pureness and the innocence of the life radiating through it. I will always remember the film 'The Green Mile' in which it was said that 'The abusers love their victims to death'. Energetically, there are two types of abusive energy. One is expressed through anger and bitterness and the other is an illusory projection of love. For example, the father may tell the child he does this because he loves him/her and through his dysfunctional state and neediness, he really believes this to be true. The child then becomes confused about the definition of love, and guilt enters into and pollutes its energy field. The child believes that to reject its father who loves it in this way, is wrong.

There is nothing worse on the earth than living a confused life. Confusion is like being caught up in a fog, whereby the light is dim and we cannot see the truth of any given situation. The job of the parents is to teach the child to distinguish between truth and illusion, but if we are living in confusion, so too will the child. The only answer is to teach unconditional love, especially to those confused children who grew up to be confused adults and who are now doing the same to their children. There is no judgment of perpetrators, only an understanding that they have got lost in the fog whilst searching for love.

The Physically Abused Child

Physically abused children have very depleted energy. Their aura often has holes and tears in it and the chakras have become so weak that the protective sheath which covers them is seriously damaged or missing. They live constantly on the edge of their nerves, as they often try to please the abuser to extreme ends in order to keep the peace. The child's whole energy can sometimes be a very dirty yellow colour due to the constant fear they live in. As fear resides in the kidneys, they usually suffer from kidney deficiency, which may result in bed-wetting, night sweats, dry mouth and even asthma attacks. At the time of the abuse the Soul is often far removed from the body and watches from a distance. This is why these children can become forgetful, distant and solitary. Each time the child is hit, a vibration echoes through its whole energy system and for a single moment the child experiences a stillness. This moment is very similar to death and it can seem timeless. This is because the energy bodies are registering the impact of the destructive vibration.

Physical violence is usually carried out through anger. The energy of anger is layers of suppressed emotion and, when a situation causes it to rise, the surging force can become extremely destructive. If an adult expresses anger towards a child, the child will then take this energy into its own energy bodies and store it up as suppressed emotion. This will often result in angry outbursts whilst still a child or it will manifest in adulthood. If this suppressed energy is not expressed as anger, it can often move into grief or sadness. The child then creates a false safe world, where very few people are allowed to enter in. They may also become suspicious of other people's motives. The side effect of anger is guilt, as after the attack the abuser often goes through a period of sorrow for their actions and the child can feel that somehow it is to blame. If the abuser is a loved one, this circle of attack and remorse can confuse the child and they may get thrown into emotional torment between hating and loving their abuser.

Due to the beatings I often received whilst living in the children's home, it was not until I reached my teens that I began to have the courage to stand up for myself and say no to the abuse. As a child I was too frightened to challenge the adults. I felt I would be even more rejected or more abused for speaking my truth. I would therefore be very obedient to the rules inside the home, but became destructive out in the streets. At one point my brother, other boys and myself had finally taken enough and we decided to run away, but first we had to acquire the finances. So we dressed my brother up as a cowboy with a mask, hat, toy gun and a tepee for his cloak and sent him into the street to mug someone for their money. Whilst we waited around the corner, my six-year-old brother pointed his gun at a passing woman and asked her for all her money. She laughed, ruffled his hair and walked on. We were so disappointed at not being able to get free from our fearful situation. Had that woman known of our desperation, maybe things would have been different.

It is often the case with abused children. Energetically, they have not fully formed, so their attempts at letting the world know their pain are sometimes hidden in childish play. As adults we often brush this off as unimportant or even as humorous, not realising the deeper meaning the child is trying to share with us. At times children can be so desperate, that they become frustrated with themselves and intolerable to be with. Their whole aura and chakra system is very damaged, clogged and open to the negative energetic influences of the earth. If the karma is too much to handle, the Soul pulls away at this point, leaving the body to be used by these influences, hence the term, 'a soulless being'. These energies that have now taken over the body are the ones which are responsible for creating a lot of the chaos we see on the earth today. As adults, these children can often be the ones who turn to drugs and alcohol or become extremely aggressive. In a sense they can take no more abuse, they have had enough, so they use self-destructive means as an illusory escape from their inner pain. All this happens because we did not love, accept and nurture the Souls that resided in our children, and still the chain goes on into the next generation.

Bullying

Many children are bullied in the home or at school by other children or even teachers. To bully a person renders them powerless and can cause great emotional distress. So why is it one child is bullied and not another? Over the years I have been fortunate enough to be friends with a huge family of sixteen children. It recently emerged that out of the ten sisters five were sexually abused by the father, three were made a pass at and two experienced no attempt of abuse, they were not even aware of their sisters' situation. Each abused sister thought it was only happening to them, so they kept quiet fearing that if they told anyone they would be disbelieved.

When I observed the energy of the five abused women, I recognised that each had brought with them from other lifetimes an inner belief of not being worthy. They then created outside situations that would challenge them to break out, to stand up for themselves and recognise their true worth. This experience was their karma. The three sisters whose father attempted to abuse them told me that they stood their ground and challenged him. Energetically, they directed energy into his aura that told him they were worthy. This made him back down. The last two sisters told me that they were the rebels of the family and throughout their life the father had very little control over them. The father had not dreamt of attempting to abuse those who were expressing more strength than he.

Let us now look at a child who has low self-worth. His energy field gives out a signal to those around him that reveals his state of being. Those who carry abusive tendencies pick up on this signal and react accordingly. Children who are energetically sensitive, but are able to stand up in the face of adversity, are maybe only challenged once or twice and then deemed too strong by the bully. Those children who do not lack self-worth or confidence are not even considered as targets for attacking forces.

A bully is usually someone who has experienced a lot of pain in his or her life. At some point they may have been made to feel worthless, therefore they usually attack weaker people to prove they still have some form of personal power. A bully may have also been brought up in a strict and angry environment. Their bullying ways may be a call for help. Once whilst walking through a park, I saw a child of about ten hit a younger child. The mother ran over and became angry. She started shouting at the bullying child until he ran off. I noticed that his energy carried a lot of unexpressed anger and the mother's reaction to him only reinforced his belief that he lived in an angry world. I wonder what would have happened if the mother had opened her heart and treated the boy as someone who needed love and understanding? I bet he would have remembered for the rest of his life that it was possible to experience love in this angry world.

Education

I am not going to give the above subject much space, because I feel the education system does not do the Soul much justice. I have yet to meet a happy teacher who agrees with it. The Latin word '*educare*' actually means to bring forth and the problem with the present education system is that we '*put in*'. Each individual Soul has experiences and knowing that goes beyond anything education could ever give it. If we understood that God is the ultimate artist, the ultimate author, mathematician, musician, composer etc, then we would be near the truth of the abilities of the Soul. The role of education should bring out the qualities that the Soul wishes to expand on in this lifetime and we can only do this by dropping the current system. I am not saying children should not learn how to read, write and do basic maths, what I am saying is that we have placed too much emphasis on developing the intellect and not enough attention on the individual creativity of the Soul.

In fact individualism is virtually non-existent in schools, for the child is immediately put into groups according to its age and then academic ability. I knew a boy at school who was a genius with his hands, yet this fact went unnoticed. I could see the Soul was heading for a life as a brilliant artist. I later met up with the boy as a man and he was completely lost. He had not received the earthly help he needed to bring forth his Soul's abilities. We therefore need to allow the *Soul* to guide us, not the rules and regulations. For example, if a child shows talent in a subject, we need to allow him to let go of other subjects where only a basic learning is required, so that he can make space to express these qualities. As a society we cannot bring ourselves to do this because we live in a fear-driven 'what if' world, so we fill the child up with useless information 'just in case' he needs it later. The Soul often takes a back seat at a time when development is important. As an adult it then has to correct the conditioning it received from its years at school.

Worksheet

If you are a parent how did you feel throughout the pregnancy and birth? Can you see the bigger picture of your child being a Soul with its own world?

1. How would you describe your childhood? What are your emotions around your childhood? Can you understand why you placed yourself in this upbringing? Can you see the underlying beliefs and fears that your childhood brought forth?

2. Have you been emotionally and mentally conditioned? How do you know?

3. Have you been neglected or rejected? How do you feel about this? What is the underlying fear? What is the belief? Can you keep your heart open to yourself and others when faced with rejection?

4. Have you been physically or sexually abused? What emotions does this bring up in you? Have you told anybody else? What does sharing your pain say to you? What is your underlying fear around your experience? What is the belief? Do you love yourself?

5. What was your experience of school? What does this reveal to you? What is the underlying fear? What is your belief?

Brainstorming

Take a piece of paper and, in a circle in the centre, write down a negative emotion such as anger, pride, jealousy or grief. On the outside of this circle write down all the words you feel around this emotion. If it is anger you may write 'frustration,' 'not in control,' 'not heard,' etc. Do this until you have exhausted your mind. Now close your eyes and allow yourself to feel the emotions you have placed around the anger. Feel your frustration, your fear of being out of control and so on. Whilst doing this try not to direct your thoughts to people or memories, just allow yourself to feel without naming or thinking anything. When you have finished, allow yourself to feel what life would be like without these negative emotions.

You can do this exercise for all the emotions that come up from within you and it is a very good way of revealing the fear behind the emotions. To heal the emotions you need to feel the fear, let it go and then feel the love in its place. In the last chapter of this book there are more techniques for healing, but first of all you need to recognise that your present state of life is the result of all your thoughts, words and actions. There is no exception.

4

The Rebellion Years

Maybe this is all that is needed to start a revolution.
The more aware we become,
The greater the revolution.
This is a silent revolution,
Where we do not have to preach to others,
Where just being silent and aware,
Brings about a change.
We are masters of our own destiny,
Can we let go of the past to be in the now?

The Effects of Childhood

The greatest realisation for a parent is that our children were never 'ours' and we can only lay claim to the genetic cells within the physical body. The consciousness and life that runs through the body belongs only to itself. This life is not ten or fourteen, but timeless and holds within it the potential for God consciousness, Christ consciousness, Buddha consciousness. It really does not matter what label we give it. It is unconditional love expressing and receiving itself. As parents, through our tribal beliefs, we subconsciously try to mould and change the child into something we are proud of creating. If we are not God realised, then this moulding is not love at its best. When the child reaches its teenage years, the rebellion and inner struggle that the teenager goes through show how our influences and beliefs have disturbed the Soul. The more anger and rebellion, the more suppressed the emotions have been through its conditioned upbringing.

The teenage years can prove to be a tiring time for parents. We need to ask within ourselves, 'Am I trying to control the situation?' for control can be blatant or it can be subtle. For example, a new recruit in the armed forces is re-conditioned to fit into a strict regime. In a sense he loses his personality and he becomes the army. The regimentation makes sure everyone thinks, speaks and acts in the same way. There is no room for uniqueness. This is blatant mind control, but subtle control pretends to allow you your uniqueness whilst manipulating your emotions from behind the scenes. Take, for example, the saying 'If you loved me, you would do this for me.'

This subtle control is often used by parents to manipulate the emotions of a teenager in order to reach a desired outcome. As parents we may want our children to fulfil the dreams that we did not accomplish. In some historically powerful families, like the ancient Egyptian royal family, the son has usually followed in the footsteps of the father and become even more powerful. At what point do we stop fulfilling our earthly parent's dreams and start fulfilling our Heavenly Father's? For only by following this direction do we fulfil the will of God.

Strengths and Weaknesses

For the child the earthly mother is a reflection of the Mother God and the earthly father is a reflection of the Father God. At a very young age the child does not separate itself into male or female, because it feels itself to be an extension of both parents. It is only as it grows that it begins to look at its physical form and understand it is more like mum or dad. This is a crucial moment for a child, for it immediately recognises the strengths and weaknesses of the male and female role models in its life. If the parents' relationship is a balanced and loving one, then the child understands weaknesses can become strengths, but if the parents' relationship is abusive or unstable, then the child learns weakness is something that needs to be hidden. If there is a lack of one parental energy and too much of the other, the child will often feel unfulfilled and may search for the missing energy in adult relationships.

Between thirteen and nineteen the teenagers begin to bring forth and experience the male and female energies from within themselves. For example, in one moment they may become aggressive, in the next moment they may become submissive. In effect, they are taking both the male and female energies to their extremes to see which level is comfortable and how its actions affect those around them. This emotional behaviour resides in the third chakra (the solar plexus) which rests at the parting of the ribs. It is this centre that allows the teenager to experience personal power. If the upbringing has not been loving, encouraging and supportive or the Soul calls forth suppressed emotions from past lives, then this personal power can become scattered or even channelled into negative pursuits. The teenager is also trying out all the learned scenarios it has experienced so far. For instance, one day he may react to his mother as his father does and the next day he may react to his father as his mother does. The teenager is actually trying to work through his parents' energy within his aura. He is basically trying on his parents' shoes for size to find out whether he wants to react to the world as his parents do or whether he wants to find a deeper and unique sense of self.

From around the age of fourteen the Soul begins to call on the growing child to turn within and search for its true self, not its learned self. The teenage years are therefore years of change, excitement and discovery. It is also the time when the Soul can take control and have a bit more responsibility to act upon its own initiative. At this point, if the Soul has been given enough freedom when it was younger, it will carry on expressing itself and enjoying the freedom as it gets older. If it experienced restrictions and inhibitions when it was younger, then as a teenager it will bring forth a deeper rebellion to try to break the restrictions. It is in the teenage years that the outer wall of the aura starts to take shape. Initially, it is very soft and not fully formed. This leaves the teenage Soul vulnerable to the external influences of its peer group, elders, music, media, books. For this reason teenagers often form their own clans, which are separate tribes from the parental tribe to which they once belonged.

The Rebellion

Energetically the Soul is now pulling away from the parent's aura in order to fully form his/her own and this usually occurs in stages. Teenagers can often become linear in their vision. They can live in total chaos and do not see the distortion around them. For example, their rooms become disorderly and they no longer help with the housework. The same thing is happening within their energy bodies, for they are trying to build a world around them which is not yet stabilised. This instability is a conflict, as they believe they are stable and that they know what they are doing. To the teenager, it is the parents who are directionless! The parents, who are the observers, can often see all the mistakes the teenager is making, and try to guide them. They sometimes even try to take over, not realising the child's rebellion is to get away from the parents' guidance and form their own.

This friction also reveals the parents' fears. For example, if the mother has clung to the child throughout its life, then when it enters into the rebellion, the mother will hold on tighter and the child will struggle even more. If the father has been rejecting, then the child may go to extremes to get the father's attention. The parent has to stand back and see what it is the child is saying to them and what it is they need to help them through this process of building their astral body. As parents, do we let the child run headlong into the distance? Or do we say, 'Be careful, look closely at these things,' and make the child aware of the situation, then leave them to deal with it on their own?

From a karmic viewpoint the Soul is now taking control, therefore we need to allow the individual Soul the space to enter in, as this way there will be a gradual releasing and not an extreme letting go. This is a time for setting clear boundaries for the child. If they make a mistake and go beyond the boundary, then they will quickly realise it and come back into the limits, so that, through experiences, they are given more and more freedom until they know their own limitations.

Through this process the parent's are allowing the child to pull out of their aura for the child to create his/her own one stage at a time, rather than the child taking a leap into nothingness. Teenagers cannot see into the future, they see only now, therefore they do not know how to plan or conserve energy. They are always looking for the quick fix, which is the desire to experience the buzz of everything right now! They may search for this in alcohol, cigarettes, drugs, and music. They have not yet learned how to pace themselves. This is because their astral body is not wide enough to hold a steady flow. Teenagers' auras may only radiate one to two metres from the body, therefore the teenagers have not expanded into tomorrow and they can only see what is in front of them. They are trying to fit all of their sensations and experiences into a small world and find it difficult to cope with the overflow. This is why the parents are still needed and must not allow children to go rampant as they have nowhere to store the experience, therefore they do not have full understanding of their actions and events.

A client I know has two children and his elder son's karma is mainly with him. Over the years the client taught his son to be very aware of his emotions and together they have worked through a lot of their issues. When his son reached the teenage years he rebelled against his father for about a month. He soon realised the rebellion was not needed and he has since blossomed into his own personal power. The father's second child is a teenage daughter whose karma is mainly with her mother, and because her mother has not yet worked through some of her own control issues, the daughter keeps challenging her by pushing all the limits. One of the ways she does this is by the type of music she listens to, which is often filled with swearing.

A lot of pop groups are made up of people in their twenties who market their music to young teenagers. What they do not realise is that these teenagers have not yet fully structured their energy bodies, so their underdeveloped system cannot cope with this older input of information. We are familiar with 'girl power' where girls of a very young age were told to 'do this and that' by certain pop groups. The young girls who followed the groups are now teenagers and they are left trying to live up to an unnatural reality that is still within their systems. These pop role models with their musical influence over children are bringing about rebellion at a much younger age. They are forcing the energy bodies to mature too quickly, which results in childhood becoming much shorter and rebellion more extreme. As an adult the Soul has additional tangled and confused energy to sort out. What these role models are unaware of is that they are karmically responsible for all of their thoughts, words and actions and the more people they influence, then the bigger the karma.

Fear of Rebellion

Some teenagers do not rebel at all, either because they have been given freedom and an understanding of how to deal with their emotions or because they are too frightened. I have met teenagers who have tried to rebel on a single occasion, but because the consequences were so severe, they never made another attempt. If, during our early years we are taught to 'speak only when spoken to' or to be 'seen and not heard' then we begin to withdraw into our inner world and we shut down our creative possibilities.

A common belief within society is that the child is always 'wrong' and the adult is always 'right!' We then expect an apology and dish out a punishment for the 'wrong behaviour' yet most parents fail to apologise to a child for being in the wrong. How can we expect our children to get it 'right' when we have followed the will of society and not the will of God? So you need to ask yourself if you are a perfect being. Do you apologise to others for your acts of imperfections? There is no 'right' and 'wrong', for what may be correct in one culture may be a crime in another. The only measure we have of understanding what is universally harmonious, is the effect our thoughts, words and actions have on the world around us. If these bring peace, then you are following a higher good, but if they bring chaos, then you need to look within yourself for the cause. If you were too afraid to rebel as a teenager, ask yourself if there is anything left unsaid. Do you have any unfulfilled dreams? Do you feel any resentment towards your parents? If so how can you release it? Your life belongs only to you and you do not have to live in the shadow of the beliefs that were instilled in you as a child. You have a right to be yourself.

The Box

Let us look at the theory that whilst growing up we live in a rectangular box, and within this box we sit facing one of the shorter walls. When we enter the teenage rebellion years we may turn and look at the longer wall and because there is more to see, we suddenly think we have changed, but we are still in the box. At this point our aura will fill the whole box and we may settle down, happy with our view. In truth there has been no real revolution, as real revolution means we have to get away from the system and this would mean getting out of our box. Most of humanity is trapped as the rebellion has only been within the box. They are confined in this small space.

Have you ever heard of the story about the fish who lived in a pond? He thought his pond was the largest and deepest water that ever was. One day a fish from the sea visited him. He described to the pond fish the vastness and depth of the sea and told him he was a prisoner in this small shallow space. The pond fish called him a liar and sent him away. The sea fish was free. The pond fish was trapped in illusion.

I have even observed people who, as teenagers, decided to travel the world. After getting out of the box to embark on an external search, they returned only to climb back into the box again! Very few people are able to get out of their boxes. To do so means reviewing their mental and emotional structures. I have met many people who rebelled as teenagers only to reach their twenties and live just as their parents did. Their houses are decorated in a similar style, they have similar holidays, eat similar food, have similar tastes etc. They never really expanded and became their unique self, which is the Soul. This way of living is what is known as 'the comfort zone'. People are so afraid of the unknown that they fall back into what is familiar. They do not realise this comfort zone is impermanent and is subject to the laws of change. The only permanence in our lives is the Soul, which is love. It is only here where we will experience true comfort and security and it is only by becoming free from our conditioning, that the illusions are revealed. When we are free from the waves of change which come through pleasure and pain, then the Soul will rise above impermanence and fly. A person can go to as many spiritual workshops as they want, read hundreds of books and visit countless gurus/teachers, but until they have looked at and changed their inner world, then there will be no change in the external world. The greatest aspect of teenage rebellion is the Soul knocking on the door for you to enter in and see what you are made of.

The Confused Parents

I have met many parents who have done all they can to give the child a balanced life. There has been no major conditioning that the Soul cannot deal with naturally and yet the child's rebellion is very extreme. We often hear of these cases in the media, where the child has gone into serious drug abuse, prostitution or crime, but the parents speak of the wonderful life the child has had. They cannot understand why the child is in this situation. Sometimes the Soul chooses to be born into these loving environments, so that it has a good foundation from which to experience its later life. Often it is karmic and the Soul has a choice to enter into extreme negative experiences to clear up and even meet people in order to repay its karmic debts.

The parents have to trust the bigger picture and understand that the situation has arisen despite all they have done for their child. In fact they have given the Soul a deeper understanding of love and the chances of the Soul coming out of the negative lifestyle is high because of the positive childhood experience. Sometimes because the child has only experienced a positive life, it sinks deeply into the influences of peers who do negative things. In a sense it is trying the other side of the coin, so it can understand and therefore master the negativity that roams the earth. Giving the child the most loving environment does not guarantee a perfect end result. What we can do is give our children good foundations, so that when the Soul takes full control of the body and begins to steer it in its karmic direction, no matter what it experiences, it knows love.

The Effects of Emotional Moulding

If a child has not been taught how to master or feel his emotions, then the teenage years can be very erratic for the Soul. It will find that although it resides on a planet of emotions, it has no foundation to work from and it can shock those around it with its outbursts. Energetically, the earth energy is rising up the spine towards the third chakra and it knocks loose any stagnant emotions in the system. Maybe for the first time the Soul is experiencing dramatic moving energy and in order to incur a shift, it projects this energy outwards. In its act of rebellion the Soul is breaking free of the numbness which was created around it as a child. It is beginning to express all that it wanted to say and feel in order for it to heal and be a free flowing being.

If the parents allow it to unfold then a great learning can emerge, but problems occur when the parents try to keep the lid on the teenager's emotions. This forcing down of emotion blocks the Soul from re-establishing connection to the mind and instead of the teenager screaming, they have a little shout, become quiet and then carry on living their life in semi-numbness. Have you ever felt neither awake nor asleep, caught up in a limbo land where everything is happening around you, yet you are not a part of it? This is a state of numbness, where we live in accordance with a set of rules. We do our daily duty and fulfil the expectations of others, yet we never feel truly alive. This is because we did not break out of our emotional conditioning. We accepted the set of beliefs we were given as a child and have lived them daily ever since.

The Effects of Mental Moulding

The mental body of a self-realised person is scintillating with gold strands and their energy is very quick and fine. This shows that mentally they are one with their Soul and everything they think is a Soul impression. This creates a clear-moving emotional body, so they are able to react to others with detached compassion and their actions create only harmony. When I have observed a person who holds mental conditioning then, depending upon the extent of their beliefs, the mental body can range from being non-existent to looking like structures or dull in colour. These structures, if backed with emotions, can often take the form on the astral plane as buildings, objects, and people and we may pass these structures on to our children. For example, we may have had an experience of being bitten by a stray dog. We then tell our child that stray dogs bite and the picture of our experience enters into the child's mental body and an emotion of fear takes root. Whilst walking in the street, the child may come across an ownerless dog. Immediately the picture comes forth, the child becomes fearful and a belief is set. Later in life she in turn may tell her children that stray dogs bite and the picture, which will have grown because her experience has now been added, gets passed to her children until finally a child down the line may see a pack of dogs chasing her in her nightmares.

This is how structures and beliefs are passed on. When the child reaches its teenage years the Soul calls forth all its belief system for it to look at and it begins to test all that it has been told is 'this' or 'that'. If as a parent you tell your child that smoking is dangerous, whilst puffing away on twenty a day, then the teenager will maybe try out smoking or alcohol, drugs, or truancy. They begin to take all the things that society said were not available to them as a child and they try them on for size. The teenager thinks it is an adult, but because they have no understanding of boundaries, everything is taken to its extreme. This causes them to lose their sensing and wider vision. They can only see straight forwards and if you ask them to look at the greater picture, taking into consideration other people's feelings, they cannot, as only *their* ideas and opinions matter. The teenagers also begin to allow their own judgments to mould them, and they start with acknowledging their parents' weaknesses, whereas, when they were small children they saw only their parents' strengths. The teenager is facing an identity crisis, for what the tribe has told them is their reality, the Soul is telling them is an illusion. This sends them into a panic and they outwardly grasp at different things to give themselves comfort in order to avoid looking within at their emotions.

Energetically the mind and its conditioning is being broken down, but because the teenager does not have the tools to face the suppressed emotions and fears, they simply replace old judgments with new ones. When they become adults, they may realise that the new judgments are not much different from those of their parents, only re-arranged. Teenagers are very vulnerable to the various forces on the earth that know how to tempt the teenager in its various aspects of life, often interfering with their free will by dangling big carrots in front of them. These forces come in the guises of drugs, alcohol, money, material desires and the pressure to fit in. Although teenagers do need to find their own boundaries and limits, they will still need the parents to provide these for them until they are twenty-one. It is only at this age that the aura is fully formed and the Soul is responsible for living its life according to its own will.

The Effects of Neglect

As in all conditioning there are many different levels of neglect. Each child will be affected in its own way, but energetically they will all have similarities. What I write about is not based on a set of rules but an observation of people's energy. When I first meet someone I can view any of the spiritual, mental, astral and etheric levels that needs attention and, from the information stored there, the person's life is revealed to me. The person then needs to go to the core issue of their emotional pain and release the stuck energy. Each person reacts differently to an experience. For example, one child may be severely neglected, yet it is able to handle it well. Another child may experience neglect on a minor level, but can become very distressed. When both the children reach the teenage years their rebellion will vary in intensity, but where it has affected them in their energy bodies will be similar. A neglected teenager is usually very vulnerable to influences from others, and unless the child is taken from the situation into a caring environment, they can fall into negative pursuits, such as crime and drugs. What they are doing is trying to find some form of personal power, but through the wrong means.

    The child's experience will also affect the astral bodies of the parents. I have often observed this in families who live in run-down areas, where the only outlet is to have a drink at the local pub or club. They take the teenager with them and allow it to drink at a young age. The teenager then adapts to this patterning and it extends to being allowed out late at night. It seems that the parents do not care and the child is allowed to go rampant. The child eventually ends up on the streets and may become involved in gangs who commit crimes. He knows no boundaries as he has tested the limits and found there is no one to say, 'Do not do that' or 'You do not have to get involved in the world of crime.' He has been left to his own devices and, because he cannot see beyond the moment, he does not think about the consequences of his actions.

Neglected children find it difficult to express themselves and often remain very detached from life. They can also enter into sexual relationships quite early as their need to belong is very strong, yet if they have children whilst still young, they often run away from the situation because they have no solid foundation of family life. Their rebellion is frustration and anger projected onto a world that has been unsupportive. Their logic in life is that they do not have to care for others because they were not cared for themselves. Underneath, these teenagers have a very deep understanding of life. If they find someone whom they can trust and who can help them unravel their true self, then as adults these children can give substance to others and life.

The Effects of Rejection

Teenagers, who have experienced emotional or physical rejection from their parents as a child, often reject either themselves or other people. Some of these teenagers enter into relationships early in order to experience love and security but, if they have low self-esteem, they can often hold onto the relationship when it should have ended. This desire to feel loved and needed may lead them into abusive relationships as adults where, in their aim to please the loved one, they forget about themselves. They may also leave home quite early. This is a form of rejecting the parents, as hidden within them is the need to hurt those who have rejected them, so that they may feel the pain of being dismissed as unlovable. These teenagers often create masks, appearing fun-loving and independent. They have an ability to gather many people around them, but can drop them instantly with no expression of emotion. It is difficult to penetrate the walls of a rejected teenager, as they have an understanding of survival and, if a parent pushes their will onto them, the teenager will just reject them.

Pride is the emotion that governs rejection, and teenagers can enter into extremes of unworthiness or superiority. They often become involved in gangs, relationships and situations where they are made to feel small, or they are the leader, abuser etc. The Soul is trying to give the teenager different extremes so that their way of reacting to the world becomes apparent, bringing to light their need to be loved and accepted. The teenager therefore tests everyone he meets and tries to find trust within people. Each time the teenager is let down his belief in rejection is re-enforced and the walls become higher. As an adult they may live their whole lifetime rejecting others before they themselves are rejected, until eventually they reach inside themselves and find the trust in the Soul and not in the outside world.

The Effects of Sexual Abuse

I cannot begin to describe the extreme effects that physical and sexual abuse have on the energy bodies. Sometimes they are so damaged that a person can end up with a terminal illness, and as I described in the childhood section, all illness is due to the state of a person's mental, emotional and spiritual balance. If a person has had pain inflicted on any of these levels either by himself or another person, then in time this will reflect in the body as minor or major illnesses. A teenager who has been or is still being sexually abused will be deeply affected on every level of his/her being.

If you are not aware of the workings of energy, then it can be hard to detect a sexually abused person, because they go to great lengths to hide it. They often channel their energy into outside pursuits that shut out the memories. The teenager usually becomes either submissive by being open to abuse from others, including prostitution, being bullied at work and suffering abusive relationships, or he/she becomes aggressive, by getting angry in the work place, aggressive on the football pitch or taking advantage of and abusing others. In this way the teenager proves that the world can no longer hurt him. Sometimes as adults they find solace in other sexually abused people, whether or not they consciously know of their abuse. This is because on some level there is an understanding of and empathy with each other's inner pain. In relationships problems can occur when one person wants to heal and reach a deeper state of love, but the other one does not. This is because when a person opens their energy bodies to release the suppressed emotions, this will cause the energy body of the other person to open and he/she will enter into an emotional crisis.

I could say all abuse is karmic, but this really does not answer the situation, for if you have gone through an abusive experience, then this explanation only leads to guilt, as to be abused means somewhere along the line you have abused others, therefore the repayment has become an eye for an eye and a tooth for a tooth. Let us look at it another way. Whatever you experience in your life reveals to you where you love yourself and where you lack self-love. If as a Soul you chose difficult parents who have helped you to bring forth your lack of self-love, then this gives you an opportunity to face your beliefs, heal them and then you never have to experience that level again. If you get trapped in the blame scene and always hold others responsible for your pain, then you will keep calling forth relationships with the same scenario until you accept your part in the game of life. It is true that most humans wait until they are on their knees and filled with much suffering before beginning to look within themselves for the cause of their pain. Another way to look at being abused is to see it as an act of love. Your Soul may have placed you in an environment where the abuser has abused before in other lifetimes, and in this life the abuser is faced with the same choice: do I abuse or do I finally break the negative pattern? For you to be in this situation shows you must have strength of Soul to be able to take the outcome of his or her choice.

An abuser did not intentionally come onto the earth to abuse others; they came to love and to be loved and the abused did not come onto the earth to be abused, they also came to love and to be loved. Until this is realised and recognised, humanity will continue along this current path of pain, lack of love, and judgment.

Energetically, sexual abuse affects the liver and spleen, which in turn have connections with the ovaries, testes and intestines. Most ill people I have come across who have been sexually abused have illnesses in these parts of the body. Through teaching a two-year healing course, I met a woman who had part of her colon removed due to Crohn's disease; she also needed walking aids due to acute arthritis. It emerged that her stepfather had sexually abused her as a child. For years she kept the experiences locked up within herself, which caused her to direct the suppressed energy of anger into her joints and the blame into her colon. These energies then slowly began eating away at her. Over the two years she faced her trapped emotions, until she could finally let go, forgive herself and her stepfather. She has since had the all clear from the hospital for the Crohn's disease, the arthritis has also healed and she is living a pain-free life. There is nothing outside ourselves. We create all that happens in order to love ourselves more, for there is only love. What we experience in this world are situations where more love is needed.

The Effects of Physical Abuse

Living in the children's home I met a lot of children of all different ages who had been physically abused and each one showed signs of outer anger or inner rage. This emotion is trapped fear. It stems from being completely powerless at the time of the abuse, not having the physical strength to be able to protect oneself. When the child reaches the rebellion years they set out to prove to the world that they now have some power, so woe to anybody who crosses their path! Behind their anger these teenagers often carry a feeling of deep sadness and a sense of not belonging, so they may latch onto street gangs, drugs, alcohol and crime. As a healer, I met a twenty-year-old man who was beaten, starved and kept locked in a cellar until he was three years old. He was then found and placed in a children's home. As a teenager he became very distrustful. If people tried to get close to him he would accuse them of doing things behind his back. He finally ended up on the streets in crime. It is sad how children base their view of love on how their parents treat them. They think that if the parents do not love them, then nobody else will love them either.

If the child has suffered extreme physical abuse, the Soul will often try to use the teenage years to break out of the cycle. It will do this by searching for people who can help it before it gets lured into negative pursuits. Often these children may latch onto a certain teacher or join after-school clubs etc. Although it does not heal the teenager, it gives the Soul time to move closer in and expand its contact with the person's mind in order to gain more control of its direction. I have met adults who have endured immense abuse as children, but have gone on to heal themselves without having to experience drugs, alcohol or crime. What is common among them is that they found support in something or someone along the way. We all need support at some point in our life and somebody once said to me, 'Treat each person you meet as if it was their last day on the earth.' How would this way of being change your life?

Career

When the child reaches around seven the energy moves up from the base chakra and into the second chakra at the navel. This chakra is the child's creative centre and it is here that they start to get into role-play and fantasise about being heroes and princesses. The Soul usually plays out its life path in childish games, and what you most desired to be as a child is usually what the Soul came here to do as an adult. The teenager in the rebellion stage loses this connection, as energetically they are unstable and they often fall into the will of society and search for financial success rather than inner fulfilment and joy. If we follow the Soul's guidance, then it reveals the ultimate space for us to expand into beyond our wildest dreams. Problems can occur if the teenager is being guided into employment that satisfies the parents or teachers. This can cause great distress to the Soul and it is only later in life as an adult, that the Soul may gain enough confidence to break away and follow its childhood dreams. As a parent we can help the teenager by talking about his deepest dreams and what he liked doing as a child. This may bring forth his creative energy, which will guide him onto the right path.

When I look back over my life there was nothing in my previous employment that made me believe I would become a spiritual teacher, but what I do see is that my soul guided me into situations where I experienced people on all levels of life. I now know this was needed, as I had to learn and understand about the deeper aspects of humanity. Sometimes a teenager may embark on a journey, which to society seems ludicrous, but the Soul is rejoicing. It knows where it is going and its path has just begun.

The Menstrual Cycle

When we look at nature, we can see she has many cycles. Her obvious cycle is that of the four seasons. She has spring, which is birth; summer, which is growth; autumn, which is release; and winter, which is preparation. As the female gives birth to creation, so she also follows these cycles. She has a monthly cycle, a seasonal cycle, and a yearly cycle. In the middle of the monthly cycle is her fertile time. At this point she is at her most positive, and instinctively she searches for a compatible partner to make her pregnant. Most women are not aware of this, but there are a few pointers. For example, she may feel good about herself, be more playful and assertive. Even if she is in a relationship, she notices other men more at this time of the month. Just as female animals vie for the strongest genes in another, so does the human female. A lot of affairs and romances start when a woman is at the most fertile point in her cycle.

The next phase of the cycle is towards the end of fertility. Here her body pauses, as it determines whether or not it is pregnant. If it is not then it begins the process of release. The week before the period is due a woman is at her most sensitive. At this point the water content of her body increases and as water contains memory and emotions, she therefore becomes prone to mood swings. The negative emotions are at their peak approximately a day before the period is due.

The female is the processor of emotional energy and because we are living on a planet of emotions, this is how she helps nature to balance the planet. If she suppresses her emotions before the period, then after the period, they move back into her system until the next month. If she becomes aware of the flow of her body, then over time she is able to clear all her suppressed issues from all her life and also help the planet to clear.

A woman's service to the earth is so very important. If she uses the contraceptive pill, she moves out of tune with the Mother God, because contraception controls the hormones of the body and alters the natural flow with the planet. This is a dilemma, because the pill helps a woman take charge of her child-bearing, but it also suppresses her emotions and stops her from being fully in service. We therefore have something external that again is trying to control the internal.

When a woman comes to know herself, and heals her emotions, her Soul fully takes charge of her life. In this process she will not conceive without consultation with her Soul. In other words she will be consciously in control of her child-bearing and will not have to rely on external sources to do it for her. We have lost this tool because we have strayed from the truth of our being. After the menstrual period, the female pulls her energy inside herself. If she has suppressed her emotions, then she will go through a restless point as the water deposits the toxins back into the cells. For a short time a woman may feel alone, as if nothing in the outside world can give her comfort. It is almost like grieving for something that is lost, but she does not know what it is. If a woman is fully aware and allows her emotions to surface before the period, then at this point she will feel at one with the Mother God instead of feeling disconnected.

If a woman becomes aware and consciously starts to work with her connection to nature, she also begins to flow with the seasonal changes. She starts to make intuitive decisions that can seem uncanny. For example, she will know exactly when to move house, when to change jobs, when to invest and so on. She will even be able to flow with daily issues. She will know what type of food the body needs, she will know what letter the postman is bringing, who is going to call, when to go out. In a sense she will know when to be active and create, and when to be still and prepare. If she follows her intuitions, then each yearly cycle will become more abundant and full. She will know what part of her needs pruning and what part of her needs encouragement. She will act in perfect accordance with both parts.

All the above describes the female's experience of dealing with emotion, but where does the male fit in? Men think that because they are physically different, they do not have these cycles. What they forget is that they are energetically half male and half female! So a male also enters into cycles, but these reflect the universe rather than the earth. Because the male energy is linked to the mental plane, his cycle is a mental one rather than an emotional one. In the beginning, humanity, by its thoughts, polluted the earth's emotional field. A woman's period is therefore a reflection of the polluted emotional energy pushing up into the mental world to be acknowledged and released.

If a man were to become aware of himself, he would notice that his thoughts go through a monthly process of quiet, positive, busy, and negative. If he is aware of his inner female, then he will know that his emotions need acknowledging and healing. His cycle is similar to the female's in that he has a period of inner reflection, which is a time of positive lofty thoughts; a birth, where he adapts his ideas and puts together a format; a growth, where it expands to fruition; and a decline, where he pulls his energy in ready to reach lofty ideas again. If all businesses on the earth became aware of the laws of birth, growth, death and reflection, then there would be a lot less confusion in the world.

A man experiences problems when he becomes stuck in his thoughts, because if he fears failure or has experienced failure, then he finds it difficult to get out of the reflection period. In other words he is always in the winter season and he cannot get his ideas to materialise in the physical. To create in the physical, a male needs to recognise his female energy, because she is responsible for bringing forth the astral energy that is needed to create. This is typical of businesses that have brilliant ideas, but are not stable enough to realise them, or go bankrupt very easily. It is because the female support is lacking in the energy of the creator or management. If a female tries to create without the male energy, then she will have the entire earthly tools at her disposal, but she will not know the direction to go in. Both energies need each other in order to create heaven on earth.

When a Soul first comes onto the earth, it is affected by the natural flows and influences of the earth, the moon, the sun and the planets. When it tries to break free, it is trying to break the control of these influences. This is played out in the cycles within the male or female life that the Soul has entered into. In the female, the energy rises up from the earth and into her lower chakras. She balances this within her centre at the abdomen. When it reaches the peak of fullness, which is just before the period begins, it then begins a descent back into the earth. In the male, energy from the cosmos descends into him through the crown chakra, and he balances this in his centre at the abdomen. This energy draws into his body all his thoughts that he has stored within his aura. After reaching its peak it then begins its ascent back into the cosmos. These natural waves are reflected more obviously within the female monthly cycle, where the energy of the earth, as it rises, pushes up emotional patterns to be observed and released. During this process if the emotions are not cleared, when the energy begins its descent, it pulls the emotions back into the body where they are stored until the next rising.

As the rising earth energy begins to fill the female, it starts to push emotional energy out of the cells, which forces her mind to become over-active. At this point the pressure of the emotions rising in the body can create what is known as premenstrual tension (PMT). This tension is often externally projected because the female does not know how to deal with her rising emotions and her negative state of mind. When the flow of blood starts, the risen earth energy begins to descend. This releases the mental pressure on

the female and thereby ends the premenstrual tension. At this point, when the energy lowers and the emotions re-stabilise in the body, she starts to draw more light into her body from the cosmos. After the period, a female can feel more spiritually connected with the Mother God. This is because as the earth energy rises, it pushes out the spiritual energy resulting in a lost connection. When the period begins, she starts to let go of the earth energy and connects more strongly with the light of her Soul.

One of the reasons for releasing the stuck emotions is that this rising of the energy will have a more positive effect. Rather than throwing up negative emotions into the mind, it will bring up spiritual energy. Emotional energy which has been faced and cleared becomes spiritualised energy. When a female reaches this point, she will not experience a lost spiritual connection. If a female becomes blocked she often retreats either into her intellect or her physical body. By becoming intellectual, she will not acknowledge the rising emotions within herself. By becoming focused on her bodily beauty, she prevents herself from joining with the Mother God. Both are an avoidance. In most females, their emotions reveal their vulnerability, but they need to understand this is also their spiritual strength.

This process gives the female an opportunity to work on herself through a monthly cycle. If she feels her period restricts her, or she sees it as an enemy, then she will start to block this flow of energy. Quite often the period will then become erratic. She is no longer allowing the energy to flow naturally, but distorting it. There are so many medical procedures that a woman can resort to in order to solve the problem that she has created through suppressing her thoughts and emotions, such as anti-depressants or the contraceptive pill. A hysterectomy is a typical example of human conditioning: 'Let us remove the organ,' rather than, 'Let us find the cause which resulted in the organ becoming damaged.' Most gynaecological problems can be linked to a problem in this flow of energy.

The man's peak will either be a positive or a negative time, according to the thought energy around him. If he has a lot of negative thoughts, he will find that his mind becomes cluttered and busy. When the energy starts its ascent, the male has an opportunity to deal with the thoughts as they start to move back out into the aura. As the energy ascends higher, the further the thoughts move away, the more positive he will be in his thinking. This cycle of expansion and contraction should flow with the moon and the sun. If a man refuses to acknowledge his thoughts, then he can also block this cycle from the mind, which results in him becoming disconnected from his emotions and physical body.

Great thinkers or philosophers often lose their sense of how to take care of their physical self properly. Their dress sense, hygiene, eating and environment can often lack attention. In a sense they live completely in the mental world and avoid bringing the cosmic energy down into their emotional and physical worlds. A male can also get to a stage where he locks the energy into the physical. He does this by becoming totally obsessed with his physical appearance, bodily strength and his masculinity. By living only in the physical he is refusing to allow the cosmic energy to rise upwards and move out of his emotional and physical worlds.

If you are in a relationship, start a diary together. The woman needs to list her daily emotions, and the man the state of his daily thoughts. Confer with each other and observe the cycle you dance together throughout the month. You can also observe on your own by keeping a daily diary of your emotions and thoughts. This will reveal to you how the male and female sides of yourself are connected, and the different changes they go through in a month. Keep this up and you will see a pattern emerging. When you have become aware of this process then begin to work with your thoughts and emotions. Become observant, allow your thoughts to flow, but do not get caught up with them. If you find yourself thinking, bring your awareness to your breathing. Your emotions should then begin to reveal themselves. Allow them to surface without using the mind. For example, if you feel like crying, the mind might tell you it is due to suppressed anger. Do not follow the mind's description, but focus on the emotion. This may seem like a long arduous process, but you cannot expect to reach adulthood and then heal all your beliefs in a week! Healing yourself is a moment-to-moment process, so throw off your apathy and start to discover yourself. The process is difficult. It takes courage and commitment, but what you will uncover is the real you - a pure illuminated diamond.

The First Sexual Relationship

The second half of this book is going to deal with relationships and how to heal them, but it is worth noting that the first sexual relationship that a teenager experiences can be the building block for every other relationship. When two people fall in love, the pink energy of love enters the heart and blasts away any negative traits to the edges of the aura. These traits might be jealousy, pride, anger, fears, desires. Slowly over a period of time the negative traits start to move back in and the flow of love becomes restricted. This is when we go through a change in the relationship; the 'honeymoon' period is over and we begin to see faults within our partner. At this point the relationship either ends or we embark on a roller coaster ride of ups and downs. This realisation that our partner is not perfect and what were once the cute bits are now the most annoying can unsettle our world, for what we are really experiencing is a mirror to our own subconscious self.

The teenager, who is at a very sensitive stage, can often experience this first rush of love as an uncontrollable and exhilarating feeling, but when the love becomes restricted, it can become the most emotionally painful time. Through this experience, the Soul registers the obstacles to the flow of permanent love. It then directs its energy towards other Souls in order to enter into relationships which will bring forth these obstacles. Our first experience of sexual love for another is therefore the foundation for healing ourselves. If you look at your own first love relationship, can you notice the stages of change it went through? Did you feel small/powerful in the relationship? What annoyed you most about the person? Have you seen these traits in other people? What does this say about you? What was your part in the break up? Can you see what parts of you annoyed the other person? Have your relationships since then followed a similar pattern? Your closest and most intimate relationships reveal to you your hidden aspects that restrict the flow of your true being.

Teenage Pregnancy

Over the last fifty years the role of the family has changed dramatically and society is in conflict. Half of society is made up of the minds of the generation who still remember the 'sunny, good old days' and the other half of society is made up of the minds of those who want to experience everything in very little time. Teenage pregnancy is very much in the middle of this conflict. In the 1800s and early 1900s if a woman was not married by the age of twenty-one, then she was in fear of becoming an old maid. At this time people also had a shorter life span, so society accepted young marriages and teenage births. We forget teenage pregnancy has always existed, but what bothers our society is the fact that today teenagers are choosing to experience sex without being married. Throughout past generations marriage was probably the most controlled aspect of people's lives, apart from religion. The children who are being born today carry within their genes all the thoughts, words and actions of all their family members before them, so the ultimate rebellion of the teenager is to break the chain of control and challenge the beliefs of society.

The most difficult obstacle for a single pregnant teenager is the lack of support that society gives her. The saddest thing of all is that the pregnancy is often karmic, so the teenager is being obedient to her Soul, but disobedient to society. This carries a penalty. We carry out the sentence by usually placing her in appalling living conditions where crime and drugs are rife. We make fulfilling her creative dreams a misery as childcare and help are difficult to obtain. More often than not the mother ends up on state welfare. If the child grows up and follows in the footsteps of the peers around him by committing crimes, we blame the young teenage mother and we say 'Well she made her bed, so she can lie on it!' If the teenage parents do manage to stay together, then usually financial struggles mean that they still end up in poverty. If they survive this together, then their Souls have qualities that the rest of society needs to take a lesson from.

One day, in the future, humanity will know the meaning of oneness. We will understand that these teenagers are showing us where we lack love as a society. When we see other people who are not our immediate family struggling, we tend to turn a blind eye or show less interest. Each time the mother or the child cries out alone, that cry vibrates through all the hearts of humanity and out into the cosmos. Usually a teenager becomes pregnant for two reasons: firstly because it is karmic and secondly because on some level she is crying out to be loved.

The Second Rebellion

It is worth writing here about the second rebellion one has as an adult. Up to the age of twenty-one the Soul's aim is to rebel enough to break free from the emotional patterning of its parents and give itself a structure to work from for the next seven years. If it does not break free by this time, it tends to hold onto the emotional content of the parents until it is twenty-eight. Between twenty-eight and thirty-five, the person enters into a second stage of rebellion and it is at this point that the spiritual search usually begins. Now the person becomes more interested in pursuing his Soul's path rather than his upbringing. The extent of his second rebellion will depend upon how much he rebelled between fourteen and twenty-one and how he has worked on the energies between twenty-one and twenty-eight.

The second rebellion is when the Soul really gains control of the vehicle and we start to let go of inherited karmic lessons that we have taken on. The person then has a choice, does he stay linked to his family patterns e.g. goes for lunch, always on the phone, fits an expected role, or does he wander off and find his Soul's path? We can see this in many religions, where people may join a monastery, become a sadhu or a wanderer. Basically, around every seven years the cycle changes and we enter into a different facet of ourselves.

We could say the Soul reincarnates into the same physical body by changing the emotional body and its conditioning. In a sense every seven years the Soul takes a step back, reviews its life so far, then comes back in with changes to make. Quite often when people look back at their past, they say, 'That was not me doing that!' This is because the next aspect of the Soul does not identify with what went on before. The seven-year cycle allows the Soul to re-align, confirm its commitment, and release the karma of the previous seven years in order to move into the next phase of its learning.

We get problems when we carry the emotional wounds in the astral body for long periods of time, so that when the seven-year cycle comes up for review, we are unable to let go of what went on before. We then find it difficult to embrace a new facet of our being because we are carrying the extra baggage. At some point we have to address this baggage, as the whole point of the Soul assessing itself is so that it can correct any imbalances. It is like a point of closure. If we avoid looking at our unfinished issues then closure becomes difficult and we cannot move on in our daily life. As above so below, if we are stuck here, then we will be spiritually stuck, so look and ask yourself, what is unfinished in your life? What are you carrying with you that is older than the seven year cycle? What do you have to do to bring about closure? Look upon those with whom you have difficulty and ask yourself, if it was your last day on earth what would you say to them? Now write this down in two letters, the first letter is to reveal all your pent-up feelings about the person or persons and the second letter is to describe what you have learned about yourself from knowing them in your life. Now burn the letters and let your emotions be freed.

Worksheet

1. What was your rebellion like? Do you feel it changed your life for the better?

2. Were you afraid to rebel? Have you since followed in the footsteps of your parents? Do you secretly wish for your life to be different?

3. Can you understand the concept of the box? Are you still in the box?

4. What stops you from getting out of the box? Is it the fear of the unknown that keeps you where you are now? How can you change this?

5. Do you find yourself doing things to please others for love and acceptance? How would it feel to say no for a change?

6. How has your childhood affected the way you react to the outside world?

7. Do you blame others for your childhood? Can you see your Soul's hidden emotional beliefs that put you in this position? How can you deal with this?

8. What was your first love relationship like? Have you re-created a similar scenario with another person? What is it that people do to annoy you?

9. What are your feelings about people who are single parents? People that live in poverty/luxury? People who commit crime? Where do these beliefs come from? Can you see the bigger picture? Have you realised yet that your beliefs add to the outcome of society?

Exercise: Our Cut-Off Points

All misused energy becomes stuck unless we are able to acknowledge it and allow it to flow again. Most people I have come across have cut-off points in their life where energy has become suppressed through not expressing their truth in a non-loving situation. This trapped energy in our past prevents us from fully experiencing the present, simply because we keep being pulled back to our stuck issues. The Soul then keeps creating similar scenarios in order for the past to be brought up and healed in our present relationships. To deal with this never-ending circle, we need to go into our emotional body to recognise and feel the stuck energy we began to store in our childhood. For example, the moment a parent either verbally or energetically communicates to a child that they are not worthy of love, then the child internally or externally begins to cry and even though the body matures, the child is still crying inside. The energy is therefore stuck. The person cannot move past this feeling until it is healed with truth and love. The only way we can do this is by bringing up the child within and facing our pain.

After reading the following make yourself comfortable, close your eyes and relax your breathing. Choose a particular age from your childhood that you wish to look at, now imagine yourself at that age standing in front of you. Without thinking, just observe yourself, send light from your heart to the child's heart. Keep doing this until you feel the child has filled up, and then ask your inner child what you need to do to make it whole again. Follow what it needs, and feel any pain that your child is telling you or showing you. You may find your child wants to hug you or climb inside you, allow yourself to merge with your child. You may have to repeat this exercise over three days. Keep doing it until your inner child merges with you, as it is this merging which shows you that the cut-off points at this age are being dealt with. You can then choose another age and repeat the process. You may also notice that you gain more energy and joy, and feel yourself becoming more complete.

If you find this process difficult or time-consuming, do not give up, because these signs of difficulty are showing you that if you can persevere, then there will be a breakthrough and a reclaiming of your energy. Only you can heal you, nobody else will be able to do it for you. If you do not face yourself in this life, then ask, when will I look at myself? Because until you do, your issues will remain with you.

The Lovers

When the love that binds two Souls makes its connection, you have to yield to its reaction, for the course of love, like the surge of a great river, follows a predestined path. To resist would be futile.

When the scent of love caresses the hearts of the lovers they are lifted to dance in the aura of the Divine. The embrace of love Divine cocoons the Souls and places them gently into life. The compassion, caring and sharing are signs that the cocoon is in tact. For what is brought together by love can only be parted by love.

The wings of joy breeze over the lovers, giving them substance for the journey ahead. To share that love with the world is the destiny of those smitten by love's calling. When the song of love echoes within all the worlds in which the lovers dance, then love will have fulfilled itself.

The tenderness of a kiss, the warmth of physical embrace and the physical oneness are its echo. It calls to the Angels as they sound their trumpets and sway to the music of the spheres. Love has come calling here today.

5

Relationships

Never think you know,
Always be open for more.
Never take no for an answer
Knock on every door and keep knocking,
You deserve to know the truth and find yourself,
Your real self, your whole self.

The Role of the Male and Female

The process of humanity is centred on relationships. In every moment we are relating to something or someone. Even the hermits in the mountains are having a relationship with themselves and nature. As nature is life and we are a part of life, then you could physically shut yourself away in a cave, but on every level of your being you would still be in contact with all of life. The belief that when we are physically alone we are disconnected is sheer illusion. A lot of people run off to solitary confinement because they fear relating to other humans, but they cannot avoid it. We fear that when we relate, we will reveal what is hidden within us. The whole point of life is to be in harmony with everything that crosses our path. The only way we can do this is to recognise what is false within us and what is real. Relationships are one of the tools that the Soul uses to do this. They teach us how to become aware of and balance our expressive and receptive aspects, the male and female parts of ourselves.

The mental plane is the plane of Divine Inspiration and it vibrates to the male aspect of the Soul. The astral plane is the plane of Divine Creation and this vibrates to the female aspect of the Soul. Before Souls became trapped on the earth through fear, they were balanced in both their male and female energies. Therefore the whole earthly experience centred on Divine Creation through Divine Inspiration and everything was formed with perfection. If a Soul chose to be physically male, he would have become externally inspirational, inspiring all those he met, and inwardly female with creative abilities. If a Soul chose to be physically female, she would have become externally creative, bringing beauty and balance to the world, and her inner male would have inspired her. These were natural states for balanced Souls who were able consciously to open and accept both their male and female energies.

Humanity is not presently at this point of wholeness. We are still stuck in the illusion of duality. We do not recognise that we have both these energies within us. Each person we meet is a mirror to revealing the imbalance of these energies. For example, if you suffer from insecurity issues in relationships, which is an imbalanced female trait, you will draw towards you people who find it difficult to commit. Instead of looking within for our weaknesses, we only focus on the external. This may cause us to view others as an object of desire, or perhaps an opportunity to manipulate and control, consciously or unconsciously. So how do we heal ourselves?

The first thing you need to do is accept the Soul aspect that you have chosen for this lifetime. If you are a man this means that your task is to master the mental plane by observing your thoughts. This will open the door to release any suppressed emotions. For a woman this means that you are an emotional being whose task is to master the astral plane through purification of your emotions. This will then lead you into becoming aware of your mental state. Over the ages men have belittled the role of female energy. They have ignored and suppressed the nurturer of life. Women have become frustrated at this and the adage, 'If you can't beat' em, join' em' came into play as women put down their suppressed roles and tried to enter into the man's mental world. She did this by overriding her emotions and entering only into her intellect. Spiritually, she has pushed through the auric bands of her emotional body without purifying them first, and burst into her mental body. By using her mental energy she has tried to compete with men in order to be loved and accepted.

If we were to split the body in half at the diaphragm, we would see how the lower half of the body, the intestines, stomach, kidneys, spleen, legs, feet etc, are the nurturing support system of our daily life. It is this half of us that represents the Mother Earth. The chakras in this part of the body are the processors of emotional energy and these are the links to the astral plane. The top half of the body contains the expressive and giving aspects of our self. This includes the heart, lungs, brain, arms, hands, thinking, communication and vision. It is this half of us that represents our inspiration and God. The chakras in this part of the body are the processors of thought and speech and they are the links to the mental plane.

If a woman shifts her female energy from the lower half of her body up into the top half where the mental plane resides, without first purifying and mastering her emotions, then she will lose her feelings of being supported and nurtured. Her lower chakras will become neglected and this will open the door to illness. A woman can make this shift by externally entering into high mental careers, becoming forceful, aggressive, analytical, mentally stressed and frustrated. Spiritually, she is trying to be in a place where her female energy cannot survive for long.

If a man avoids contact with his mental body, by not regularly having lofty thoughts, and chooses to lower his energy into the emotional part of his body, then he will become apathetic or totally absorbed in physical pursuits. With apathy he may lose his drive, his direction, his hopes, and he may become depressed. If he becomes totally physical in nature, then he may only look towards bodily beauty. He may even be capable of committing serious crimes without any apparent thought or emotional attachment. If a man lives totally in the mind, by ignoring his feelings, then he can become ruthless, domineering and ignorant, denying God's existence. If there is no reverent connection to God or lofty intentions in a man's daily thoughts, then he will find dealing with his emotions difficult. It is the mind that belittles the role of the emotions and says that God does not exist. Therefore the female energy finds it easier to *love* God without needing proof of His existence, because it is centred in the emotions. The male energy finds it easier to *know* God, as it is centred in the mind, which has direct contact with the Soul. The aim of the human being is to unite the male and female within itself. Through this it will *love* God and *know* God.

A woman needs to balance and clear her suppressed emotions before she can raise the energy in her body up into her higher chakras. This way she will secure her foundation before fully opening her male inspirational energy on the mental plane. This process teaches her to focus her thoughts on the love of God. A man needs to direct his thoughts to God and master his mind before he can enter into his emotions. This way he will find that the Mother

God directs and supports him through the astral plane. This way he will feel safe and live totally for the moment.

Nature reflects this process. The Mother Earth's energy, which is drawn up through the soles of the feet, flows up the spine and into the heart to meet with the Divine energy, which has travelled down from the crown. Symbolically, a woman has to reach up for God and the man has to reach down for God's support.

A woman is always searching for a man who loves God, whether she is consciously aware of it or not. From within she recognises that he carries God's inspirational energy. If she has not awakened her male side in this or previous lives, then, by meeting a man who consciously loves God, this will bring about a shift within her. It will open the door for her inspirational energy to awaken. She then creates only for God, delighting at all the beauty she can manifest with His inspiration. She becomes like the glass that holds the water or like the earth that holds life.

Man, on the other hand, is always searching for a woman who loves Mother Earth and is fertile to embrace God fully. If he has not awakened his female side in this life or previous lives, then, by meeting this female, he will be supported and nurtured, so that he can enter into his emotional, creative world within himself. We need to understand that there is nothing external which we cannot find within ourselves, but if we need help to open up parts of ourselves, then the internal doorkeeper can present itself through an external person. One of the greatest things we can have here on the earth is someone to share our journey with, for it is this sharing that is true love.

The role of the female energy is to reflect the Mother God completely, and her teacher for this is nature, for nature is the manifestation of the female within God. The role of the male energy is to reflect the Father God completely, and his teacher for this is the physical result of his mental thinking. Ideas that have been created without love, support and nurturance are manifestations of chaos. For example, I recently purchased a new vacuum cleaner and I immediately recognised that it had been designed by a man without the consultation of his female side, for it had so many design faults and short falls that using it proved difficult. Humanity has created many things without consulting Mother Earth. Our manifestations have given her chaos and destruction, making Her job of purification very difficult.

This has also extended out into the family, because like the Mother Earth's energy, the woman's female energy is the foundation; it is the purifier of emotional energies. The man's male energy is the expression of these emotional energies, which he then extends out into the world. If he pollutes them with his mind, then he pollutes the female, the family, humanity, earth and beyond. The male energy is responsible for making God available to the female energy. This is a major problem for humanity, because until man finds and falls in love with God, then a woman will try to enter the mental world, so that she may find God for herself, but bring only frustration, neglect and maybe illness.

The male energy gives life to the female energy. He brings God to her. She takes this life within her and gives birth to Divine Creation. The female then gives this creation back to the male who inspires it to grow into the love of God. This can occur within each of us or unravel as an external relationship. Either way we are always reaching to unite with the love of the other half of ourselves.

A woman is like the musical instrument that is perfectly tuned to the seven notes of life, and man is the composer. If he is in realised oneness with the Divine Inspiration of God, then together they will create heavenly music. If, however, the instrument is not tuned and in harmony, or the composer is not in love with God, then only discordant notes will be heard. An instrument is only as good as its composer. Its composer is only as good as its instrument and neither could have been created without the love of God.

The Mirror

The adult years are the Soul's way of looking at its relationship to the world around it. By observing its thoughts, words and actions that occur through its interactions with other energies, the Soul learns whether its reactions are triggered through fear or love.

Basically, relationships are used as mirrors for the Soul to see the truth about itself. Over the centuries we have become more and more flippant about our emotions. We are now saying that it is acceptable to have negative emotions and express them onto some external source. Many of societies institutes have grasped the need for the healing of the emotions and the mind, but they have left the most important ingredient of the soul out. This includes some counselling models and the teachings of psychology. People are encouraged to own their feelings, but they are also encouraged to place the focus of those feelings onto the external. For example, they might say, 'Oh it makes me angry when you do that'. What we need to realise is that for anger to be triggered in us, then there must have already been anger there, caused by suppressing our truth in other experiences. Looking within for the root cause of the anger will take the focus away from what is being externally done to us. The Soul put us into this situation to experience an emotional response that needs healing. No external source can ever be blamed for our emotions, as all our responses to external experiences reveal the state of our inner being.

Example
A man running for the bus accidentally knocks another man to the ground. The man stops and tries to help him up, but the fallen man shrugs him off and expresses outrage by shouting and cursing at him. The experience brought up the man's suppressed emotions. A second man also experiences a similar incident, but he accepts the help to his feet and his response is not one of anger, but assertiveness, as he clearly points out the effect of the man's actions. Therefore his emotions are centred and his mind is clear. The difference between the two is that the first person is not aware of his inner world, so he blames all his emotional reactions on the incidents of the outside world. Whereas the second person does not have anger in his system and he can remain aware and assertive in the moment.

It is not what is done to us that matters. It is our emotional reaction to it, and we need to be able to look underneath our emotions to the beliefs we have held onto. Whilst counselling, I met a woman who was very angry with her father-in-law at the abusive way he treated his wife. She finally acknowledged to herself that as a child she and her mother had suffered abuse at the hands of her father, but because he had now died, she was transferring her suppressed feelings onto someone similar. When she decided to look within herself for the cause of her anger, she saw a reflection of herself in the mother-in-law. This revealed her deeper feelings of worthlessness. This understanding of her fear of not being loved and accepted set her suppressed emotions free. She now understands the bigger picture, and her father-in-law no longer brings up any anger from within her. She has realised that it is the belief systems of her mother and father–in–law, which have placed them together in a relationship.

I could now say that you can let go of everything which has happened to you in the past. This is simply because we cannot change the past, as we can only work with what we have in the present. This means working with what is happening to us now in each and every moment. For all our karma, childhood and teenage years are being played out in our present relationship to the world. For example, imagine yourself standing in the centre of a circular room and all around you are labelled doors, i.e. one is career, one is mother, one is father, one is partner, etc. Everything that comes through these doors demands a response from you and each response you give reveals what emotion is stored within you, i.e.

anger, jealousy, pride, desire, joy, love, etc. Therefore whatever you are relating to on this earth is showing you deeper aspects of yourself. There is nothing outside of you. Only you can create your reality by your inner responses to external experiences.

If only the counselling and psychotherapy industry understood that it is not the anger or guilt etc, which a person needs to accept, but the underlying fear which has trapped them for maybe many lifetimes. If only doctors understood that a failing liver is not just a medical condition, but also an organ full of unexpressed words and emotions eating away at a person, then healing would not only be a chemical journey, but an emotional, mental and spiritual journey back to wholeness. Let us now look at our different aspects of relating.

Relationship to our Partner

As an adult your most revealing relationship is the one you have with your partner. In the previous chapter I explained what happens energetically when two people fall in love. In this period of time we experience what it is like to live without fear as an obstacle to love. It is later on, when the emotional issues come back to us, that the real work begins, as we start to see some aspects of ourselves mirrored in our partners. At this point we have a choice. Do we realise it is an opportunity to see our patterning and assist our partner to see theirs in order to grow, or do we leave the relationship? This is an important moment in a relationship, because in today's society, when problems arise, it is easier to file for a divorce or find a new partner, than it is to look at our part in the drama. What we have to realise is that we carry with us our pattern of learning. Each soul that is presented to us has come to teach us something and if we do not get the message from one, then we will attract it through somebody else. We will take the same issues into all our intimate relationships until they are looked at. The most important thing is to recognise that our partner is not a mind reader, so we have to convey the message we are trying to put across. A lot of relationship arguments occur because our partner does not react in the way we want them to. For example, they do not put the top on the toothpaste tube, or they do not put their dirty clothes in the wash basket. We need to communicate our requests rather than expect them to know.

It is also worth becoming aware of the agendas within the relationship. For instance, one of the partners might want to reach the top at work and spends most of their spare time pursuing this goal, while the other person may not be so career minded, therefore is happy to come home and watch television. What you then have is two different people pursuing two different courses of action. This may result in one person feeling unloved and unattended to while the other is pursuing personal goals. This feeling needs to be conveyed or problems will begin to arise in the relationship. If the feelings are conveyed, then the couple will be able to support each other in their growth; but usually, instead of honestly speaking our truth, we begin to criticise, we say, 'Oh you don't love me any more. You are always at work. You spend all your time on the telephone'. The most important thing is to say what you think or feel and take quality time out with your partner or with your family. If too much energy is put into other goals and not enough into the family, then the family will not survive because it ends up in conflict. The family is crying out for love, but because the unit is not completely balanced in energy, then it becomes open to breaking down.

The whole of humanity has this agenda problem. What we need to realise is that our partner is also a Soul learning lessons. Even if you know it is a big mistake for them to strive to become top in the business world, still support them in making their mistake. Yes, we may be able to see what is round the corner because we have learnt that lesson in other lives, but they still have to learn it, so we need to support them in their growth. Even if they do not want to hear your advice, let them have the space to see how their actions are affecting you, so that they may be able to understand the effect of their desires.

We know that due to our childhood conditioning we often place ourselves in relationships that reflect our known zones. For instance, if your father beat you when you were a child, as an adult you may enter into a relationship where the man beats you. It may be that your parents made you feel small and worthless, therefore you attract to yourself a person who constantly criticises you and makes you feel as small as your parents did. Whatever intimate relationship you are in, on some level you will be trying to heal your childhood, whether you are consciously aware of it or not. For it is our karma which places us in our upbringing, but it is our distorted beliefs that trap us as adults. To become aware of our issues we need to begin to observe how we feel around our partner's actions. For example, do you often react as a child to your partner, seeing your partner as the parent? Or maybe you are the parent and your partner is the child? Do you feel you are treated as a doormat? Worthless? Rejected? Vulnerable? Do your partner's actions make you feel insecure? Jealous? Angry? What is your belief behind these emotions? Is it that you fear not being loved? Not being in control? Lack of support?

Often the Soul chooses a main emotion which becomes the focus of its life. For some, this may mean they are trying to master pride, anger or jealousy, etc, so most of their relationships have a common underlying thread. Julie is a friend who has spent most of her life struggling with the emotions of jealousy. As an adult, she would enter into a relationship and everything would be wonderful at first, but when her partner wanted to spend time with his friends, she would sit at home consumed with jealousy. By the end of the day, her mind would have created all sorts of scenarios in which her boyfriend was being deceitful. This increased her feelings of insecurity about his love for her and devoured her trust. Her desire to be his only focus in life always left her feeling that she was not adequate. She began to compete with his world by doing things that would please him to keep him near. In a sense she became his ultimate fantasy, but because desires are subject to change, keeping up this charade costs valuable energy. When someone else's actions bring about feelings of not being good enough, what is the fear that is hiding? Is it the fear of not being worthy, or that what we have to offer is not unique enough? Be honest with yourself. In the final chapter of this book there are a few techniques that show you how to remove the energy from your energy bodies and be free from your stuck patterns, but first you have to become aware of your emotional and belief patterns.

Most of what I have just explained to you has probably already been written about, so we need to look a little bit deeper in order to understand our being. If we are here on the earth to integrate our male and female aspects in order to become whole, then we could say our partner is an outer reflection of our opposite inner energy. For example, if you are a female and you have attracted to yourself a strong male who makes you feel unloved or taken advantage of, then look at what this is saying about the inner you. Where have you not loved yourself? Why is your male side taking control of your life? Where does your life lack freedom and creativity? What you need to do is get in touch with your needs by spending time loving, treating, complimenting and nurturing yourself. You will then begin to break out of your old patterns and bring your female energy into harmony. This will bring down your male side into balance. You may find that your external relationship changes. He may become softer or you may part from him and attract a more balanced person.

The same applies if you are male and you have attracted to yourself a female who is controlling you. What is it within you that is suppressing your male assertiveness? Why have you allowed your female side to govern your life? This will make you avoid problems, confrontations, saying no and being active. Therefore get in touch with what is right for your male energy and what will make you grow and progress in life. Assert yourself by first tackling the small things, until eventually you balance your male energy. Your outside relationship will then change to accommodate your inner change. It will either become more equal or fall away.

By viewing our partner as the other half of our energy we can see things so much more clearly. It actually reveals where the receptive and expressive aspects of our self need balancing. Where do you need balancing? Would you say your male side overpowers your female side? Or your female controls your male side? Write a list of your negative traits. Which ones are receptive and which are expressive? Can you see how these traits play out in your relationship? How would you describe your partner's negative traits? Now look within yourself and see how these affect you emotionally? What are your beliefs behind your feelings? Nobody said becoming whole would be easy. The key is the awareness that everything that is occurring on the external is a reflection of your inner being. The only exception to this awareness is that when you have become fully integrated, you then become a clear mirror for others to see themselves without affecting your own balance. This means you no longer react from fear, but from a space of love.

Another example of being able to view our other half in a partner was a couple I met at a workshop. The woman was very creative. She wanted to be a writer but she lacked inspiration. In other words, she was active on the astral plane, but she could not reach up into the mental plane. This reflected in her body because she suffered from acute alopecia and headaches. The man was very inspirational. He had great ideas and he started his own business, only to lose it in six months because he could not pull the physical together. In other words, he was active on the mental plane but he could not reach down and materialise it on the astral plane. Now you would think that each of them would be able to come together and make a whole, but this is not what being whole is all about. She needed to see how to activate her inspirational energy through him and he needed to see how to activate his creativity through her. As neither of them had a deeper understanding of their self, they built their foundations on fear. They were both too frightened to let go of control. She felt that if she gave herself to her male side, he would take over and devour her creativity. He felt that by allowing his female side access, it would suffocate his inspiration with rules and regulations. When we try to control and run our lives through how we think it should be, we run into all sorts of problems. It is usually because we are trying to hold one side of ourself down. Have you ever tried to hold an inflated ball under water? It is impossible because it will fight you all the way for release! Resistance is futile, so why not let go and let God take over?

The most joyful aspect of a relationship is in the beginning. The most painful aspect is at the end and in between it is a mixture of both pleasure and pain. Is this not what we are inside, a mixture of darkness and light? If this is true, then the point of being together is to help each other transform the darkness into light. There are two spiritual reasons why a relationship breaks up. The first is that a person may find the relationship is too challenging. They are being shown aspects of themselves which they do not want to see. This may be externally revealed through affairs, abuse, habits, constant criticism, etc. The other reason is that one of the partners has outgrown the other. When we meet we are both teacher and student to each other. In one moment you may be the teacher, in the next the student, but often the relationship can become unbalanced as you may find that one is always being the teacher and the other the student. At this point it is time for the teacher to break away so the student can find another mirror that will bring up different facets of their self. Externally, this often reveals itself in two people being together but living separate lives or involved in affairs. Problems can occur here if the student does not want to let go. If we are in this position, then we have to realise that there is an opportunity to let go of something which is no longer beneficial. We can then be free to embrace another experience where we will once again be a teacher to another.

We have become so caught up in the idea of security that we often mistake this as a foundation to a relationship. If we were to see ourselves as free beings not needing, depending or desiring anyone else to give to us, then we would set our partner free on so many levels. How many of us try to control the comings and goings of our partner? If our partner said to us that they felt the need to go to Africa tomorrow, how many of us would say, 'No, you are not?' It is amazing to realise how we stunt the growth of other Souls, and we call this a relationship of love. True freedom comes when we can share a relationship with someone, which allows them to experience what their Soul needs, without any control from us. If you find this difficult to do, what are you not trusting? If it is your partner, then what deeper part of you are you not trusting? What emotion does this bring up? What is the fear? Can you let go and let God direct your life?

Example

Julie has spent all day preparing a surprise dinner for Rob. She has bathed, changed into her best clothes, cleaned the house, lit the candles and opened the wine. She is feeling happy and excited about spending an evening of intimacy with the man she loves. Suddenly the phone rings. It is Rob. He tells her that his friend Pete has asked to meet with him in the local bar, as he needs some help through a difficult patch. Julie tells Rob of her plans. In response to the guilt he now feels, he tries to make her disappointment better by telling her he will only be gone for half an hour. She reluctantly agrees, but feels agitated, as his previous record of keeping to his word is wanting. By ten o'clock Julie is still waiting for Rob whilst Rob, who has not been out for a while, is enjoying his friend's company and has forgotten about his promise to Julie.

Both have acted out of a space of love. Julie for Rob and Rob for Pete. In the initial intent of Julie and Rob's plans there is no wrong, so where did love become exchanged for pain. It was in the emotional response from both. Julie did not want him to go, as from her past experience she knew he would not keep to his word, but she did not speak her truth either. Rob was caught in the middle. He did not want to let down Julie or Pete, so instead of making a decision which was based on truth and not on guilt, he led her to believe he would fulfil something which he had no intention of carrying out. This led Julie to an even greater disappointment.

Let us now look at this energetically. Both of them have difficulty communicating with the opposite sides of themselves. Julie finds it difficult to trust her male side to follow through on decisions. Externally, she will attempt to follow through on something only to let herself down. She needs to assert herself and create boundaries as to what is acceptable treatment to both sides of herself. Rob finds it difficult to be assertive. He tries to keep his female side happy by appeasing her with false hope. He will then do the opposite of what is expected and often feel guilty. He therefore needs to become honest about what his true intentions are. In the external relationship they both need to communicate to each other fully, Julie her worth and Rob what he is really intending to do.

Is this familiar? What do you feel is the solution? Has your partner ever chosen something else over you? How did this feel? What was the fear behind the feeling? Was it that you felt less worthy? What does this say about you? How can you communicate more worth in your life?

Example
'You make a lovely couple' said Karen's mother to her whilst out shopping together. 'Phil is such a good lad. He came round and fixed my washing machine the other day and he is going to help Aunty move house this weekend. It is good to know my daughter is being looked after.' It seemed to Karen that everyone liked Phil. If only they knew him like she did, but if she told anyone she felt sure

they would not believe her. Later that night Phil came home drunk again. He pushed her for not making his favourite dinner and threw the food at the dog. Abuse poured from his mouth. He called her a whore and then the beating began. He was always careful and never hit her face. It was usually the arms, legs and stomach. She had silently lost two babies this way. When he had exhausted himself she sat in the corner and cried. She could not understand it. When he was sober he was the kindest man you could meet, but when he was drunk he was the nastiest man you could meet. She knew tomorrow he would cry at the pain he caused her. How can she leave this love/hate relationship?

Is this scenario familiar? What do you feel keeps them in this relationship? What do you feel is the solution? What does your answer say about you? Have you ever experienced a relationship where your partner's personality changed through the use of alcohol or drugs? What was your reaction? What did the relationship say about you? Through my observations in life I have met men who are very feminine inside, but to cope with the world, they often portray themselves to be masculine. They do this by sometimes fighting, entering gangs, the army, turning to drink, etc. This is simply because the male society finds it difficult to accept feminine men, so these men can find it difficult to balance their energies here on the earth.

Some men who suppress their male energy become abusive when they are intoxicated with alcohol. The alcohol relaxes the hold on the inner suppressed male and then it rises to take control. In their sober moments they are usually governed by their feminine energy. A man often suppresses his masculine side if he has a lot of unfinished issues. This suppressed energy can emerge as anger, sadness, bitterness and violence. If he has attracted to himself a female whose inner belief is worthlessness, then often after alcohol, his suppressed male energy is played out within the relationship. After the abuse, when the man becomes sober, he is once again his female side. He then feels deep remorse at what he is capable of doing. These men usually have issues with their fathers. They often suppress their male energy for fear of being like their father. It is this fear which will lead the man into situations that bring up his conditioning and beliefs, so he can acknowledge them and begin the process of healing.

The female in this abusive situation needs to acknowledge she is suppressing her male side, as when he does emerge, he is degrading and abusive. She needs to ask herself what it would mean to take control of her life, rather than hoping that one day everything will work out. She is costing herself valuable energy waiting for the external man to realise her worth, love her and live happily ever after. The woman lives in fear and she is constantly checking the energy her partner is expressing. The relationship is showing her that she needs to assert herself and find her worth. She also needs to face her childhood by looking at her beliefs and fears of being a female, which leave her open to abuse from her male energy.

Through our most intimate relationship we can now see a picture of what it is we do, but we are also beginning to see a solution that shows us a way of knowing ourselves better. To begin with you need to be honest with yourself and your partner about your feelings, not by projecting your stuff onto your partner, but by saying, 'Hey, I'm feeling sad right now.' Begin to ask yourself what is your part in the drama? What is your underlying fear? Then look at your agenda or what it is you want from the relationship. Finally, through your emotional responses, be aware of any male/female imbalances from within.

Sometimes when I meet people it is as though they have a label stuck to their forehead, which may say, 'I am worthless, therefore it is alright to treat me in a worthless manner.' These people enter into relationship after relationship always coming out battered and bruised with a stamp on the label which says, 'Yes, confirmed worthless!' Until we learn that we are not worthless, but beautiful, loving and gifted, we will keep entering into scenarios with many different people who will fulfil our expected role. When a change of belief occurs and we accept the truth of our being, then these types of relationships fall away. This freeing of our energy will lead us to enter into more balanced experiences.

Relationship to Parents

Our mother is a reflection of the Mother God and our father is a reflection of the Father God. What does this mean? If our partner reflects our hidden relationship to our self and the need to become an integrated Soul, then our parents reflect our hidden relationship to the Divine. Behind the Soul lies God. On our returning journey to wholeness, we have to turn and face the beliefs that we have created around God. We have to take down the obstacles and boulders that we built in our external search for what has always been there within us. When I was a child I felt as though God had rejected me. I felt unworthy of His love, as I was given no parents to take care of me and was placed in an unloving and abusive environment. Over the following years I had a deep conflict within me. I had to face my beliefs and tear them down. I had to realise it was not the Mother God who had rejected me, but it was my beliefs that made me feel unsupported, unworthy, uncared for and disconnected from life. I then had to acknowledge my beliefs around the Father God and know He did not abandon me, punish me or withhold His love. It was I who did it to myself. I have since found out that my parents' relationship to each other followed this same pattern. My mother felt very lonely and worthless and my father would abuse her and then abandon her to cope alone.

If we now take what we know about our childhood, look deeper at our experience and see what beliefs our parents brought forth, we will find we have reflected similar beliefs towards the Divine. If you were sexually or physically abused, what does this say about your relationship to the Divine? Do you feel spiritually powerless? Do you feel as though God is punishing you? Do you feel unworthy to receive love from God?

If women are severely abused often it is because they do not recognise the Female God, therefore they feel they have no spiritual essence. Do you recognise this in your mother? In yourself? If you were rejected or neglected, what does this say about your relationship to the Divine? Do you feel unworthy of love from the

Mother God? Do you feel uncared for and unsupported? Ask what stops you realising and becoming one with the Mother God. I have given many lectures and talks all over the world, but the one thing that stands out is that many people have no knowledge of the female aspect of God. They believe She does not exist. In many religions it would be preposterous to suggest that the female essence of God is equal to the male. Many temples do not allow women into the inner sanctuary to pray because the men believe that women are less important. The Mother God is very much alive. Each time we care for, nurture, create beauty, sing, laugh, play music, dance, paint, meditate, enjoy nature etc, we are being held within her energy. How can we dismiss the importance of this joy-giving energy? Most people on this earth are searching for joy and happiness. In essence they are searching for the Mother God.

I have also observed that if our parents die before we have a chance to heal our beliefs, we often transfer our beliefs onto our in-laws or someone whose actions resemble those of our parents. It takes great honesty from ourselves to recognise this. We have become so used to blaming the actions of others for our pain that we find it easier to see the fault in another than see it in ourselves. If you do find your relationship with your in-laws is difficult, look within you for the emotions that their actions bring up, then go behind the emotions for the belief. When you find your truth, become aware of how, in order for issues to be healed, you have transferred them onto your in-laws. For example, if your father-in-law belittles what you do for a living and you become quietly angry, then look at your belief of unworthiness and see if this same scenario was played out with your own parents. If you recognise an imbalance, then use the techniques from later on in the book to let go of your suppressed emotions. You will then find that the external relationship will reflect your change of energy.

When the Soul comes to the earth it takes on many labels and roles. By natural means the three things it cannot change are the colour of its skin, its sex and the fact that it is somebody's child. It is these three things which have given birth to culture and race separation, obsessive sexual issues and nations that arose and fell through the genetic family line. Until humanity accepts its culture as one, its sex as a reflection of God, and that the children we raise are Souls in a human form, then it will continue in the belief that I am 'this' and you are 'that'. In other words separation. It is important to therefore heal and let go of all our suppressed emotions about what our parents have done or still do to us. Only when we realise that we have placed ourselves with them in order to bring forth beliefs from other lifetimes does a clearing take place. Through this process we will begin to see the face of God.

Now ask yourself, what is it you want from your parents? Can you communicate these needs to them? What is it you need to change about yourself? Is it that you need to forgive your parents and yourself? If your mother or father only had one minute left to live what would you say to them? If God were sitting in front of you what would you say to Him? What obstacles have you placed before God to stop the flow of love? The beliefs you have about your parents are the same beliefs you have about God. Even the atheists who do not believe in God are saying there is no one to support me and love me for who I am. Open your heart. See your parents as Souls who have come here to learn about how they stop the flow of love in their lives, and then be thankful that in their struggles they are also revealing your own obstacles to love. Is this not true service?

Relationship to Siblings

If our parents represent the male and female aspects of God, then our brothers and sisters reflect our relationship to all others on the earth. We often rate how much our parents love us by measuring the material things and affection our brothers and sisters receive. This then extends out into the world and we judge how much God loves us by what others receive. If others get more than we do we say, 'God is punishing me.' If they get less than we do we say, 'God loves me.'

When my parents put me into the children's home, they held onto my brothers for a while longer. This made me feel I was less worthy of God's love than they were. It is strange how we make ourselves small enough to be into put into boxes with labels on that say, 'fragile', 'waste' or 'heavy load'. We then become upset when people treat us according to our labels! Have we not yet had enough of this merry-go-round? It is time to realise that we came from love, and it is this love within us which is waiting for us to let go of control. It can then extend into its limitless space. So why are we always limiting ourselves with such small ideas? What labels would you say are on your box? How do you live your life in relation to them?

If your brother or sister brings up anger, jealousy, pride, guilt, sadness, etc, then look at what that is saying about you and your relationship to the Deeper Self, which resides within you. Now ask yourself if you feel that your parents love you more, or less, than your siblings? What is the underlying belief/fear? What does this say about your relationship to God? Do you feel God loves others more or less than you? Do you need to share your feelings with your siblings? Can you let go of your beliefs and let more love in? When you stop blaming others for what is going on inside you, life becomes liberating. Facing the obstacles you have placed on your path to God makes you realise His love is the same love He has for everything. There are no varying degrees!

Relationship to Children

The previous chapters explained about the energetics of childhood. If we have children of our own then we have probably seen a little of what we do to condition their lives. It is difficult to admit that even though we have done our best, the outcome of our children's lives may not be what we would have wanted for them. Maybe they made the same mistakes we did. Maybe they took an unexpected route, or they may seem to be very distant from us, yet there is another way to view our children and the effect they have on our lives. Children often represent the innocence of life. This innocence reflects our own connection to our inner joy. Our children therefore show us our own inner child. If we have obstacles to inner joy, then these will also become revealed. For example, if your child brings up anger in you, then where did you experience anger as a child? If your child brings up jealousy in you, as a child where are your issues of jealousy?

There is a woman who attends my courses who has two small sons. The elder son is very angry towards her and the younger son has a carefree attitude. The first child brings up her anger. The second child does not show her any attention and he brings up her feelings of not being loved. When she decided to look at her emotions she began to see her own childhood issues around her mother. These were her feelings of anger at not being given any attention or love.

Our children reveal to us where and through what emotion we first felt difficulty receiving love. This is why people who have been severely mistreated in childhood often find it difficult to raise children, as in a sense they are facing themselves as children again. Sometimes these people avoid having children altogether, because sub-consciously they do not wish to face this hurt and vulnerable inner child whom they have shut away. If they do become parents and they are able to recognise within themselves the need to love, then often they will shower their children with lots of affection. This will change the generations to come, but they sometimes run the risk of over-protecting them through fear. This can reveal itself as a tendency to control the child's life and manipulate it into safe territory. The problem here is that it becomes stifling for the child and as a teenager it may rebel in extremes to break the control. This control is often based on the fear that no one is trustworthy. A female friend of mine, who was sexually abused as a child, is married with two daughters. Within the marriage her suspicious mind kept secretly eating away at her. If her husband wanted to change the children's nappies or bathe them, she would create negative mental scenarios. Instead of talking about her fears, she projected accusing energy onto her husband, which would often make him feel guilty for wanting to share precious moments with his daughters. She then began to manipulate and control the energy around her. She became obsessed with her children's safety. She could no longer relax and enjoy being a parent. She also began to see herself reflected in her daughters, one of whom was timid and the other was angry. She realised that as a child she was too frightened to speak out about the abuse. She felt she had not been in control of the situation. This made her very angry inside, which led to suppressing it in her internal organs.

There are also people who cannot have children, yet medically they are given the all clear. Energetically, there is often a deep-rooted fear around facing the inner child. Sometimes when these people adopt, they go on to naturally have children of their own. By facing the fear with the adopted child, the fear has become broken down, releasing the energetic blockage. What are your feelings around children? What are your fears around children? Can you see your emotions reflected in your child? Can you see your own childhood? What could you not say as a child?

Sit down and write three letters. Each letter will be to your parents. The first one will be from you as a child, so write down all your feelings and everything you wanted to say as a child but could not. The next letter will be from you as an adult. Write down everything you still need from your parents and what it is you want to say but cannot. Your last letter will be a letter of thanks. Write down all the wonderful things you have experienced with your parents. Now burn the letters and let your emotions follow the smoke.

Another issue we need to look at is how parents react differently to each child according to its sex. Have you ever noticed how the father tells his teenage son to go out and live life, but often becomes frightened of letting his teenage daughter experience freedom. This is because he knows what other males are thinking when they look at his daughter. The mother often teaches her daughter from a young age to wait for love because she knows how a young girl is not in control of her emotions and can throw caution to the wind. This hidden sexual agenda is in conflict, as we have the saying 'go and sow your wild oats', but with fear of the consequences. This shows us the basis of human life, which is a man's quest for the fulfilment of desires and a woman's need for security. When we begin to raise our children with an understanding of how to master desire and how to find inner security, then there will be no need to have these met externally. Life will then be experienced from a space of peace and there will no longer be chaos.

From my observations, I have also understood that the majority of parents try to give their children a better standard of living than they themselves received. This often brings a struggle to provide for material desires and many people end up in financially driven careers or in debt. It is as though the parents sacrifice their dreams in order for the child to fulfil theirs. If the parents are still struggling with life after the child has grown up to be successful and financially secure, then often resentment from the parents can display itself. If the parents need to ask for help from the child, they can also feel guilty. It is as though the parent is now the child and the child is the parent. They may feel that after years of maybe working in a joyless environment, they have been left behind, forgotten and even powerless.

Most parents I have spoken to have told me the giving they shower upon a child is done without needing to receive, but they often find that when the child leaves home they feel empty and exhausted. There is also an unspoken energy. After providing the child with an opportunity to follow its dreams, it is now time for the child to return the giving to the parents. This may be through financial help, getting married to the right person, grandchildren, DIY jobs, visits, etc. If the child does not offer its help to the struggling parents or rejects their requests, then the parent begins to begrudge the years of giving. What we need to do is recognise that a parent's role is to give unconditionally to the best of their ability. If we have feelings of resentment then we need to look within at what this is saying about our unresolved issues. We need to ask how we feel about our children's success? How we feel about not fulfilling our own dreams? What we sacrificed in order to give? Where we lost our joy? What are we really asking our child for? What is our inner pain around struggle? Are we frightened to ask for help? What is our belief? What is our fear?

Relationship to Pets

There are many different worlds which reside upon the earth. We have the mineral kingdom, vegetable kingdom, plant kingdom, the insect world, the human world and the animal kingdom. All these worlds reflect life experiencing itself through physical existence.

The nearest in likeness to the human emotional world is the animal kingdom, especially those animals which we term as pets, i.e. the dog, cat, horse, rabbit, etc. Not only do these animals respond to our affection but they also give it back in return. Although we train them and mould them, they still belong to a different world. Therefore they must follow their own evolution through the collective animal Soul.

We have pets for many reasons but most importantly for company. What we need to do is look within ourselves and see if our pet is filling a gap within us. If we are using our pet as an aid to receiving love and comfort, then know that aspects of the pet will be reflecting you. If it is stubborn, are you stubborn? If it is disobedient, what authority are you challenging? If it is submissive, what part of you feels unworthy? When we mould pets to behave how we want them to, then they become a mirror.

Most of us cannot resist a puppy or a kitten. If we allow them to grow according to their collective Soul, then they become unruly according to the human world. To own a pet is to understand it is not a human. It does not have a mental or emotional body with the extent of capabilities that we do. The line between walking the journey of life with your pet and moulding it is very thin. Let us imagine for a moment you are a dog. Your instinct is to hunt, to be around those who are like you, to run free, procreate and sleep. Instead you have been taken by a human who has uprooted you from others like you, put you in a closed-in area, who feeds you, controls your toilet, your procreating, and you can no longer run free.

I am not saying it is wrong to have pets, what I am asking is how much is your pet expected to fit a role of what you think it should be? Become aware of your relationship with your pet. Really question your motive for owning one. If you find it is a need within you, then face the emotions and the hidden fear. If you find your relationship with your pet honours its own kingdom and you are the observer of life in another form, then this is the true relationship between man and animal. This way we are not possessing, moulding and conditioning, but sharing and observing something, which in its own world is perfect.

Relationship to Friends

Our parents and siblings mostly define us by how we have been in the past, whereas our friends define how we are today. There is a saying 'The Prophet is not recognised in his home town.' This is very true, simply because our family find it difficult to let go of the person they recognised in the past and accept the person of the moment. How many of us still feel like children in front of our parents or act out a different version of our self in front of our siblings? We have many facets of our being. What we do is split ourselves and we present different parts to different people, so the boss may see the efficient side of us, the children may see the nurturing side of us, the partner the romantic side of us, the employees the powerful side of us, but it is our closest friends who see the side of us which brings all these other facets together. For example, in a single conversation we may tell them of our day at work, our problems in our relationship, or we may compare child notes. Our closest friend is often able to cross more barriers than any other person in our life. Energetically they reflect the aspect within us which enables us to seek inner advice. It is our Soul looking at our facets and showing us how to act. Externally, problems arise when our friends have their own agendas and we cannot get a clear mirror to look into. Even this says something about the inner state of our self.

It is also interesting to note how the male and female energy acts differently with friends. The female energy seeks female energy for emotional support, so they are more concerned with feelings rather than strategy. The male energy seeks the male energy for mental action and requires strategy without any input from the emotions. Conflict can often arise between friends of the opposite energy when they cannot understand each other's way of resolving issues. This occurs if the male energy cannot get in touch with its emotions and the female energy cannot rise to understand mental concepts. For example, John has a problem with his secretary's standard of work. His friend Pete suggests that he has a talk with the secretary to get to the bottom of the issue, whereas John was looking for a contract clause to fire the secretary. John was looking at the problem from a mental level, whereas Pete was looking at it from an emotional level. If we look at balance then both the mental and emotional areas need attention. Avoidance in any of these areas externally, reflects an inner avoidance at looking at our own issues.

I have a friend who constantly worries about what others think of her, so she tries to make everything she does perfect with no room for faults. One morning we took a trip to town together and she passed a comment about the state of her hair and that she was not wearing her best coat. When she came out of the bank she looked a bit flustered. She explained that she thought the bank teller was thinking her hair needed styling and the cuffs of her coat were dirty, when in reality this is what was going on inside her. It is amazing how we project our thoughts onto others because we believe we are not perfect. We then believe it is they who judged us! We think to have faults is to be imperfect and to be imperfect is to be unworthy of love and acceptance. An Islamic carpet maker always makes one mistake in his carpet. He does this in reverence to God, as they say only God can be perfect. What thoughts and feelings do you have about yourself that you believe others judge you on?

Friends are mirrors for our problem solving, but we also need to be aware of the feelings they bring up in us. These feelings are our unresolved issues that block the communication with our own Soul. For example, you are driving in the car alone and you are lost. As you come to a junction you have a feeling to go left but you turn right instead. Twenty minutes later you become more frustrated at yourself as you realise your feelings were right. Now let's look at that again. You are driving in the car, but this time with your friend and you are lost. You come to a junction and you have a feeling to go left but your friend says turn right. Twenty minutes later you are angry with your friend as you realise your feelings were right! In the first scenario, you knew that not following your Soul's direction cost you time and energy and there was only you to answer to. In the second scenario, you knew that not following your Soul's direction cost you time and energy but, the difference is, you projected the blame onto another instead of accepting you only have yourself to answer to. There is nothing outside of your self.

Relationship to Strangers

Not all relationships are karmic, but we may still be affected by people with whom we have no karma. For example, in the office where you work there may be a man whose attitude to you is sexist. What is the definition of the word sexist? It is when another dismisses, abuses or belittles your human form. Although you have no karma with this man, for his karma is with the company, he is still bringing up a response from within you. Now you can do two things. You can either play his game by reacting to him or you can become observant, which is awareness without judgment. In this observation, you will begin to see what is behind the human man. You will realise he acts out his scenarios to make people feel fearful and uncomfortable. These acts empower him, but disempower you.

There are many people in the world who have lost most of their contact with the Soul, and what takes the Soul's place are very low energies or entities. These entities have become earthbound and they feed on the negative thoughts of humanity. They create chaos wherever they can by using the vehicle of the human body. Their intent is to render you emotionally powerless through fear, which leaves your mind open to abuse. This allows the entities to influence you into creating negative thoughts. This traps you in a vicious mental and emotional circle, as they feed off your Soul's light. While reading this it would be interesting to note your response and to ask yourself, are there energies upon the earth that do not have my best interests at heart? Observe your daily life and become aware of your mental and emotional states. Notice how you change your way of being with different people and in different environments. These changes are the influences energy has upon you. For example, if you are with a person who has a lot of anger in his system, then the energy will penetrate your system, find your anger issues and expand them. If you have unresolved issues, you will affect people in the same way. Observation of yourself and others will reveal the truth of all seen and unseen energy.

It is also interesting to note how differently male and female energies respond to strangers. A woman is very aware of the male emotional energy around her. This is because she searches for any negative desire or intent, which would render her physically vulnerable. The man however, is more aware of any mental threatening energy, which reveals if he needs to physically defend his territory. For instance, if a woman is walking in the woods alone and she sees a man coming towards her, she will immediately have a vulnerable response. Her mind will create all sorts of scenarios and she will send out a fear signal. However, if the man says, 'Good morning' and walks on by, the woman feels relief because her fear of being vulnerable has not been physically played out, yet it was played out on every other level! How many times have you felt vulnerable? How do you feel about being a female? What is the worst thing that could happen to you physically? What is the fear behind this? It is true that physically women are the weaker sex, but the conditioning and beliefs go deeper than this, as some women feel that being weaker on one level means they are weaker on all the rest. If as a female you come into your power on the mental and emotional planes, you would reflect this in your way of being on the physical plane. If you then come across a man who has a negative intent, the forces which reside within him would recognise your light and he would pass you by looking for an easier catch. Your vulnerability is your strength, in that you can use it to become aware and awareness is power on all the levels of your being.

If a man met another man while walking through the woods, he would react differently, because the signal men send out is not emotional but mental. In a sense the two men would be having a power struggle on the mental plane. This would decide who has the stronger force. If the threat is big enough then it is played out on the physical plane. I have met many men who are small in stature and some of them feel very similar to women in that they are physically vulnerable. They may become scapegoats for larger men or they become violent and vicious, fighting to prove they have strength. Saying this, I have also known men who may be small in stature, but have very clear and powerful mental planes. These men are able to blast the minds of those who would create chaos and often render them physically unable to take action: it is as though the fight goes out of them. As a male have you ever felt vulnerable? How do you feel about your physical stature? How do you defend yourself? What is the worst thing that could ever happen to you? What fear is behind this? We only have to look at the role model of Gandhi to see that male energy does not have to gauge its worth by physical power, but by inner strength, perseverance, and facing adversity with wisdom. This is what led India to freedom.

Relationship to Any Me?

When we realise we are connected to all life, then we understand that to dislike another reflects disliking a part of ourselves. The term 'any me' is an awareness that all other human beings on this planet are within you. They can be any part of you. To reject or dismiss any part of you will become an experience in your external world. When you love and accept your whole self, then you no longer see the earthly experience as something negative, for all darkness and 'enemies' become integrated into the light within you.

What is an enemy? We usually denote an enemy as somebody we hate. What is hate? It is a space where love does not reside. Only the mind can create a thought which contains no love. The only way it can do this is by becoming detached from the Soul, which is love. An autonomous mind separates. It cannot bond things because its sole purpose is to prove it has total control. It does this by trying to dominate other minds. We often hate others who try to overpower our minds, or those whose beliefs and actions are the opposite of our own. They are not under the same umbrella as we are therefore they pose a threat to our beliefs. We defend ourselves by thinking they are wrong, and we hate them for not conforming. This is so blatantly displayed in business, religion, wars, cultures, race, families, etc.

The one thing an autonomous mind abhors is the fact that it is not superior to the Soul. In other words it cannot control love, for love cannot be controlled. Love requires the mind to be its tool for expressing and receiving love. The mind in its defiance begins to create external wars, diversity and division. It tries to prove that love does not conquer all, yet it forgets that karma is love and a Soul will not leave the realm of earthly lives until it has become fully integrated, proving in fact that love does conquer all. How the mind spends its time trying to pursue a pointless goal! If you hate something or somebody, then what is it you are asking them to believe in? What have they done wrong? Can you look at the emotions it has brought up in you? Can you see the fear/belief behind them? Do you want justice?

The justice system punishes those who seemingly commit unloving acts. If we are the victims, we feel anger because we have been unable to tell the perpetrator of our pain. The role of the solicitor is to get the pain communicated to the judge and jury who decide if the perpetrator should pay a penalty for incurring an effect on our energy. Most of what happens to us is karmic, but this does not help with our pain, as we often hate those who cause us to feel pain, especially if a loved one's life has been taken from us. Can you see your enemy as someone struggling with earthly life? Can you recognise the good in your enemy? Can you forgive your enemy? Do you recognise that they may see you as the enemy? Can you see the love in you? Can you forgive yourself? Do you recognise that it is an internal conflict that has brought about an external conflict?

We see so much conflict in the world. Every day in the news we are being updated about the latest fighting and combat deaths. Many people say wars are evil, ugly, wrong, and yes, they bring immense pain, but we also need to understand that wars are not what we think they are. They are not just about humans killing humans, but they are unseen forces fighting through humans. Sometimes these forces can only be released and cleared through extreme actions such as a violent war. In New York on September the eleventh many innocent people were killed, but we also need to note the reaction it brought up. Some people became angry and wanted to get revenge. Others became fearful at the prospect of a war. Those that committed the act were jubilant at the outcome. They really believed that what they did was right. If two leaders declared war on each other, but nobody came forward to fight, what would happen?

I am not saying that all wars are negative forces fighting negative forces. Whatever happens in the physical world has already been played out in the spiritual realms. This means a physical war can be the reflection of a battle between the light and the dark. We need to take out all judgments and beliefs in order to see the truth of the forces that are at work behind the scenes. We need to understand that negative forces are able to work through humanity to bring destruction and chaos, simply because we are not masters of our own emotions. 'Love thy neighbour as you love yourself.' Jesus spoke these words two thousand years ago and they have a very powerful meaning. There is probably no greater teaching on the earth than this. Every Muslim would agree, every Hindu, Christian, Buddhist, Jew, etc. So when you look at your enemy, see him as your neighbour, see him as a Soul learning. Try to understand that he has got stuck in his learning, for he wants to be loved just as you do. Remember this. The most evil man or woman was once a baby in its mother's arms.

Relationship to Homosexuality

Homosexuality is such a controversial subject within society. Some say it is acceptable and some say it is unacceptable. It is so easy for us to judge another when we have not experienced life in their shoes, and so hard to come to a point of true compassion. Karma has a way of putting us in similar situations to those in which we have judged others. These can be in this life or in future lives. As a race we have become so trapped by our beliefs that we can no longer see life from a whole perspective. At a workshop, I met a young man who was homosexual. He asked me if God still loved him, as his family and society had shunned him for choosing to live his life in a different way from what they expected. I told him that in this life he had retreated into his feminine energy and he was trying to heal his male side, not through finding a partner who was a dominating female, but who was a dominating male. He was reaching out for someone to show him what he needed to see. I have also observed this way in gay females. If they are very male in their energy then they tend to seek the female reflection of themselves and they often find it in other females.

The Soul is not interested in the beliefs of society. Its only focus is to come back to wholeness and if someone of the same sex has what it needs and can help it, then it accepts the teaching. Ultimately, we are both male and female and there is no wrong or right in love. The only true emotion is love, so how can a person be judged for loving?

If you are homosexual, then take out the guilt, for guilt arises in thinking you are not pleasing others. Accept that this way of being is following your Soul's will to heal itself. Embrace the love you feel for another and observe it from a whole perspective. See any imbalances between your male and female side, and use your external relationship as a tool to heal these aspects. As you become whole, your external relationship will either become more enriched or fall away, opening the door to someone who will reflect who you are in a much clearer way.

Relationship to Religion

Although on the surface religion seems to unite people in a common belief, it also creates division as it sub-divides us into groups. We become Christians, Buddhists, Hindus, Muslims, etc and we proclaim that our God is the only God. How wonderful it would be if, even in our different groups, we recognised the unity of all things and we saw this unity as one God. Some beliefs say there is no God, yet they talk of the spiritual path to enlightenment. Is it possible to be spiritual and not believe in God? Yes, some aspects of Buddhism highlight this belief. If there is not a God within your belief system, then you need to acknowledge that there is love. The source of this love can be called God, Angels, Universe, Allah, Shiva, etc. It really does not matter, as ultimately there is only love. Until we learn this and accept it internally, then we will continue on this path of division.

Love unites. It does not separate. Therefore we should honour our brothers and sisters who pursue a belief system different from ours, because in a sense they are seeking the same thing. They are still seeking God. They do not want to keep being told that their beliefs are wrong. We are constantly fighting over belief systems and the whole of humanity is caught up in this battle. What we need to observe is that a belief system is something we believe in because we have been told to. It may even sound right to us or feel right to us, but do we really know it and understand it? The most important thing in all religions is to find out for ourselves. Just because we read a book and it says something is right, how do we *know* it is right? Let us find God within us. Let us find the Christ within us. Let us find the Buddha within us. Let us find Allah within us. Let us find within us the essence of what all these great people and writers have spoken about. Let us not just believe because we have been told to! We are told that fire burns, but if we do not go near the fire and feel the heat then how do we know fire burns? We have to experience for ourselves, and some people may even have to put their hand fully into the fire, others their finger, and some only need to feel the heat to understand it.

Each Soul has to quest for itself. Do not let your religion divide you. Do not let your religion say, 'I am right, they are wrong,' because this is inadequate for the world. It is this way of being which has created all the conflict. People are fighting only to keep their belief systems in place, whether it is a country, a religion or a philosophy. The only way a fight can stop is through acceptance. This acceptance is being able to see things as they really are, which is that each Soul on the earth is on a journey of learning and growing. Only when you are observing without judgment can you see the truth of their struggle. We all believe in love and although we may have different ways of obtaining it, it is still love we believe in.

In recent years many people have looked for gurus. Well, there are very few teachers on the earth who understand the energetics involved in accepting students, and it is not always favourable for the Soul to join a group or Ashram. I once observed the energy of a guru in front of a praying crowd. He accepted the devotion to himself, but I ask you, where is the freedom? How is it a person can devote that much energy to another Soul without devoting it to his own Soul? We have missed the point. We say these gurus are the embodiment of God, but *we* are also the Divine.

The true teacher recognises the different levels of awareness within each person he meets, and it is as simple as that. A true teacher knows how much you are connected to the Divine spark within your own Soul. They know this through your level of obedience to the promptings of your inner voice. It has nothing to do with your obedience to the teacher or how much you devote your energy to him in prayer at his feet. When a true teacher meets a person, the person is often oblivious to what stands before him and in the silence, which may mean without any spiritual talk, much work is done. Just by the teacher being pure in his thoughts, words and actions, will many levels of stuck energy be lifted from a person's energy field. You may consciously know what is occurring or you may just feel very light and happy after an encounter with a seemingly ordinary person. A true teacher helps you to stand and does not keep you at his feet with a promise of a glimpse of him every morning at ten o'clock! It is always wonderful to meet someone external who knows the road better than you, who can help you shift the boulders and obstacles, but ultimately there is nothing outside of you. The external teacher is only a reflection of your own internal teacher. If that teacher demands your devotion, worship, prayers, energy, etc, but does not help you see your God self, then this is something else. It is something that disempowers you and does not empower you.

I have met many so-called teachers on the path. Those who say 'you must do this to reach enlightenment' or 'this is the only way' are delusional. The true teachers who have graced this world, Jesus, Moses, Buddha, Krishna, Muhammad, etc, all had one thing in common, which was, 'Go within to know yourself.' Whether it meant through loving your self, looking at your desires, devotion, strengths, etc, it really does not matter, for each one leads to the truth. What they never said was, 'Search outside yourself for the answer.' Each teacher taught a varied system, but each one had their foundations built on pure thought, pure words and pure action. Who do you look to for your answers? Before you ask anyone for advice, ask within yourself first and then wait for a sign. It may come through nature, an ordinary conversation, you may hear it within, get a feeling, or you may wake up in the morning with a solution. We have become so used to relying on external guidance that we have forgotten to realise the only true guidance comes from within ourselves. We think other people have more of a connection to God than we do. We think they know Him better than we do and we say, 'We are not worthy enough to be graced by God.' We then hand over our personal power to others. What is your relationship to religion, gurus, teachers? Does the teaching bring you growth? Are you more connected to life, nature, God, love etc, as a result of the teaching you have received? If not, why do you feel you have not grown? Does your religion, teacher, guru take you within yourself, or do they teach you that God is up in the sky? That He is in sacred places? Or that you can only reach Him through them?

Not long ago I read a book that described how women could not reach enlightenment. Well, for all you millions of females out there you need to know that God sent out rays of himself, so that each ray would return consciously knowing its God-self. He did not say only males could return, females are not allowed entry! A fully enlightened person is someone who has integrated his/her male and female self and become God-conscious. In other words the Soul is fully functioning as a creative and inspirational being while residing in a physical body. Some forms of spiritual practice are so one-sided. I have often observed the energy of monks and nuns and seen that they are lacking or avoiding their own opposite energy. Each sect refrains from contact with the opposite sex, believing the way to God is through cutting off their male or female energy. This way of living reflects their inner world, which is non-integration of the opposite sides of themselves.

Another example of our beliefs around females and spirituality is the story of the Virgin Birth. If I was to say to you that Mary was an enlightened Soul, who, through her marriage to Joseph, who was also enlightened, gave birth to Jesus by the normal route of making love, what reaction would this bring up in you? I am not writing this book to prove to you that any of this exists, only to bring up reactions within you so that you may look at your deeper beliefs. If we were then to say that because of Mary's inner awareness, she was able to help bring out of Jesus his creativity, his love of nature, his ability to be aware and master his emotions, what reaction would this bring up in you? This way of looking at Mary means she is no longer some far off, unreachable virgin, but the role-model for every woman on this earth. This makes her a Soul who came to the earth as a woman and mastered every aspect, including making love and childbirth.

Mary was a silent teacher. So silent that we put her on a pedestal, which makes it impossible for women to reach. Is this not man's doing? For it certainly is not God's. What is your belief around women/men and spirituality? Where does this belief come from? If all the structures of religion, spirituality or new age philosophies were taken away, what would feel right for you to do every day that connects you with love? Are you already doing these things?

Not long ago I was watching the programme Lonely Planet and the woman presenter was in Egypt. After touring Luxor she decided to visit a so-called enlightened hermit living in the desert. When she approached him they talked about life for a while, but when she went to enter into his dwelling he said, 'You cannot come in here because you are a woman!' When will humanity understand that to deny the female or male energy on the outside is to deny it on the inside. Until there is an inner change to bring forth a balance, then the outside will always reveal a conflict.

One of my greatest observations in my workshops is that many people have suffered because of the beliefs in their religion. These religions are mostly male dominated, which leaves an imbalance and often people have rebelled. Some of these people have then turned towards the 'new age' concept or Celtic, druid or earth mysteries. In a sense they have gone to find the deeper meaning and understanding of the female earthly energy. One thing that needs to be made clear to these people is that if you deny the male religion in order to only accept the female religions, then you are in conflict, because there can be no denial. There must be an acceptance of all forms otherwise it creates anger and bitterness. In essence, the male has denied the female and now the female is denying the male. We are creating a conflict and in truth no one is better than the other. If you are currently studying one of the great earth religions or beliefs, then you need to remember that this is not everything, so you must experience and find the truth for yourself.

There are many new age ideas, colour therapy, aromatherapy, crystals etc: but ask yourself, how many true crystal healers really know exactly one hundred per cent what a crystal does? Very few people have the vision and the knowing to understand precisely what the crystal is doing on every level of our being. They probably do not see the energies that surround the crystal. If they do see the energy glow as a colour, can they see the evolving mineral entity of the crystal? If they can see it, what happens when that entity comes into the aura? It is time to ask questions and not just believe. On workshops do not just accept that when you use a crystal this happens and that happens. Find out for yourself. Not only observe what happens in the moment of using crystals, but also monitor the results throughout your life.

We can see this reflected in the western system of dieting. So many people go on yoyo diets moving from one diet to another. Some people find eating just raw food works, but for others who try this they may become ill. Some people believe eating carbohydrates is a good diet, for others it is not. There is no one system. We have to observe everything. What is your relationship to alternative therapy? If you are a therapist, do you know your field because you have read about it or because you have found out for yourself? Are you in denial of alternative therapy? Why? Are you completely immersed in the earth and denying the male aspect of God? Are you immersed in religion and denying the female aspect of God? How can you balance this?

Relationship to Nature

Nature is the manifestation of the female within God. This earth sustains all life that resides here. Each day she brings forth gifts that reflect the love she has for us. It may be the birds singing, a golden sunrise, dew on the grass, a gentle fall of rain, the wind blowing the leaves from the trees, or even the magic of a white carpet of snow, yet the majority of humanity falls out of bed and does not even notice. It amazes me how many people say God does not exist, yet everyday He showers us with visible miracles. What are we waiting for? Maybe a man with a white beard sitting on a throne? You only have to watch nature's changing of the seasons to see the whole point of life. She teaches us about growth, the breath, reincarnation, love, joy, peace, balance and the male and female energy of God. Nature is the reflection of the pure teacher within, for she has no hidden agendas, no expectations, no attachments, no judgments, no fears and she will teach you according to how open you are to receive her. How open are you? Look out of your window right now. What do you see? It is a true fact that we become similar to what we surround ourselves with. This is because our energy moulds and fits to whatever space we live in. What space do you live in? Is it full of tall grey buildings? Or is it filled with nature and space? Are you happy in your current environment or do you feel it is time to move? What stops you from moving and getting closer to nature?

At some point on our path back to wholeness we will have to address our relationship to nature, for she reflects the female aspect of ourselves. Her present state of chaos is a reflection of how humanity treats the female energy of every form on the earth. When we first came to the earth, nature was all ready here, but because we contaminated the space around us with our thoughts, this was reflected in the changes in our environment. As the male mental energy became more dominant, nature became something to use and her protests were drowned out. Over the last hundred years, as women also began to pull away from her and move into the intellect, she has started to revolt. What message is she trying to give us? Do not underestimate the power of endless giving through love and creativity, for her power is such that because she is held within the palm of God, then we are subject to Her seen and His unseen laws, but as a race we have been disobedient.

If the Mother Earth was a woman, then let us ask what have we done to her? We have fed her chemicals, which have polluted her blood stream and her organs. We have taken her against her will and then forced her to give birth to hybrids. We have analysed her assets, practiced our new combat techniques out on her and destroyed things about her that we did not think were perfect. We have performed surgery on her and taken away parts of her and made them extinct. We have given her our garbage and expected her to eat it, process it and clean it and finally when she cries out in pain and anguish, we say, 'Stop crying you pathetic woman!' We must be so proud to be the human race.

In the beginning science was a means of understanding nature. This knowledge enabled us to work alongside Her in harmony. Science is therefore man's way of connecting the heart with the mind, but what we have done is left the heart out. Recently, I was watching a documentary on cloning where one of the scientists was very excited about a possible breakthrough in being able to produce an embryo and create a human baby outside a mother's womb. He gleefully proclaimed, 'We, and not nature, will be in control of our own evolution!' What are we doing? When we look at it from a spiritual angle, or with the involvement of the heart, we will see that the baby will be without a proper environment to nurture a Soul. The karmic package is connected through the energy fields of the parents into the womb of the mother and then into the energy field of the baby. If the baby is formed outside this spiritual process, then a spiritual process does not occur. Now ask, what will then occupy the body of the child? All that is left are the low earthly energies and entities that we have created with ideas like these. It is ludicrous to think that in the future we will be able to pop along to the baby shop and order a clone of ourselves to be picked up in nine months. Wow! The world is going to be full of even more Soulless human beings! If we took this idea and began growing apples in labs by means of artificial feeding, artificial light and added chemicals, would you still eat it? Yet scientists get excited about creating something artificial when the real thing is pure beauty and a sheer miracle.

What I am going to write about next may shock you, but I am not here to prove that reincarnation exists, nor am I saying you have to believe in all my words, for this would be creating a belief system. I only wish to share something with you through my own inner knowing. Many thousands of years ago, there was a time in the history of the earth when women were the dominating force and men were subject to slavery. As men were extremely sensitive to their emotions, the women controlled them through the emotional centre. They were then treated as the weaker sex. What occurred was a revolt, as the man's ploy to escape the control of his emotions was to come into the mind or be purely physical, even brutal. The women were weak in these areas. They could not match the intellect or brute strength. To compete they began using the physical body as their weapon, either through being body beautiful, or in muscular competition with the man. The male has since become the dominant force of the sexes, but recently another revolt is beginning, where the women are starting to become stronger, but what we do not want to do is reverse the roles, as this would start the process all over again!

Balance is the only way. This is achieved through each individual looking within and accepting they are made up of both sexes, which heals the inner conflict of power between these two forces. This will also reflect externally in our oneness with the earth, as we will consult with her on every level of whatever it is that we wish to create. We will also become one with the universe and consult with the God within, as to what ideas are harmonious to create. Nature reflects our inner conflict with ourselves. As we become more at peace, we will begin to see her in a different light, and we will wonder at all her magic that has been there all along, but we refused to see it. How would you describe your relationship to nature? What can you do in your daily life that makes you feel at one with her? Have you tried walking in nature and just listening? If you live in the city, can you reach out to her in your spare time? How can you clean up your own personal environment to reflect your love for her? How can you give to nature? You will be amazed at how a close relationship with nature can change you.

Relationship to Culture and Race

Being raised in a children's home, I was very fortunate to have been brought up with children of mixed races who became some of my closest friends. This allowed me to observe their culture. At the time I did not understand that there were black and white races. One day I was walking to school with my black friend when I saw my first adult black man riding past on a push bike. Suddenly in sheer delight I shouted to my friend, 'Wow look, there is a black man!' My friend turned to me and said, 'Yeah, he looks like my dad!' I then realised my friend was black. It had never dawned on me before.

Society has separated people into sections. If you are white you are in the Western group. Those who are black are in the African group and those who are oriental are in the Chinese group and so on. Along with the splitting, we label them and we say, 'Because you are this race, then you have to behave in a certain way.' In general, when you look at another human being, they have two eyes, ears, two arms, legs, a body, etc, and it is only the colour of the skin that is different, yet we are constantly judging. We may judge them because they do not believe in the same things that we do or they pray to what appears to be a different God, but inside they are still a Soul who is learning. We no longer see people as a unique Soul, which is love, because we see them only according to what they present to us externally.

When I look energetically at the races on the earth, I can see the male and female principle in them. The white race leans towards its male energy, as it is expressive and very much in the mental plane. This is why the West has invented much technology, but it has also become prideful, in that it comes across as superior. We can see this reflected in how we have treated our black brothers. The black race is a feminine race, in that it works with the creative aspect of itself, but instead of becoming one with this energy, the Western group have used it, abused it and repressed it. When a male energy becomes too yang (male), it reaches a peak and then begins to lose its power. In a sense it starts to soften and become female. The Roman Empire is a good example of being very male and powerful, only to lose it all. When a female energy becomes too yin (female), then it becomes hard and unyielding. It becomes male. This scenario is currently being played out in many cultures where a male race has tried to dominate a female race. The female will take the worthlessness for so long, then she will begin to turn her energy into male energy by expressing herself. This is the danger, because when two male energies compete, then war breaks out.

England was once a very male and powerful society. Over the last hundred years we have allowed in creative female cultures. If we had worked with these cultures, then England would have become very balanced in its energy. Instead the male energy has repressed the female and we have placed her in poverty or in ghettos out of the way.

There is an external conflict simply because in each of us there is an internal conflict. Tradition plays an important part here, because many people leave one culture to enter into another, but they still try and live their lives according to a set of rules from another place. What does this say internally? That we hold onto the safety of the old, rather than trying to understand or embrace the new. We think our way is right, therefore another race or culture has got it wrong. We then get angry if they do not convert to our way of living. This gives way to hate and ignorance.

What is the solution? To heal the external we need to look at our internal beliefs, because if we can greet our brother with no judgments, then instantly his beliefs are opened up to be healed. It will then be a Soul-to-Soul contact, which extends far beyond culture and colour of the skin. What are your experiences around other culture and races? If they were negative, then how much of this is showing you your beliefs? What are your beliefs? What are your fears? Where did these come from? The culture of humanity is a two-fold energy. It is male and it is female. Until the male stops being superior and the female stops being worthless, then in all the corners of the earth, in every human, in every country, every city, town and village, this fight for balance will continue. It is about time we stopped blaming other cultures for doing *this* to us, or not doing *that* for us, and started healing the male and female within, for this is the culture of the Soul. One day humanity will see exactly what it has done. That day of vision will come at the end of each life. We will then have to recognise that the slave driver becomes the slave and the slave, the slave driver, until the healing of the male and female is completed.

Relationship to Addictions

We have many addictions: food, tea, coffee, alcohol, cigarettes, shopping, obsessive cleansing, money, drugs, sex, routine, etc. Behind every addiction lies an emotion, and behind every emotion lies a belief. Years ago, I worked with a woman who suffered from obsessive cleansing of her hands. Each time she touched someone she felt she had been contaminated. She was aware of what she was doing and she tried to stop herself from washing her hands by overpowering her mind with a new thought pattern. Although she stopped washing her hands, she started to wipe down everything before she touched it! There are so many workshops that centre on changing the patterns of the mind for another pattern. Have we gone mad! Have you ever tried to stop smoking by using only the mind and then found you have channelled the desire into something else: eating more, chewing gum, chocolate? Our original mind pattern is created from our beliefs. A belief will extend through all the energy bodies. To try and change only one energy body will bring confusion and conflict from within. The woman above finally realised that her obsession was related to her abuse as a child. She felt she had been contaminated by humanity. She had to face her emotions and her belief of worthlessness, until eventually she forgave both herself and the person who brought forth her belief.

Addictions are suppressants of our emotions. I always laugh at the way the English make a cup of tea in the middle of a crisis! If you are a habitual tea/coffee drinker, ask yourself what is behind this act? Is it boredom, stress, loneliness, sadness? Could you give it up right now? If not, why not? Where is your dependency? When you start the inner work, you may need to give up things so that the underlying emotion which was being suppressed, can rise to be cleared. After this period, you may go back to doing certain things. The difference is they will become an enjoyment rather than a necessity. It is also very beneficial to do internal cleanses, colon cleanses, liver and kidney cleanses, etc. This deep tissue cleansing helps to flush out toxins from the system. There are lots of books available on the subject. If you decide to take this route, it might also be beneficial for you to seek the advice of a herbalist.

To heal our addictions, we first need to become aware that we have an addiction. It is no good constantly telling a person that they are an alcoholic. They need to see it to take the first step. The next step is to become aware of thoughts that are linked to the addiction: 'I need some chocolate' or 'I want a cigarette', then become aware of your feelings. Before you reach for that cigarette or chocolate bar, ask what it will bring? Is it comfort? Is it relief? False joy? By using it, what will I be avoiding? Can I stop for a moment and feel the underlying emotion? If you can feel the emotion that is attached to the desire, then can you look at the underlying fear and ask, if I do not have it, what will happen? What is my fear? How have I not been allowed to be myself? Where have I not been loved? How can I let this go?

After going through these steps, if you still feel the need to follow your addiction, then become aware of your thoughts and feelings whilst in the act. One of my weaknesses is a desire for chocolate! I love the taste of chocolate! One day, after rooting in the cupboard for a stray piece, I sat down in front of the television and devoured it whilst my mind was on something else! I was not aware of my thoughts, my feelings, the taste, my body or what it brought to me. I was mindless. How many times have you acted out your habit without full awareness from every level of your being? Can you follow the above steps? What is your experience? Or is it that you cannot be bothered? What is behind this emotion? Keep looking. There is no hiding place!

Some addictions can be hereditary. I read about scientists who were researching the possibility of taking out genes that carried addictions and illnesses. What we need to understand is that if we start to mess around with DNA, we are taking away the choice from the Soul. We are interfering with karma on a very serious level. In one family of two adults and two children, the genetics may carry the illness of leukaemia, but only one of the Souls may need to bring it forth for its experience in this lifetime. The Soul may have chosen this family simply for its genetic coding. We think we are just physical beings, but our human form is a result of our Soul's energy. What we see or experience is only the tip of the iceberg and there are very few people who are able to see the bigger picture. We are like children passing a time bomb to each other thinking it is a ball! Even when those who are spiritual adults tell us that what we are playing with is a time bomb, we still carry on, sniggering to each other about the adult's ignorance! It is not our mind or our human form that is in charge! It is time we realised that we are the physical effect of all our thoughts, words and actions, since the beginning of light.

It is time to face what you do with your thoughts, words and actions. Where you are, what you are doing, where you are going, are all related to the thoughts that you think consciously and subconsciously, to your apparent and underlying emotions and the fears on which you have built your foundations. The key is Awareness! Awareness! Awareness! on every level and in every moment. Your addictions are your friends, because they are showing you what you need to look at and how you can reveal the issues you want to avoid feeling. Ultimately, the best relationship you can have is the relationship with yourself.

Relationship to Money

Money is energy. It is our mental and emotional reaction to it that determines its effect on our life. There have been moments in my life when I have lived in poverty and there have been moments when I have been wealthy. What amazed me most was how I felt in each situation. When I was poor, I initially felt worthless and trapped at the lower end of society. When I had money, I felt fearful of losing the money and becoming worthless again! I went round and round in this circle of loss, gain, then loss, gain, until eventually I realised it was my inner state of being that was trying to show me my belief system. Somewhere within me I did not love myself enough and have faith in the bigger picture. Even those who are living a 'middle class life' are still trying to reach a 'better' standard. In other words they still want to be more worthy in the eyes of society.

When I look around I see so much struggle upon the face of humanity. It is all because we fear not being loved. This is the root of our problems. Society has tried to answer our inner pain with money. Therefore our collective minds made up a system that separated people into worthless and superior. Even within each separate unit a fight for worth can occur. Many who are wealthy compete against each other to prove they are superior and many who are poor are just as keen to register the lower status of those who are less fortunate than themselves. Did you ever watch the film Pretty Woman? One of the reasons it was such a big hit is because the tycoon let down his barriers and let love enter into his life, which brought him an understanding of others. The prostitute began to realise her worth. Even at the end, when she went back to the poor area where she lived, she had decided to leave and do something worthwhile with her life. They both realised that money was not the answer. Love was. It was this realisation which gave them the strength to face what they had thought was real and understand their fears, which were the obstacles to achieving a better life. What is your relationship to money? How do you feel about those richer/poorer than you? Who do you blame for your present situation?

Example

Desire is the cause of all suffering……………………………..

Matthew owns his own software business. He lives in a six bedroomed house with acres of land just outside London, yet each morning he wakes up with an ache inside himself. He cannot describe this feeling, so he pushes it aside as he puts on his business mask and leaves for work. He knows deep down that money cannot fill this hole nor can the comfort of his wife whose demands on him for more things keeps him working long hours. He registers that she unknowingly must be feeling a similar ache, yet he is too frightened to stop this merry go round. He fears being deemed worthless in the eyes of his family, friends, competitors and society if he does not achieve success. This fear of failure is what makes him carry on… Does this sound familiar?

There are no victims………………………..…………………………

Marcy wakes up to the sound of the children arguing downstairs. She has slept for ten hours, yet she still feels tired. Oh, the dreams she had for herself! Instead she is stuck living in a back-to-back house in the middle of a run down housing estate. As she gets dressed, she ponders on this inner conflict within herself. Here she is in a life that screams, 'You are nothing!' Yet inside she feels she has so much to give. 'What is this pain within me? I am so alone'. As she leaves the house to take the children to school, she decides tomorrow she will enquire about college…but tomorrow never comes. When she reaches the gate, her battered car stands without any wheels. 'Why me?' She cries… Does this sound familiar?

There are similarities in these two situations. Each person is registering that something is not right inside. This creates a reaction in their outside world. In their own ways they are both struggling to love themselves. When an animal gets trapped, for a moment it becomes still. It does not struggle. In that moment it is aware of every sensation that is around it. In this state of awareness the animal immediately knows its fate. This is our way out of the traps of illusion. It is by becoming still and aware on every level of our being. We may think that money is the answer, or changing the government. In truth, if you were given a million pounds tomorrow, your fear of not being loved would perhaps wear different make-up, but it would still be the same.

The Soul lives only for the moment, simply because it has no concept of time. It lives in a timeless realm where past and future have no meaning. Its first experience of time occurred when it formed a mental body. When it became a physical being, it understood that a thought does not instantly form on the physical plane, but takes many moments to come about. The Soul has since got lost, because what the mind thought about, even lifetimes ago, is only just being manifested. We then presently find ourselves in situations that do not seemingly reflect who we think we are. When we become aware of our self in the moment, this will reveal to us what our mind is trying to manifest and the state of our hidden emotions. There are several ways of doing this, e.g. being breath conscious, body conscious, non-attached to thoughts or opinions of others, etc. The one exercise that helped me become aware of my relationship to money was carefully listening to people's words. Every time someone mentioned money or material gains, I would observe my feelings and reactions. Clarity began to form, as each time I heard a fear in someone else's words, I recognised it as my own. This understanding of my inner beliefs set me free from the wheel of worthlessness and fear of failure.

If you had a magic ring, what would you wish for? Would it be for wealth? A big house? A sports car? World love? World peace?

Two thousand years ago Jesus said, 'It is easier for a camel to pass through the eye of a needle than it is for a rich man to enter into the kingdom of heaven.' If we are masters at obtaining all the jewels and money the earth can offer, but we are not the master of ourselves, then we have nothing. We are in a state of true poverty. Therefore you do not need a magic ring. You can turn within and become wealthy, become love, become peace and have everything you need to support you in every moment. We believe we are not lovable until we have gained the status of material wealth, so we work externally to create externally. This is subject to change, as it is impermanent. If we work internally everything will follow externally. This is true wealth and permanence. For material wealth can be taken away, but the riches of the Soul can never be taken away. Look at your life. Are you focused on the internal world or the external world?

Relationship to Occupation

Over the years the most popular question I have been asked is 'what should I be doing for a job?' The answer is simple. Your job is anything in which you can love and be loved, for this is what will bring you happiness and fulfilment. If you are in a career where you are not happy, then you need to look at it. Some people get joy out of bringing pleasure to others, yet there are also some who get joy from making others suffer. If bringing pain to others is where they want to be, then leave them there, but it does not mean you have to be in that space as well. What you really need to ask yourself is this, 'Does what I do benefit myself, humanity and the environment? Or is it destroying myself, humanity and the environment?' When choosing a career think of your life purpose and ask, what do I want to do? Now become aware of your emotional response. Have you dismissed your dream as unobtainable? Have you laughed at your fanciful idea? Are you afraid of the changes it might bring? Are you afraid of upsetting other people in reaching out for your dream? Now imagine barriers before you, describe them. What do they represent? Are you sure these are not excuses for not obtaining what would make you happy and fulfil you? Now imagine pushing the barriers over. See a clear path between you and your dream. How would you feel if you obtained it? How would your value of life change? Would you feel at peace?

When we are young, we often play out our deepest dreams. When we reach adulthood, these childish ways get swept under the carpet for more financial and material desires. What happens then, is we reach a peak where we realise this money-making, gadget-collecting habit leaves us cold inside and we start to feel restless. At this point we either break out, or we remain static, often losing our ability to be inspirational. Our heart has gone out of pursuits that do not bring us joy from within. We have become frustrated at the endless collecting we do externally. It is amazing how, as an adult, we neatly fold away our inner child into a hidden drawer within us. It is only after years of trying to live life according to external rules that we decide we have lost our joy in life. We came here to love and to be loved. We came here to serve. It is only this that will bring us true fulfilment. Therefore take out your inner child, unravel it, and find out what it was that you so wanted to be as a child. Then take a look behind the emotion of this. Was it to bring joy, to help humanity, to support nature, to create beauty, etc.? Start by taking a step in the direction of your heart, which is love.

If your dream was to help others, then you also need to understand desire is the cause of all suffering and to be of service will bring you suffering. You will see the sadness and the bitterness of humanity, but you will also have the joy of knowing that you are doing what you came here to do. The Souls, who are living a life in service to help humanity, are here because they heard the cries of the Mother Earth and the trapped Souls. These Souls offered their assistance to ease the pain. If you have felt the call to change your present career into something that will uplift the heart, but you have ignored it because of the fear of change, then you are adding to the pain of the planet and not to its healing. It is difficult to be free of desire. No matter what you are doing on the earth, it will have some form of desire attached to it. Even the desire to be desireless, is still a desire! In whatever career you choose, be true to yourself and give to the world the best you have and the best will come back to you.

When I was very young I used to sit in the church and listen to the stories of Jesus and the Apostles. I noticed that the stories always related to the past. My thoughts were, 'I wish He was here now, for I would not have done those things to Him that other people did,' yet my whole life was about doing the things that these other people did! I denied Him, I swore at Him a few times, but I always had a sense of wanting to help people, to heal people, to make people better. Now I feel that I have fulfilled my desire. I have fulfilled the dream that was in me as a child. By the time I was fourteen, this desire within me became a quest, it became a deeper knowing that my life was about my love for Our Lord and that everything I did would lead me to love and be loved. What stands in your way to loving and being loved?

Relationship to Business

Example
Doug is supposed to work a forty-hour week, but he finds that because he also takes his work home, he can work an additional ten to fifteen hours every week. Inside he is beginning to resent the pressure. He feels that to tell his manager he needs help will deem him incompetent. His main fear is that the company will favour another as more able and he will be replaced. His family life is starting to suffer and his wife has warned him that if things do not improve, she will consider a separation. What does he do?

Does this sound familiar? Are you afraid to ask for help at work? Are you afraid to say no to an overload of work? Would it not make sense for the man to approach the manager, explain what he is mentally, emotionally and physically capable of, and then leave it up to the company to employ additional help? Yet we find it difficult to honour ourselves in this way because we fear losing our job. The real fear underlying this is the fear of being judged as an incapable human being. How can we ever deem ourselves worthless when the Soul belongs to the Ultimate Creator and is built in His image?

Over the years I have helped many people to start their own business. The two main things that I have observed are firstly, that it is people who create the business and secondly, for the business to be recognised not only on an earthly level, but also on a spiritual one, all products should be worthy of being sold to God. Before selling a car, a used car dealer should ask himself if he would sell that car to God. If the answer is an inner yes, then the sale will not create negative karma. If the answer is an inner no, but it is sold anyway, then it will create negative karma, because knowingly he has passed on faulty goods. When a person creates solely for God's use, then he acknowledges the worth in his clients. This way of being attracts to him spiritualised energy, which teaches the world the true meaning of service through business.

Over the last hundred years companies have become huge and personal contact with employees has diminished. More often than not the focus is on the end result rather than the process. When a person first has a business idea, they collect around themselves the energy they will need to make the idea physically manifest. This may include a person with experience in the selling field, a person with typing skills, a person who is able to handle the buying of the parts to make the product. When these people come together a business is formed. Problems can occur when the business is energetically imbalanced. It may become too male if it becomes ruthless and forgets that it is the people who make the business. Or it may become too female by being relaxed, which allows the people to become inefficient and no longer dynamic.

Problems occur if employees are not able to use all their skills in their work. For example, the secretary wants to not only type, but also share her ability to supervise people. If the secretary is refused, then she may feel rejected and unhappy. Trying to keep the equilibrium within the business is very difficult. The business world is built on competition. There is competition between companies selling the same product, competition between employees to get promotion and competition within ourselves to prove ourselves against others. There is a space for everything in this world, but we think that if we do not get our product out first, or if we do not corner the market, then we will become extinct. In a sense we are saying that if the world does not find what I do worthy, then I will no longer exist, therefore I need to be the top dog. I need to be reassured that what I have to give is worthy.

If you own a business, then look closely from the management right through to the employees and question what your way of working says about you. Do you honour the process? Do you value those that work for you? Do you take into consideration their individual needs? Do you expect more input from them than they are paid for? Do you recognise their input and your output should be an equal balance? Question whether what you sell will bring unity to the planet or help to destroy it. Ask Mother Nature from within if it helps with her process of giving life or does it hinder it. If you do find any imbalances, then ask yourself what you can do to make these imbalances become harmonious. It might mean becoming organic, changing your chemicals, recycling your waste, using biodegradable products. Whatever it means to become in line with heaven and earth do it! Do not sit back and comment on the amount of money it will take to change your current process. For what is money? It is energy, so you will need to put energy back into your business to purify it. If you are really willing to be honest, you know how your product affects the world. If it is harmful then you have karmic responsibility, which you will have to face. If not in this lifetime, then certainly in another one. You will have to put right any negative impact you have upon this planet and humanity. There are no exceptions!

Relationship to Sex

There is sex and there is making love. What is the difference? Sex is a release of built-up energy. Making love is a sharing of purer energy. When we perform anything without love, then it is not love that comes back to us. We are energy, and through the act of an orgasm we open our chakras and release energy. If our energy consists of negative thoughts or suppressed emotions, then this is what we release, but where does this energy go? If you are male, then it enters into the chakras of your female partner. If you are female, then it enters onto the chakras of your male partner. The act of sex itself reveals to us the state of our mental and emotional conditioning around love. Two Souls who make love to express loving feelings towards each other on every level, will feel recharged and at one with each other. This form of sex is total sharing, because their minds are completely empty and their emotions are centred in love. They have entered into the moment.

If we have sex to reach an orgasm for the buzz, or every night through habit, then this is not love. It is a way of ridding ourselves of negative energy by dumping it onto someone else. When we have sex we let go of our barriers. This puts the female in a position of vulnerability, as the nature of her female energy is to receive. This can leave her fearing the intrusion of the male giving energy and the negativity that may come with it. Afterwards, she may feel violated or empty. This is because subconsciously she knows the energy she has received is not pure. The act of sex renders us more vulnerable than at any other time, therefore we have to stop using our partner as a storage vehicle for our pent-up energy.

If sex is a means of relieving tension, controlling another, possessiveness, fantasies, power and lust, then know that the act has brought about a negative effect within the energy field of your partner. This act has not been through love, but through fear. Sex is a sharing of energies, so you need to think about whom you are sharing your energy with. In this sharing you will receive into your energy bodies not just the positive aspects of your partner's world, but also the negative. People who have casual sex need to be aware that during the energy exchange, we place cords into the chakras of our partner and we receive a connection to all the other people they have slept with. Physically, you may only be with one person, but energetically who knows? Would you go outside and roll about in raw sewage? Yet we constantly pollute our energy bodies and give others permission to join in with the pollution.

The other alternative, which is a taboo subject in society, is masturbation. To admit to self-satisfaction raises many eyebrows. There are endless beliefs as to why we should not take part in this perfectly normal function:

If you masturbate, you are dirty!
If you masturbate, you could cause yourself an injury,
If you masturbate, you will go blind,
If you masturbate, you are unattractive, desperate, a failure,
If you masturbate, you are bad,
If you masturbate, you should be ashamed.

The list is endless! If you do not make love regularly or release yourself, then the base chakra, which sits at the genital area, will become charged with negative particles that it picks up from the earth. This energy will build up and slow the chakra down in vibration. This affects the other chakras on the spinal column. Regular orgasms are a spiritual function for the health of all the energy bodies, so when you feel you need sex, i.e. a release, then you need to masturbate. You could masturbate first and then make love afterwards. This will allow the release of the built-up energy to disperse, leaving you ready for deeper intimacy. Making love and sex are two different things. Making love is a total sharing and coming together and the purer we can become in thoughts, words and actions, then the closer we will become. The idea is not to pollute your partner, and we do not have to, because masturbation is a tool for keeping ourselves clear.

Wherever We Think We Are

We have become conditioned to believing that we have to look to another human being for relief of our sexual urges. It this belief which has caused us to become obsessive about sex. A young man came to see me for a consultation and he complained of feeling ill. He said he felt very strange internally. When I looked into his aura I could see many different energies of other people. He told me that he had recently posed nude for a gay magazine. On looking closer, I realised that he was being used as an object for people's sexual fantasies during sex and masturbation. People, who were thinking and focusing on him, were actually directing perverted energy to him. I have also seen this in quite a few women. Once, I was helping a friend to paint the outside of his house. When I reached his teenage daughter's window, I was bombarded with sexual thoughts. I realised these were boys at school who, whilst masturbating, were thinking about her. All around her window was the energy thought forms of these people. It is important to realise that, if, during the act of sex or masturbation, we send thought forms to another person, then this is where a good portion of our energy goes.

If you are single or have a different libido from your partner's, then you need to take control of your sexual energy, and masturbation can help you, but you also need to take control of your thoughts during the act. If while masturbating you direct your thoughts to the person of your desires, or pornographic material, or past scenarios, then that's where your energy will go. If you are feeling lonely, depressed etc, then you will also project these feelings to where your thoughts are. To be thought-responsible whilst you are at your most vulnerable, can ensure that your energy is not polluted and that you do not pollute the energies of others. You can do this by directing your thoughts into nature. This process will liberate your need of having another person to fulfil you and it will ease the sexual pressure within your relationship. The idea is to direct your energies into a more wholesome way of being. Have fun exploring your preferences. You may visualise sitting under a waterfall or lying on soft grass in a sunlit forest, etc. Only you can create an essence of freedom and peace to explore the natural side of yourself. Masturbation this way becomes one with the nature of your being. You will feel re-charged and refreshed afterwards, as nature is the ultimate purifier.

Can you imagine how much this way of being will free us from the obsessions we have around sex? It may even change the dynamics of your partnership. A man may become more relaxed around his libido and a woman may feel more nurtured and cared for. The focus on our needs during sex will become less controlled, as we begin to give more to our partners instead of fulfilling the desire to receive. What is your relationship to sex? Could you give without receiving? How do you feel after sex? If you feel tired and heavy, where has your energy gone? If you feel unfulfilled, what is this saying about you? I have met many people who try to avoid sex with their partner, either by going to bed early, feigning illness or even starting an argument. If you recognise you are avoiding intimacy, what is the emotion behind it? What is the belief? Can you share your feelings with your partner? If we cannot communicate on every level of our being with our partner then we may hold back during sex. Do you hold back during sex? Do you feel vulnerable?

What we do with our thoughts during sex is crucial, because if you are thinking pornographic thoughts, thinking of past lovers, desires, etc, then this is what you are inviting into your energy bodies and chakras. This is polluting you, when the process of orgasm is to cleanse yourself. Once again we have conflict. If you can channel your thoughts into nature then the sex will change, as the heart will open more and the connection to your partner will be more complete. It will be even better if you can lose yourself in the total act of giving, which is a clear mind, open heart and pure selflessness. There is the lower form of sex and the higher form of sex. The first form engages only our desires, but the second form engages the Soul through the opening of the heart. Do not take my word for it, put the teaching to the test and find out for yourself.

Intimacy

People often tell me that they do not touch their partners because it always leads to sex. I have noticed that if a child is not hugged and kissed by its parents, then when it is touched as an adult, this leads to sex. We need to learn to touch each other and share moments: perhaps massage each other's feet, stroke each other or hold hands. So much energy is exchanged in these moments, that often the act of making love is not needed. We need to realise love can be shared in many ways. Touch is an amplification of love.

After a couple have had children the sex drive can be affected. This affects the female more because she has gone from being the lover to also being the mother, and in society a lot of people have difficulty around mothers having sex. In fact we may have problems accepting that our own parents have sex. This is because of the belief that sex is dirty, rude or naughty, etc. How did you feel when you first realised your parents had sex?

It is often believed that to get close to God you have to become celibate. Monks, nuns, priests, popes, cardinals, gurus and their disciples refrain from sex. Somewhere inside is this belief that sex takes you away from God. This is because lovemaking has become confused with our need for release and release has been denied as an unnatural, dirty activity. When we make love in a clear and pure way, where we are completely open to our partner in a state of love, we unite with God.

If we are addicted to sex, we need to realise that we are using it as a means of release. As with all addictions, it may be important to refrain for a while until you understand and gain control over the emotional desire for sex. Then it is possible to obtain the perfection of love and total sharing.

Some women believe having sex brings their man closer. It is sometimes the only way of feeling intimacy and attention. After sex, the woman wants the intimacy to extend into hugs and words of love. However, the man often turns over or falls asleep. Energetically, when a man has an orgasm, he gives his energy away to the woman. He therefore feels empty and he has to rest to regain his balance. A woman can often feel more energetic after sex. This is a result of two things. Either her energy has been polluted by the collected energy from the man, which makes her want to get moving to clear it, or she has received pure loving energy and she feels inspired to get moving to create. In your relationship are you afraid to touch your partner in case it leads to sex? Do you have issues about being touched? Can you find the hidden emotion? The fear? What are your beliefs around intimacy?

Why Do We Have Affairs?

The heart chakra is the centre where we hold our cords to those we love. This is what is meant by the term 'affairs of the heart'. When we enter into a sexual relationship with a person, what we are saying is that you have a deeper connection to my heart than any other. If all our chakras and energy bodies are clear and flowing, then our relationship will be honest, liberating and free from expectations and control. If we have blockages, negative beliefs and expectations, then our relationship will often run into problems. Affairs occur simply because we cannot be our true self in our present relationship. What we fail to realise is that the affair will only bring us a short-term relief from looking at our issues, for ultimately this state of being will run into the same problems. We cannot escape from what is going on within us, as we only transfer it onto the new scenery. What is really going on is that we are frustrated at not being able to be ourselves.

I have met many couples who blame each other. They blame it on the other's restrictions, control, sexual issues, growing old, fading looks, career, money issues, lack of support or understanding. The list is endless, but how often do we ask ourselves, what are my emotions around my present partner? What is my fear about the relationship? What is my part in all this? How can I change? Instead we turn in another direction outside of ourselves for the answer. Some affairs are also karmic in that the third person helps the couple to see what is going on in the relationship, and many couples have gone on to become stronger. However, the hurt partner often cannot forgive, and the anger of being lied to gets projected. They see themselves as the victim. If for just a moment they stopped and looked at their part in it, then they would see their hidden fears. Often we fear rejection, not being loved, and we feel we are not enough.

There is a saying, 'Hell hath no fury like a woman scorned.' When a person is scorned by another, they may go into extreme anger and frustration. Basically they are saying, 'I was not loved completely' and they react negatively. The person may go out of their way to destroy what was built. They may return the love letters, cut up clothes, involve solicitors, damage property or cars. They react in a way that says, 'I want justice,' so they set out to hurt the pride of the person who hurt theirs. In a sense they are doing unto the other as they feel they themselves have been done to. At the time we really think this is the answer, simply because we have let our emotions, instead of the soul, rule our being. We do not always understand the law of karma and that our situations are there to teach us. Therefore we need to ask, what is it I am being taught?

A man can be very physically strong, even fixed in his thinking, but a woman can destroy him and turn him into putty with just one dig at his emotions. He may respond by going into his shell, not communicating with her, or perhaps going out to the pub. A man cannot defend himself emotionally, and a woman cannot cope with a mental attack, as it damages her emotional body. If a man betrays a woman she may respond by buying new clothes or acquiring a new hairstyle. They both need to look within rather than reacting to each other.

Question your deeper issues. Look at your fears and find out what it is within you that has brought this experience to you. Nothing has been done to you. Your Soul has created this situation in order to find the true you.

Who Do We Blame?

Awareness with action brings about permanent change.

We blame others for our suffering. We blame others because they do not do what we expect of them and we blame others because we have ended up in a certain position in life. The opposite of blame is

forgiveness, or we could call it acceptance, but in the end it really does not matter what label we put on it, for it is love. The most important thing is not to blame others for the position you are in, but to see what it has taught you about you. Do not dwell on what it has *done* to you. You may feel hurt and you may feel embittered, but what is the inner cause that has made you feel this way? Is it anger? If it is anger, then what is the seat of the anger? If it is fear, so what is the fear? Is it that you cannot speak out? That you cannot say what you feel? That you cannot be yourself?

What we have to strive for in life is to take out all the judgment and blame. These two run hand in hand. If we strip these down, then what is left? All that is left is love, because there is only love. To reach liberation we have to get rid of what has attached itself to us, only then will there be love, which is what we really are. You do not have to love what is attached to a person, but love the person for who they are, which is the Soul.

Blame is a form of projection. We see them as 'the bad guys' and say, 'you are this and you did that.' What we are doing is telling them that they are not love. We are confirming their worst fear and what do you think this will do to the person? Do you think they will turn around and say, 'I accept that I am bad. I'm a sinner and I am not love?' No, they will defend themselves because, just like you, inside they are crying out for someone to confirm their Godliness. Even if what is attached to them is far from harmonious, somewhere within them lies God, waiting for the door to be opened by another who does not judge them, but accepts their mistakes as a yearning for love. Before blaming another, look for what it is that they have taught you about yourself. Do not judge in anger by saying, 'They have shown me nothing, they have only hurt me.' What is hurt? It is the fear that we have not been loved. We always have to bring it back to an emotional level, simply because we are living on a planet of emotions, and behind the emotion lies the belief which is the fear. Fear makes us deny our part in the drama, either as a mirror to another or as a participant, responsible for our actions and reactions.

When have you blamed another? Can you now see your fears? Can you forgive them? Can you see them as a Soul struggling with their fears? Can you help them by accepting them and opening the door to love? Free them and in the process you will also free yourself.

A while ago I wanted to send a letter to someone, which would convey my feelings of support around a difficult time they were going through, so I wrote,
Dear Jenny,
Love Mike.

Jenny then phoned me and said you forgot to write the letter! I replied I did not need to sympathise, empathise, reflect or point things out, for instead I sent you the universe. Look at your fears and use the only solution there is to heal them, which is love.

Self-Blame

When we blame ourselves for the outcome of a situation, we may as well put on a pair of boxing gloves and beat ourselves senseless.

This is what the energy of self-blame does to the Soul. The point of life is to master our emotional responses to situations and not be subservient to them. If we make a mistake, but hold onto the negative aspect of it, then we have not taken the prize of the experience, which was to know the outcome of our choice between love and fear. Self-blame keeps us in a negative circle of self-sabotage. It takes our light and makes us feel guilty for any pain that we may have caused another, or received. If we can accept the event, learn from the experience and move on, then it becomes an enlightening moment.

If a person already has a low sense of worth, they take on the blame for other people's actions. Many people who have been or are being abused take on this form of self-punishment. They believe that somehow they created the scenario for the abuse to take place, therefore they are to blame and deserve the punishment. Even after leaving the abusive situation, people will continue to blame and punish themselves. The abuser has gone, but now they are abusing themselves, keeping the negative programme in place. We are not responsible for other people's actions; they are responsible for their own. We only need to answer to our own Soul and not to the demands and desires of other human beings. When we answer only to the inner call of the self, we become blameless. This way of being will cause conflict between yourself and others, simply because it will highlight where the human manipulation is trying to get a hold.

The Soul only knows love. It has taken a human body upon the earth in order to experience the lessons of duality. If we give it a chance, it will learn from the situation and then move onto the next lesson, putting its new found knowledge into action. If we are aware of our part in the scenario, we can take all judgment out of the situation and know that we do not have to make the same mistake again. If we get stuck in the negative energy of self-blame the Soul cannot move forward. It will keep creating the same scenario until we realise that we can take no more self-beatings. Life is a school of learning. We choose our lessons and we choose our reactions and we will stay in the classroom of self-blame until we choose otherwise.

Where have you blamed yourself? What was the lesson in the situation? Can you feel the emotion and look for the hidden fear? Have you blamed yourself for other people's actions? What does this say about you? It is now time to let go, forgive yourself for any mistakes and then move on.

Resentment

Resentment is very similar to blame in that it eats away at our being as a feeling of something being unfair. We often feel resentful towards another person for doing something which does not please us. Resentment also stems from having expectations that are not met. For example, you do a favour for someone, but when you ask for a favour in return, the person refuses you. A feeling of resentment then emerges and you begin to begrudge that you did the favour for them in the first place. Energetically, you have closed your heart. The energy of love with which you did your favour has become distorted within you, as now it is conditional. It is tainted with a hidden agenda of expectation.

The feeling of rejection is our fear of not being loved. The solution lies in being able to keep our heart open in the moment. This will allow us to see the bigger picture. We may then realise that our request was turned down because others are struggling with something else. What then stops us from helping the other person to solve their problem in order for them to have more free energy to fulfil our request? Fear makes everything personal and small. Love reveals everything, making our understanding complete. Whom do you resent in your life? If you saw life from their angle, what would change within you? What are your beliefs around giving? Do you give to receive? What is your fear if your requests are declined? Look back over your life and pinpoint areas where you begrudged giving or feared asking for help.

The Saboteur

What is a saboteur? It is someone who is self destructive and obstructive to the forward moving force of hope, love and joy. It often appears in the form of negative comments, i.e. I can't...I give up...I'm not good enough...If I do act, then I shall fail...etc. It is the voice of the mind within us that is obstructing our growth. The saboteur is often in deep conflict, for they struggle against the flow of life. This leaves them constantly asking others for help, which gives them hope and a direction, but then out comes the saboteur and mixes the positive advice with negative questioning.

The saboteur fears failure and when an opportunity arises for positive change, it does not act and remains static. It looks at everything negatively, therefore the glass is always half empty. It is the male energy within us that gives us the ability to be assertive and face any obstacle as it appears. When we are lacking in yang (male) energy, then we fear taking action. Therefore the saboteur does not live in the moment, as it is always focused on the pitfalls that the future might offer. In this moment right now, we do not even know if these pitfalls exist, but the saboteur can create mountains out of molehills! What our thoughts create here on the earth reflect what we are building as our spiritual heaven. There is no separation.

The saboteur is often a worrier and it expects to be disappointed, rejected or deemed not good enough. It is a reflection of our relationship with the Father God. We are saying that He is not protecting us and that we are out of the fold of Divine support. We believe that to fail is to be bad. Therefore we avoid any attempt to try and reach for our highest potential.

A saboteur lives in doubt that God resides within himself. He can have the most inspirational ideas, but does not act upon them as he feels he does not have the power to materialise them. The mind will belittle who he is, telling him that his ideas will fail and that they are out of reach. The saboteur can be known as the second mind or that of the inner parent. It is the mental thoughts that hold all the beliefs from the family, society and country that the person was born into. It renders a person inactive.

To heal the saboteur we need to look at our issues of rejection. Where in our life were we deemed not worthy or loveable? When we are rejected we often answer by rejecting other people and our dreams. We destroy the moment. The saboteur brings the past into the present and lives their life still believing that something, which happened maybe even life times ago, is still relevant in the now. They put darkness into the moment with their fears and destroy the light.

The observation of our thoughts, words and actions, will reveal if we are being self-destructive. If we are prone to analysing, justifying and taking apart inspirational ideas, then we have the saboteur within us. Once we see how we are reacting; we can thank our saboteur for the teaching, let go of the negative patterning, and take action.

When we travel further along the spiritual path, the life issue which the Soul chose to work on, becomes more apparent. In effect, we are facing the major obstacle that we have placed before God. This is an initiation into greater freedom. This means that if you have taken on jealousy, pride, anger, the saboteur or apathy, etc, as your life lesson, then the experience of it can appear to be so overwhelming that you feel engulfed by it. The unveiling and uprooting is done by constantly being aware of your thoughts, words and actions. This is the final battle and God will be the conqueror.

Soul Responsibility

How many times do we hear the saying, 'You need to take responsibility.' Yet there are very few people who really understand the term 'responsibility', as most of us become responsible through guilt. We take things on because we believe that we need to uphold something to please others or gain a sense of worth. The Soul's understanding of responsibility is purifying its thoughts, words and actions so that its effect on the world is pure. If we break down the word responsible it actually means to 'respond to kin'. What we need to do now is understand how we are responding to our kin. Is it through fear or is it through love? When we respond through fear, we say yes to things when we mean no or we carry certain burdens because society says it is time to. By following fear we are ignoring the Soul, who may be telling us that we do not need to go into these scenarios.

When a child reaches the teenage years we say to them, 'Now, it is time for you to be responsible.' In a sense we make life seem serious and we destroy the joy. We teach the child that being responsible means taking work, family, commitment, relationships, problems etc, very seriously. We tell them that even if they find no joy in these burdens, they must carry them for it is their duty. It is very rare to find a child, a teenager or an adult who has been guided to take inner responsibility. This is the awareness that their inner response to others releases the burdens of the external life. Would you describe yourself as a responsible person? Write a list of your responsibilities. Which ones are a burden? Do any of them bring you joy? Do you take on responsibilities through guilt? Duty? Being forced to? Which ones benefit your Soul? Which ones benefit society? If you were to let go or share the responsibility, who or what would it affect? Look beneath the responsibility. Do you perform it through love or fear? If it is fear, what do you fear will happen if you let it go? Your first responsibility is to your Soul. If you allow it to guide you then everything you think, say and do will be a pure response to kin and to the world.

The Soul understands that thought is the first step to creation. The second step is emotion, which is the desire or intent, and the third step is the action it needs to create on a physical level. For example, in the office a woman meets a man and she finds him attractive. She discovers that he is already involved, but she still secretly desires to be with him. Now she is at the third point. Does she take action towards him or does she look within herself at her desires and become aware of her thoughts. This is being Soul-responsible. If she decides to make a move without consultation with her Soul and he accepts, but six months down the line a lot of people become emotionally hurt, then she has created karma. She responded to a situation not through full awareness of herself, but through a single-minded desire. When we act from our Soul's prompting, then all that we do will be karmically right. If the woman consulted her Soul and was prompted to make a move, then she is fulfilling karma. The end result will therefore be a clearing of something and not a creating. Responsibility is about tuning our thoughts to the higher good, mastering our emotions and acting when both of these are in harmony. Being truly responsible for our own actions may result in going against what society believes we should carry, as living through our Soul means we will be living a guiltless life.

No More Lying

Be True to yourself, you deserve it!

Often when I observe people speaking I can see the colour tones of the words. The energy that surrounds these tones can then reveal whether a person is telling the truth or not. It amazes me how some people think that because they are solid matter it means they are not transparent! We think that we can get away with lying, but we forget that our energy bodies are connected with everything. If we tell a lie to someone then it is immediately registered in the other person's energy field. One of the main reasons we lie is for protection. This may be to protect ourself from personal consequences or to avoid hurting others. People who are perpetual liars often weave worlds where they present themselves as worthy in order to cover up their feelings of worthlessness. There are others who have become so accustomed to lying that they no longer register it as a fault. Their lying has become automatic.

Energetically, in each moment our Soul presents us with energy to express. If we ignore the Soul and follow the mind's conditioning through fear, the energy that is expressed is no longer pure. It has become distorted. When we lie we need to ask ourselves what would occur if we told the truth? Would it mean change? Or will someone see us as not perfect? If it would bring another person pain, then how can we tell the truth with love? How can we begin to recognise when our actions create chaos? If we tell lies to feel more powerful, then how can we take a pause and see our life as it really is? How can we recognise our worth? Do we have any unfulfilled desires?

If lying has become second nature, then we have to look back at the first time we can recall needing to protect ourselves from pain. Children often learn how to lie at a very early age. This is because they live in the moment and they have not yet learned that there are consequences for their actions. If a child is naughty in the morning and the mother says, 'Wait till your father gets home,' by the time the father arrives home in the evening, the child may not fully remember the event, so the punishment has a more damaging affect on the energy bodies. Children learn through the ways of pleasure and pain. They realise that they have to discover some aspects of life in secret. If they are caught out, they will deny it in order to avoid the pain of being reprimanded. Lying then becomes a way of life. The ultimate fear is pain, and behind pain resides the belief that according to others, to experience some aspects of life is 'wrong'.

Our Intentions

Behind everything we think, say, and do, is our intent. This intent is linked to acquiring the fulfilment of a desire. We have many intents and some we use as goals, i.e. I intend to be the manager in twelve months or I intend to get that woman to notice me, etc. Ultimately, there is only one pure intent, which is to align our thoughts, words and actions with God's will. Any other intent has some aspect of selfishness attached to it, no matter how sweetly it is displayed. So how do we recognise whether our underlying intentions are from the stream of love or fear?

Over the years I have met countless healers, mediums, spiritual teachers and new age philosophers. The one thing they all have in common is the desire to help others, but their hidden intent will be different. Some help others in order to receive money, some to give and receive love, some to receive devotion, others to confirm that their beliefs are right and others to assure themselves that life goes on after death. Yes, I have met mediums who are afraid of death! Underneath each of these intents lies a fear. Pure intention, however, lives in the moment. It does not think about an outcome, nor does it move things around to achieve results. For intent that flows from love, knows it does not need devotion from others. It does not need to be proved right. It knows the deeper aspects of death and it knows that all its needs will be met. Pure intention has no attachment to results, only that it is walking in the footsteps of love.

Look closely at what it is that you do and recognise what you want from the person or situation. Do you compliment others to get what you want? Do you use others for what they can give you? Write a list of all your goals. How do you intend to achieve them? If you need help from other people, what act are you going to put on to receive it? By looking at our hidden intent we can begin to change our life into living in a world where we have no demands or expectations from others, only an understanding of what we need to do in the moment to stay in the flow of love. We can measure this love by the inner peace we feel whilst living in a fast world that lives on the edge of a quick fix.

Stop today and really define your intent. Why am I doing what I am doing? What will it bring me? What am I giving?

Denial and Acceptance

They say the only thing that is constant is change; but the only constant in this world is love. This love causes anything which lacks love to change. For love is sufficient unto love and all that lacks love must be exposed.

What is denial? When we cover up an inner energetic message with the mind, we are, in effect, preventing the truth from surfacing, because we believe the truth is more painful than the illusion. When we turn within and face the inner message, the truth will tear open our wounds and allow the poisonous toxins to flow. This will then allow the comforting healing balm of love to enter in to us.

When you go through an experience that lacks love, the first energy you encounter is shock. If you do not move out of this energy into anger, it becomes denial. When you touch anger and move through it by facing the truth, you enter into sadness. This is where you comfort yourself for the pain that was inflicted upon your being from another who is also struggling with life. After sadness comes acceptance. This is understanding the bigger picture. Acceptance is a form of compassion for yourself and others.

When we get stuck in denial we are avoiding the truth, either consciously or unconsciously. For example, if your friend asks you if you are OK and you answer yes, even though you are fully aware that everything is not OK, you are in conscious denial. Unconscious denial is when you are asked how your relationship is with your mother and you answer it is fine, but you are not aware of a deeper issue. Many abused people have lived their life in denial of the abuse they received. They may paint a rosy picture of their upbringing, covering over the pain. After a while the mind actually believes all is well, but the inner being is sending a message of suppressed issues. Later in life they may enter into a crisis of rage or anger as they begin to face their denial. To deny your inner messages is to lie to yourself. Most illness and disease is caused by blocked emotion, which is a denial of the truth.

The first step to healing denial is to admit that what you experienced was not a situation of love. You did not receive or express love. The pain you will feel may raise itself as anger. Allow yourself to enter into this emotion, but also recognise that you are angry with yourself for not being able to handle what occurred. Let go of the guilt, for all experiences are a learning. There is no 'right' or 'wrong', just love or fear. If you need to feel sad, then give yourself this healing time, but do not enter into the mind and torment yourself with the past. Let the feeling rise and let the memory go. When you finally reach acceptance you are free, because acceptance is love, it is forgiveness. You have acknowledged the pain of not being loved, but you have also accepted that it is painful not to give love, and there is no greater pain to the Soul than not being held within the flow of love.

The Crop Circle Exercise

The crop circle is an exercise that will help you to look at what stops you from having perfect relationships with every aspect in your life. Copy the example on page 261 and place your name in the centre circle. Starting from the twelve o'clock point on the far outer circle put the title 'life purpose'. Following round in a clockwise direction put the name of your mother in the next one, then father, partner, male children, female children. If you have only one child or no children, then place the name of your siblings in these circles. Proceed with work, home, finances and prominent friend. If there are any circles left, place what you feel is important in these.

Starting with your mother, write in the inner circle what stops you from having a perfect relationship with her. It might be that she is controlling, bossy or unresponsive. Even if one or both parents are deceased, still write what prevented you from having a perfect relationship with them, as the suppressed energy will still be in your system. Move around the circles focusing on each different issue. When you have finished, draw another crop circle diagram. Fill in the middle circle with your name and the far outer circles in exactly the same way as the first one. In the inner circles start with your mother again, but this time look behind what you originally wrote to find the hidden fear. For example, if you originally wrote, 'my mother shows me no affection,' in the second crop circle, you might write, 'I fear not being loved and accepted by my mother.' Do this for all of them and then look at how you relate to the different facets of your life.

You can also do a crop circle that focuses on your desires. Put in the outer circle at twelve o'clock 'life purpose'. Follow it clockwise and put in the next one 'perfect relationship', in the next, 'dream home, dream job, perfect finances, dream car', and any other which is relevant. In the inner circles write what your relationship to having these things is. In the next crop circle, as before, write the hidden fear in the middle circles. You may find that time is your issue and you will need to ask what the fear about time is.

Observation changes everything. By doing this exercise you have observed what is going on in your subconscious. These beliefs are what stop you from manifesting perfect relationships and dreams. Coming to an awareness of the fear behind your beliefs will change your energy, enabling you to take action. If you were to repeat the crop circle exercises in three months' time you would find that most of your obstacles had diminished. You will find love resides in the place of fear. If however, the same issues still come forth, then your observations did not result in action. Awareness leads from realisation to pure thinking, pure words and pure actions.

The True Dynamics of Relationships

The Crop Circle

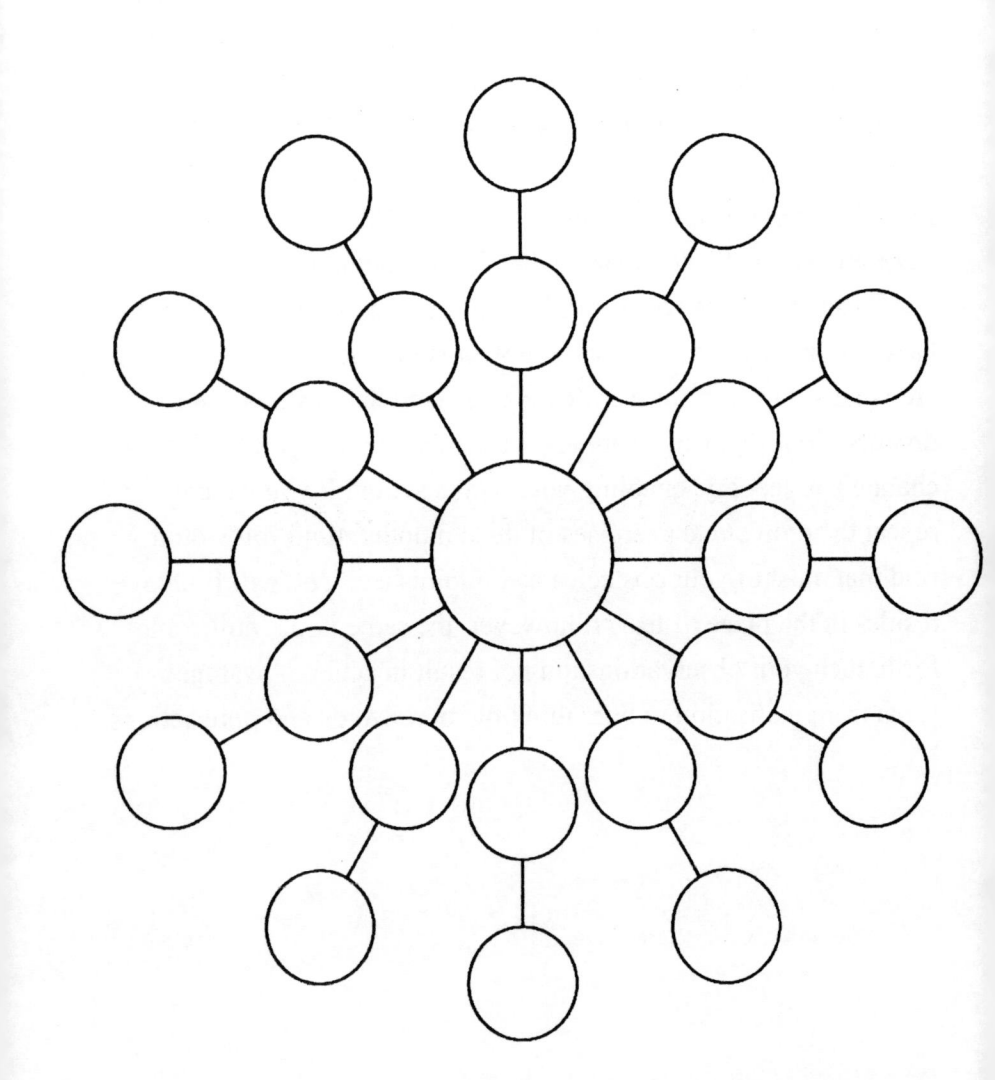

Part three

The Journey Home

Part Three

The Journey Home

6
The Wisdom Years

☼

All over the countryside the crops are being gathered,
Autumn has come calling.
The stubble wheat casts its golden carpet
For all who gaze upon its beauty.
The geese begin to honk in the distance,
Changing the silence yet creating a beautiful effect.
In life we reap what we sow.

The Aged

When I was a child I thought twenty was old. When I reached twenty I thought forty was old. When I reached forty, I started to think that when I reached seventy then I *will* be old! The truth is at every age we still feel youthful inside. I have spoken to many older people who suffer because the mind wants to go faster than the ageing physical body will allow. There is huge conditioning within society that as we age past our physical peak, we become less vital to the community. We can see this reflected in employment, sports, media, modelling, sales, etc. one exception is in politics! And it is amazing that we do not want our country run by a twenty-five year old, yet we dismiss the older generation as something to sweep under the carpet. Why do we do this? It is because each time we look at an aged body shuffling its feet around the supermarket we cringe, because we know that this may be us one day soon. In other words by not facing our physical decline, we think we will avoid death.

If we look at age from a spiritual perspective, we will see that a physical decline does not reflect a Soul's decline. In fact it is at this point that we are at our peak of giving to the world. What better teacher could there be than someone who has lived their childhood, come through rebellion, understood and healed their relationships and is fulfilling their life path? Two thousand years ago in Israel there lived a community of people called the Essenes. These people understood the true meaning of age, that through experience comes wisdom. The elders were therefore highly valued as important members of the community. They were often given the job of teaching the meaning of life to the younger generation.

In our present day we have a habit of making the elderly redundant. There are so many lonely older people out there, yet their Souls probably have a wealth of knowing that could help the younger ones who are stuck on life issues. Instead we put our troubled Souls on shows like Jerry Springer and then laugh when their hurt and pain causes them to hit out. What I aim to do in this section is reveal the stages of growth a Soul goes through as it reaches the final section of its earthly life and to make clear that right up to our moment of death, we can be a valuable and unique gift to the world.

Life Review

In every moment we have choices and each choice we make tells us the state of our inner being. Ultimately there are only two choices. There is love and there is fear. Thoughts, words and actions born out of love bring peace. It may seem that this statement puts love over as something gentle and mild, but love is the most dynamic and powerful energy there is. It created the earth we stand on, the sun, the moon, the planets and universes, yet we have this belief that love is passive. Love can only be passive to love, as passive means able to receive. Therefore if you avoid telling the truth to others because you think it will hurt their feelings, then this is not love, it is fear. We have this fear because we believe that to be truthful renders us vulnerable to being rejected and not loved. Humanity lives in this false world of believing it is not lovable, believing that here you cannot be yourself (being yourself is love), because to be love here brings only pain. When we reach the latter part of our life, we begin to see what choices led us to where we are now. We can then do two things. Either avoid our part in past experiences by blaming others, or we can face them and change our patterns while we are still in a physical body. It starts with being truthful.

Whilst reading this next paragraph, note what emotions and thoughts rise from within you.

A fifty-five-year-old woman that I know met a man when she was eighteen. This man was the love of her life and she became pregnant. Her dominant religious father refused to let her see the man again and when she gave birth to a girl it was taken on by the woman's parents as their own. The woman, in her anger and frustration, fell into the arms of the first man that came along. She married him and then left home before realising he was an abuser. She had three other children, whom she energetically rejected because she had not been able to let go of her first child and make room to love the others. The suffering for all of them continued for eight years, until the man finally left for another conquest. The woman then struggled on her own for a while before meeting a gentle man whom she married. He materially gave her everything she needed. She did not tell her new husband or her children of the first child and this firstborn daughter thought her mother was her sister. The woman kept a major part of her energy stuck in the past.

She was still very angry and bitter inside, which began to damage her present relationship with her husband and children. She was not being truthful to herself, her children or her husband. She was living a life of pain.

At fifty-five the woman felt she had left things too long. She found herself reviewing her life because she now had a desire to put things back into harmony. Energetically, they all knew the truth! It is only that the woman had spent years of wasting energy keeping it under wraps. She feared being judged and deemed not worthy of love because of the choices she had made.

How do you feel about this issue? Now look back at your own life and see where you have made choices out of fear. Look at the energy it has cost you to follow these choices. How can you heal your past? Can you let go of blame? Can you forgive yourself and others? Who do you need to be truthful with? How can you be truthful to yourself? If we look at the inner aspects of this scenario, we will see that the woman's life issue has been with the male side of her self. She has allowed her male side to dominate, abuse and control her life. Her anger comes from feeling powerless to stand up for herself. All this was acted out externally. Can you see the imbalances of male and female energy in your life? How can you rebalance this?

We have seen how the Soul reviews its life every seven years, but if we do not let go of the old then the new patterns do not fully enter our energy bodies. The fact that a part of our being is still stuck in the past seriously hinders our present moment. Therefore we cannot share our being with others while anger, bitterness, jealousy, sadness, etc, keep getting in the way. Behind these emotions is a fear and a belief that we took on board as children. Unless we face them, feel them and let them go, then the Soul will keep taking us into situations which will bring up these emotions. It does not matter what age you are, the Soul is always working for freedom. It does not stop because we become seventy. We do not go into Soul retirement! If anything the older we become, the more obvious the effects of our choices are to us and it is in old age that they catch up with us!

As teenagers we look forward to being of age. When we are of age we look forward to marriage, career and children. When the children leave home we look forward to grandchildren and retirement. When we reach retirement, we fear death. We are always running into our life, yet when we reach the second half of life we try to run away from death. There are two types of people on the earth: those that fear life and those that fear death. Those that fear life do not usually get involved with living. They may refrain from drinking alcohol, do not have sex, do not smoke or they may have strict eating regimes. They may even want to live in a cave or a monastery, yet how can a Soul become a master of its lower pursuits without facing and experiencing them. Those that fear death become dependent on others. They no longer experience for themselves but believe what others tell them. There are some religions that believe if you die fighting for a cause, you will sit with God. Then there are other religions that teach us that by not fighting, you will sit with God. Who is right?

When will humanity realise that life is for living and you alone are responsible for all your thoughts, words and actions. If you choose to experience something, then understand the Soul's focus is to master it. If you decide to have sex, then the Soul will direct you to higher spiritual sex. If you choose to eat meat, then the Soul will show you the consequences of this action. If you choose to drink alcohol, then the Soul will master the desire for it. If you choose to live in a cave, then the Soul will master its life of solitude, but you will still have to master a life with humanity. Every choice you make is a learning. There are no mistakes, for everything is showing you whether you acted from a space of love or fear. Are you afraid of living? Do you avoid living for fear of being judged? How can you turn every experience into mastering your thoughts and emotions? If you look back over your life can you see the times you feared death or followed others instead of your own truth? Do not wait for tomorrow, look at yourself today.

The Cause and the Effects

One of the things that hinders the ageing body is illness. What is illness? It is the result of something that is going on inside of our mental and emotional worlds yet, because we cannot see these worlds, we think illness is something that accidentally happens to us. We cringe at the thought that we brought it upon ourselves! Scientists would tell us it is invading bacteria or a changing of the cells, but the forces of our emotions and thoughts govern the cells.

The sooner we realise illness is a message, the quicker we can acknowledge and harmonise the imbalance. There is no judgment, just awareness. For example, when the car will not start, we look for the cause of it in the engine. When the TV does not work we look for the cause of it in its electrics. We have many people who sort out these causes. We have the electricians, the plumbers, the mechanics, etc, and when we are ill we have the doctors. What we do not realise is that, although the doctor will say the cells have been affected, they do not look at the cause behind the effect being played out in the cells. In truth behind every cell lies its programmer: our thoughts and emotions.

Many people live their lives totally unaware of the unseen world. We think that because we cannot see our thoughts and emotions floating in the air, they do not exist. Therefore we believe that the space around us is empty. A friend of mine started work in a hospital. He told me that during the first two weeks of his new job he fell ill. Two years later he is still suffering from periods of illness. He remarked it was a known joke that when you work in a hospital you become sick! Energetically, he was constantly being bombarded with polluted energy coming from the illnesses that patients were suffering from. These energies were carried in the air and, by intermingling with his energy field, they broke down his tolerance barriers, polluted his thoughts, affected his emotions and brought about an illness of his cells. When you first live or work in a negative environment and you become ill, you should know that it is the mental and emotional state of the place that is infiltrating your energy bodies and affecting your cells. If you do not detect this and change your circumstance, then after a while you begin to think and feel in a similar way to those around you. This will bring the vibrating force of your essence to a lower plane.

Scientists will tell us we have picked up a bug, but remember anything that wishes to destroy your health and leave you weak is a negative force. Never underestimate what you cannot see. Negative energy will eventually materialise in the physical world, either through a world crisis or through illnesses, but by then we have already been energetically polluted. You need to become constantly aware of where your thoughts are directed and your moment-to-moment emotional state. Awareness is your personal power, so start to become strong by not giving this power over to negative forces. I have met very few true teachers, but one that I did meet often became ill. When I looked into the aura, I understood this particular Soul came here to take on the forces of negative thoughts and emotions that surround this planet. The teacher was able to pass the negativity through the body and purify it as her way of service. This is an exception. The majority of humanity is still caught up in creating these forces and the only way out is through increasing awareness.

Age is not only a physical process, but also a reflection of our inner state. It is never too late to clear and heal yourself. The cold showers, mentioned in Cleansing of the Energy Body, chapter 7, will help you process the thoughts and emotions of others around you that do not belong in your energy field.

You have a spiritual right to claim your auric space. You can start with looking at your current state of health. All cells vibrate.

The tone at which they vibrate determines how they come together to form a shape. Every organ in the body follows this process. A clear organ will vibrate harmoniously, and as vibrations form colours, each organ will energetically appear as a different colour. If the thoughts and emotions that enter the cells are negative, then they change the vibration and colour of the organ. This change slows down the organ, making it unable to process energy and give us the right response to a situation. We have now become polluted on every level of our being. When the organ is first affected we are immediately alerted. We may feel a slight twinge or pain. Minor childhood aches and pains are often the first signs of this inner imbalance. If we do not acknowledge it at this point, it becomes more deeply embedded in the body's tissues.

Most people usually sail through their teenage years and early adulthood feeling relatively healthy, but if we continually fill the cells with negative thoughts and emotions through these stages of development, then the pain and illness may materialise at an older age. When we are at our peak of vitality we can usually keep the energy suppressed and controlled. As the body declines in vitality, we no longer have the strength to keep the suppressed negativity from breaking out and devouring the remaining healthy cells and organs. All illness is an external effect from an internal cause.

Even when we seem to innocently catch a contagious illness, we need to question what is going on within, because the invading force can only take hold if we already have a weakness within us. I feel I also need to mention karma here, as you may live a life where you only give your best in every situation, yet you still become ill.

This is because you either live or work in a negative environment, or it is your Soul's way of clearing accumulated energy from past lives. This is a service to yourself, as you must be ready to face and deal with the issues for your Soul to bring it forth, therefore there is no judgment. Another aspect we need to realise is that the more inventions we create that pollute the planet, the more external forces we give birth to that will affect every level of our being. The more negative forces there are, the harder it will become to remain pure in thought, word and deed. The chances of then becoming a God-realised being are very slim. Humanity has a choice. It can either remain on its present path of illusion or it can take charge of its self and wake up to the truth.

If you have become ill in your older years then know this is due to the thoughts and emotions you have accepted into your cells. There is no blame here. There have been so many books written on illness and healing that I do not feel I need to give another definition of what is stored in each organ. In the next chapter I have described a technique that allows you to enter into your stuck emotions and release them without having to intellectualise or think about the process. If you are ill or suffer from pain, can you recognise the thoughts and emotions that caused the illness? Looking back over your life, can you see where you held your truth in? Do you understand that by not expressing the truth of who you are, you have brought about an inner pain? Write a letter to the organ or area where you are experiencing pain. Describe how it affects your life, how it affects your emotions and what thoughts come up around your suffering. Then write another letter from your pain to you. Let it tell you why it is there and what you can do to heal it. Finally burn your letters and follow the advice of the pain.

The later years of our life give us an opportunity to face the effect of how we have lived. If you find yourself in negative surroundings with negative people, then do not judge yourself. In that moment of awareness, you have touched the deepest part of your being. Nature teaches us that there is a bottom to everything and when we reach this lowest point, then the only way is up. By thinking that you have reached an age where what you do does not count, you are only feeding negative energy. The only thing that wishes to keep us at our lowest point is the negativity, which thrives and grows on the pain of humanity. You cannot be in the arms of Angels whilst whining from the bottom of a pit! You need to make an effort to climb out, only then will you be offered a hand. If you put your absolute best into life, but it only achieves 20 per cent of the needed effort, then your Soul will give you the remaining 80 per cent. You may have felt this occur when, after putting in a lot of effort, things do not seem to move. At the point of giving up, something wonderful occurs and everything falls into place effortlessly. This is the realisation that something big and powerful has the ability to make things happen. You are with yourself twenty-four hours a day. You are the greatest influence in your life.

Menopause

Menopause is the cessation of the menstruation process that people always associate with women. Men also go through a menopause. Counselling and psychotherapy have now begun to work with this theory. It is important to realise that the menopause is more than a stopping of a bodily function. It is also a changing of a spiritual function.

The Soul's focus is to become whole. It chooses to enter the earth as a physical being who is outwardly one sex and inwardly the opposite sex. When a female child reaches puberty not only does she start to menstruate, but this is also the point where she has taken on all her childhood karma and is ready to begin working on it. She is now a creative being, responsible for all her thoughts, words and actions. The same principle applies to the male child, who goes through a voice change. This is the point at which he becomes an inspirational being, responsible for all his thoughts, words and actions. From now on the Soul is responsible for processing its emotions and mastering its mind.

When a woman reaches the menopause, two things can occur. She can either sail through it because she has purified her energy bodies or she experiences an internal battle. In one moment anger is the victor, in the next it is jealousy, in the next it is sadness, in the next it is joy and so on. This can go on for months or even years. Scientists have described this as a hormonal change where the oestrogen in the female greatly diminishes causing irritability, tiredness, depression and hot flushes. Their answer is to provide women with a synthetic oestrogen pill, which counteracts this process. If a woman is given oestrogen only, it puts her at risk of endometrial cancer, so she is also given progesterone, and this hormone therapy is known as HRT. Not one chemical in the body can change without the Soul's knowing. The menopause is a purifying cycle that the person goes through in preparation for its new life. It is almost like a mini death from the old into the new, as the female lets go of her ties to the earth, purifies her emotions and enters into the mental world. A man purifies his thoughts, lets go of his mental world and enters into his emotional self.

The menopause is a tool that the Soul uses to balance out the opposite side of its self. Often women at this point become more interested in career pursuits, while men may take up creative hobbies. It often shakes up the relationship and both may have affairs. I met a couple who had been married since their teens. The woman was a very strong force, whereas the man was meek. At the time of her menopause he had an affair. He realised inside himself that he wanted to take charge and be the assertive one, whereas she was softening and becoming more creative. The affair allowed them to see that they were in fact switching roles. It took them two years to come to terms with this process and, as long as each one was willing to let go of control of the other, their steps became leaps. Has this happened to you? Can you see your own change during the menopause? Can you see your partner's? I have also met couples where one has flowed with the process of change, but the other has held on to the old. These couples have parted because one has grown and the other has not. Can you recognise this in your own relationship?

Problems can occur if the woman has avoided her emotions and suppressed them throughout her menstruating years, because the menopause will bring them all to a head. If during the menopause she continues to avoid her emotions or uses synthetic drugs, then she will not enter into the new phase of her life. In other words she will become stuck and frustrated. If the man has avoided his mental state all his adult life, then, at his turning point, he will try to avoid it by turning to external pursuits, e.g. affairs, money, power, etc. If he avoids facing what it is he has created with his mind, then he will not enter into his emotional side and he may feel as though he has failed to achieve something. It can take just one life for a Soul to become whole. It does not need hundreds of lives, sometimes as a male and sometimes as a female. This came about because we created karma. You can use your female and male polarities to clear up large amounts of negative energy by becoming conscious of the dynamics of your life. The Soul uses this halfway mark of the menopause to enter into its other half for this process.

Women

How would you describe your menstrual cycle? Is it emotional? Overwhelming? Heavy/Light? What beliefs do you have around menstruation? Where do these come from? What was your menopause like? Can you see what your emotional issues were? How has your life changed? Did you flow with it or avoid it? If you avoided it, then how can you start to face it? What do you fear will happen if you let out your negative emotions? Can you understand the role reversal concept? Can you relate to this concept? Have you become more assertive? Softer? Has your partner changed? Have you changed towards your partner?

Men

How would you describe the state of your thoughts? Are they mostly negative? Critical? Positive? Doubting? Have you experienced a male menopause? If not, have you experienced an internal struggle between what you are doing and what you want to be doing? How did you resolve this? Was the answer external? What would the internal answer be? Do you feel you have failed at anything? How has this affected your life? Can you understand the reversal concept? Can you relate to this concept? Has your partner changed through menopause? Have you changed towards your partner?

Mid Life Crisis

There is much literature on the subject of mid life crisis, but one very important factor is missing. A panic occurs in a person simply because they realise they have not done what they came here to do. In other words they are not on the path of the Soul. It is this realisation that we have completely lived our lives according to an external conditioning, which leads us into a crisis where we throw everything out in order to find a solution. The problem arises if we focus on the external. We say, 'It is my relationship that is wrong. My job is unfulfilling. I am not getting what I want/need,' etc. We then uproot things or take drastic action without first going within and finding out where we really should be. A friend remarked to me that he felt mid life crisis was now happening to people in their twenties. I feel this to be a result of children experiencing things earlier and therefore becoming dissatisfied with the external more rapidly. They are finding that they are not where they should be much sooner than previous generations did. The way out of the crisis is through change. The only permanent change that exists is internal change and anything else is subject to the external laws of seasonal change.

I have met many people over the years who think when you hit forty life starts running out. It is between forty and forty-two that the Soul looks at where it is and where it needs to be for the second half of its life, hence the phrase 'Life begins at forty!' If it is not on course, then it pushes out all the emotions and thoughts that are in the way. These are our conditioned beliefs. The Soul then calls in other Souls who will help it challenge these beliefs in order for them to be shifted. Externally this may result in affairs, redundancy, career change, going back to college, divorce, late pregnancy, illness, etc. It might even be more than one of these at one time, so if we have not progressed in our earlier life, we are pushed to our limits during the crisis! The point is not to judge ourselves, for it is a way in which the Soul is helping us with our growth. If you try to resist, then the crisis will only become bigger. All crisis situations show us where we need to strengthen our alignment with our Soul and once we become aligned, the crisis smoothes out. New patterns then emerge from within and begin to shape the external world.

Have you experienced a mid life crisis? How did you deal with it? What were the emotions? What beliefs were under these emotions? Have you cleared these beliefs? What were your fears in the crisis? Do you feel you are on your Soul's path? If not, why not?

Write a letter to your Soul describing all the dreams you had for yourself as a child. Tell your Soul about your ups and downs as an adult and what you would have wished to change. Finally describe where you are now and what you still feel is missing or needs to be done. In a second letter, write a reply to yourself from your Soul without thinking about it beforehand. What has your Soul told you that you need to do? Now put it to the test and try it.

Retirement

What is retirement? If we look at it from an energetic point of view we may see that for most of our life we have put our vitality and inspiration into the external world of production. Whether this has brought love or chaos to ourselves, humanity and the planet, is something which the Soul contemplates during the retirement phase. I have met many people who cannot rest in this period for fear of what might be revealed to them if they stopped and observed the activities of their life. Some people die shortly after retirement. This is usually because the Soul's karma has finished for this life and the retirement is a reflection of this ending. Sometimes the Soul stays on to reflect, other times it leaves the physical body and reflects shortly after death.

If you were to look at retirement as a tool that helps you reveal where you have expressed love in your life or where you have expressed fear, then it takes on a different meaning from society's view of it. Many people become ill after retirement. They often feel that society no longer needs them, so they give up. Others believe that retirement is a time to spend in the garden. They find that this is OK for a while, but boredom soon sets in. Many aged people suffer from senile dementia and they lose their vitality. The message society gives is that when you reach a certain physical age your mind and emotions decline. This cultural belief becomes absorbed in our energy bodies as a pattern, so when we reach this age, the cultural pattern comes forward and we politely accept that we can no longer give valuable input in the world. Upon retirement we stop exercising our mental inspiration and instead of using our time to be more connected to the Soul, we become bored and apathetic.

The West is in fear of death, as it holds anything aged at arms length. We only have to see the continuing trends of fashion, technology, toys, films, etc, to see how we are constantly seeing worth in the new and dismissing the old. In the East there is a fear of life. People hold onto the old and mock the new, by believing blindly in external authority and closing themselves off to new ideas. The answer lies in accepting both life and death as one. If the West accepted death, then they would release immense amounts of wisdom into each individual and the community. What is wisdom?

It is God. If the East were to accept life, then they would release immense creative power into each individual and the community. What is creative power? It is God. The East is a reflection of the female who has to open up in strength, stop being dominated by the male and allow her creative essence to flow. The West is a reflection of the male who has to stop running away from the female with his changing ideas and open up to rest in her sacred wisdom.

It is time to look at our beliefs around retirement. We need to understand that physical aging is about stepping into wisdom and our young people need to learn about the footsteps of wisdom. A world without wisdom will be the cause of its own death, for to let the unwise rule brings only destruction. The young have to understand that they need to open up and listen to the wisdom of those who have trodden the path before them. In this act of listening they can inwardly choose their own course of action. In this way, the aged are no longer redundant and the young are not struggling in the dark. Life thus accepts death and death accepts life. What is acceptance? It is love.

How do you feel about retirement? If you have retired, how did you deal with the change? Were there any fears about giving up your working life? Some people who have loved their jobs find it more difficult to let go. Did this happen to you? What did your working life mean to you? What emotion is behind this? What belief is behind the emotion? How has your life changed? Have you reviewed your past? Can you see any unfinished business? How will you deal with this? To some people retirement feels like waiting for death. Does it feel this way to you? What can you do to bring vitality to your mind and emotions? What is your belief about being old? Do you resist the aging process? All through our life we are constantly entering into the unknown. We change jobs and fear the new situation. We move house and fear the new people or environment. We change our hairstyle and fear the response from others. We get wrinkles and fear being old. Underneath every fear resides the ultimate fear of not being loved. It is our choices that bring a mixed response from others. This sets a pattern for our state of self-worth. The one thing that we cannot control is ageing and ultimately death. Do you fear growing old? Do you fear death? How will you deal with this fear?

Death

One of the biggest fears humanity faces is death.

Fear is usually of the unknown. We become frightened to take steps because we do not know what will happen. We are frightened to speak out because we do not know what reaction we will get and, because we do not truly know and understand death, we fear it. Even in the great religions, where they talk about reincarnation and seem to understand it, there is an immense fear of death. Sometimes it is the thought that you have to pass through various planes. Sometimes it is the fact that you have to review your life and relate to the emotional content of its essence. Ultimately death seems to symbolise something that is final and certainly from a physical human experience, it is. I could write another book just on death alone, so here I would like to give a brief outline of what death is.

Death is letting go on a human level. I could tell you that consciousness continues, that as Souls we live on. I could tell you that we reincarnate, and this you might take on as a belief system. This is not a true knowing. You need to find out and know for yourself. To know something is to take it beyond belief, to be certain. I feel it is very important that we inquire into death, because, when you know it, you no longer fear it. You know the outcome. It is really important to understand the whole concept of fearing something or avoiding facing it. For example, take the case of the firewalker who walks through fire. In the process he may face, feel and allow the fear to pass through him as he walks across the burning coals. Another firewalker may restrict his emotional body. He does not feel the fear, because he is able to emotionally cut himself off. Each firewalker appears successful, but internally they experienced it differently. One no longer has fear and the other is full of suppressed fear.

If you truly look death in the face and see it for what it is, then it can be so liberating. Rather than saying, 'I believe I live on after death,' imagine what it will feel like to say, 'I know I live on after death.' Some people go to spiritualists or mediums for proof of an afterlife. These people can pass on messages from relatives and loved ones. Scientists would look at this and come up with another analysis! The most important thing is what you feel inside yourself.

Because only when you have looked at death and seen it, will you understand that life is eternal. We are all here for a purpose. We are here to learn and at some stage we grow and then we move on.

The human race is so addicted to the earth, that when we leave, we often stay quite close to her out of fear. This is because we are limited in our vision. Whatever we believe while we are living is with us when we die, but because of our addiction to fear, we often hook ourselves onto people who are still alive here, such as our relatives or friends. There is no separation at death. This is an illusion of the mind. We cannot see air, yet we know it exists. We cannot see the Soul or the Spirit, but do we know they exist? We do not know if it is a belief system! We do not even know if air exists! Scientists tell us it does and that it is made up of different particles from carbon dioxide, helium, oxygen and nitrogen, but do we know if that is real? We cannot see it; we just believe what the scientists tell us. More importantly, the question is not, 'What is out there?' But, 'What is within me?' For when you truly know yourself, you instantly know about the universe and the gods. Through this understanding, you will know whether your Soul and your life is eternal.

The energy we call fear sits all around this planet. It surrounds and penetrates the energy body of a person. A psychologist may say that fear is a reaction from the brain, but why is there not just a thought, but also a feeling attached to it? We feel emotion. Fear is an emotion that sits outside the body and permeates throughout the body. Quite often the mind locks it into the body rather than allowing it to move on through. This traps the energy in the internal organs, muscles and meridians until we literally become full of fear, which is unexpressed emotion.

We have become addicted to this feeling. In death we become very radiant and alive, but, because we cannot take the brightness, we often hover back down to remain in the earth's atmosphere. If we break free from fear whilst we are living here on the earth, then we are free when we die. What is above is so below. By living close to the earth in death, we then live a parallel life. We still have streets, cars, buses, houses etc. Some people even go to work! But ask yourself, 'Is there a place beyond this?' The Buddhists say there is. They practice non-attachment through strict disciplines. Their aim is to break free from any attachment to the influences of the earth in order to move on when they die. Other people like the attachment. When they die they go home to where their mother, father and grandparents are or they stay close to children that they leave behind here.

To be truly liberated and break free, we have to become unattached here on the earth. Not by renunciation, but by working through the emotion of fear and freeing ourselves from its addictive tendencies. It is similar to giving up smoking. As you master the addiction, your whole body becomes alive. Your sense of smell and taste becomes sharper and you become more responsive to emotions. Some people find it so vibrant that they cannot take it. The same happens when people die. The new world is so vibrant that we cannot take it, so we stay close to the earth and our 'comfort zones'. You can read this and accept it as a new belief or you can see if it resonates with the inner part of your being. The reason humanity does not move on is because of its addiction to this energy we call fear. We do not even know we are addicted to it. We do not even know that it permeates every cell of our being, so how do we become free of it? We need to recognise that everything we think, say and do is through the fear of not being loved for who we truly are. Until we realise this and become free, then life will be a constant cycle of death, rebirth, death, rebirth, death......... In every religion we can find evidence of the fact that we come back!

Throughout this whole book I have described the astral/emotional and mental planes that are the male and female energies. If these planes are not clear of all negative obstacles, then at death how will you move through these planes and return to be one with your Soul? If you find there are obstacles on the first plane, which is the astral/emotional plane, then how can you reach into the mental plane, which is higher in vibration? I am not saying there is this level and that level or this process will occur and that process will occur. What I am saying is, if you fade from this life carrying mental and emotional beliefs, then you will not suddenly become all knowing in death.

Yes, you feel more expanded, but you will still have the same obstacles there as you have here. There is no way around it! The whole process of this book takes you stage by stage into looking at your obstacles so that you will clear your emotional and mental worlds. In death you will then be able to move through these worlds and fully re-connect with your Soul. Whether or not you follow the teachings in this book is your choice, but believing in life after death or not does not stop death from occurring. When you do start the process of your own healing, then it will be your Soul that connects with you and directs you to the quickest route possible, for its only focus is to become whole. It cannot leave any facets of itself stuck on any of the astral/emotional or mental planes of energy. A path to wholeness is just that, a reintegration of the splintered parts of itself collected through life and death, a path to Holiness.

At death there is no point relying on your external wealth, worldly power or fame to be able to bargain yourself into a better position. At the point of death your emotional and mental state will determine the sum total of the life you have lived. The average life span may only be between seventy and eighty years, but in death it is timeless. Who knows how long it will take you to become the master, instead of the servant, of the levels of your being. What we need to remember is that when all the external is taken away, there is only the internal left and we shall stand naked before truth. In death we can no longer hide, as all the levels of our being are there for everyone to see. While we are still in a physical body we need to ask ourselves, 'What is the most important thing that will bring me freedom?' If it is the latest bone china dinner service or impressing the boss, then make sure that along the way to attaining them, your thoughts, words and actions are pure. This is all that matters in the greater scheme of things. What is your relationship to death? What emotions does this bring up in you? What beliefs and fears are behind the emotions? Where do you feel you will go? Have you become free in this life? If not, why not?

The Loss of Loved Ones

There is nothing more painful than watching those close to you die. When we are children there is a sense that life goes on forever and we will always know our friends. When we become aged, we realise just how short and precious life really is. We lose our parents, friends, spouses, even children and this leads us to question the frailty of life. We begin to wonder what will happen when we die. Will we meet up with our loved ones or will we be alone? Funerals often bring a sharp awakening as we realise that death is no longer just a word, but it is real.

What we need to understand is that losing our loved ones reflects our deeper feelings of separation from the Divine. We believe that if our loved ones are not here physically, then they no longer exist. This is the greatest illusion, because wherever our thoughts are, that is where our energy is. If you think about your loved ones, then you will energetically connect with them. If you open your heart up to receive, you may even begin to feel a presence or remember poignant moments that you shared. This is your loved ones energetically responding. When we lose our loved ones we realise we are not in control of our own life, that there is a greater force deciding our fate, even down to the last beat of our heart. Really look within yourself at your beliefs of separation from God. Ask what fears and emotions are behind the beliefs. Question your feelings around control or helplessness. Know that what you believe around loss is the same belief you need to face around your illusions of losing contact with God.

It is important not to get caught up in the new age spiritual belief that you should not grieve. You have lost a great friend, so it is important to let your feelings out. At first you may experience shock and disbelief. After the funeral, you may experience anger at your loss. Maybe the loss was sudden, violent or long and arduous. You may not have had enough time to say goodbye and express your last parting words. The loss of loved ones through a suicidal death can bring forth a lot of frustration and helplessness. Not being present at the point of a person's deepest despair can bring forth feelings of guilt and shame.

If you allow yourself to express your anger, then a deep sadness will begin to emerge. Here, you will reflect upon your relationship with your loved one. You may remember the joyful times and even the difficult times. The fact that you can no longer physically hug and touch your loved one is the hardest part to accept. If you keep allowing yourself to experience the feelings as they arise, and then let them go, you will move to a point of acceptance. It is important not to get caught up in the mind by becoming stuck in your thoughts of the past, as this will prevent you from moving forward. From acceptance comes the realisation that you shared a journey with a unique Soul. This journey can never be repeated in exactly the same way with anyone else, but you can put all the good things that you learnt from your relationship with your loved one into other experiences. For example, out of two sons, a mother may lose one to an illness. Rather than living her life from the past and emotionally shutting herself down from her family, she decides to accept the lessons that her departed son taught her and use them to enrich her relationship with her remaining son.

The same process can be reflected in our relationship to God. Are we numb to Him? Are we angry with Him? Do we feel sad and alone in our pain? Do we accept God? Do we realise that we have a unique relationship with Him? Every experience is an opportunity for us to look within at our inner self for the truth of our being. The Phoenix will always rise out of the ashes.

The Life Path Exercise

When you have read this exercise through, sit comfortably and close your eyes. Focus on your life today and then slowly go back through your life year by year. If you can pass them by easily, keep going until you find a year where you stop. Look at what happened here. Find the block and now observe the scene. Be careful not to get caught up in thinking, but just observe. When you have had enough, start travelling back through the years again until you stop at another scene and observe again. You may find that even though you have observed a scene you cannot go beyond it to another year. This means that the energy stored at the time of the experience, is still blocked and will need more observation. You will need to do this exercise daily until you can go beyond it.

To help you visualise, you could see yourself walking back down a road, which has signposts with the years on or maybe you have a book in which each page represents a year of your past. Turn the pages until you stop and then observe that year. You could even visualise a film projector and view each year as a reel of film. When you have found a helpful visualisation then follow the above observation.

This exercise reveals where you have set up beliefs through experiences. The key is not to judge yourself or others, but to observe, because by observing you are loving. It is this love which will break the block down. You may find then that your external life starts to change. The dispersed energy can no longer keep you trapped in a false way of living.

7

Your Personal Relationship to God

Think of Me and I'll Think of You,
Remember Me and I'll Remember You.

May the perfume of Love Divine caress your heart
As we all grow as buds upon the branch of Life.
May the wind of truth bring healing balm to your Soul
As you remember your worth.
May the Sun that resides within your heart
Be truly blessed by His gaze,
For to dance upon His ray
Is the only way home.

The Journey Home

There are many worlds within worlds. When we start the inner journey we find a world greater than any we can find externally. From within you can travel to the hidden depths of nature or to the wonders of our universe, the sun, the moon and the planets where you will meet other forms of life. From within you can even go beyond this universe and explore many more, because energetically you are connected to everything that is created. When you start to clear your trapped emotions, lift the chains of beliefs and face your foundations of fear, you become free. You begin to recognise the workings of God. You could not recognise it before because your eyes were focused externally and the external is only a full stop on the page of eternity. Do you wish to believe that the full stop is all that there is to existence? Or do you want to discover words and sentences which reveal the truth of who you are? The only way is through the exploration of the inner self.

Scientists have spent many years trying to discover the workings of the external. In a sense they have taken the full stop, split it, assessed it, re-shaped it and then they have declared their findings as the truth for the whole page of eternity. All based on one full stop! Yet if they took a moment to enter into the inner, then the worlds that would open up before them would tear down most of their findings, as the expansion would reveal layers of unexplored energy. It is amazing how a person will look up and wonder at the planets, but not at the state of their inner organs. They will look up at the burning sun, but not at their own inner emotions. We are constantly focused on the small external world. No wonder humanity has an issue with smallness and worthlessness. It is true that when we enter into ourselves our greatness is revealed. We are God. It is as simple as that. Maybe it is being God that we fear the most?

In this chapter I aim to give you tools and share with you techniques to explain some of the ways in which we can clear our obstacles and become free from the traps of fear. This chapter is probably the most difficult of all, because it takes dedication and courage to first face ourselves and then do something about it. I have met many people who say, 'Yeah, I know I do that,' but then do nothing to clear their patterns. It is one thing to acknowledge your beliefs. It is another issue to heal them. It is like climbing halfway up the world's highest mountain and then sitting on a ledge for the rest of your life. Yes, you may be able to view life from a higher vantage point, but you will not have a full view of all sides of the mountain. Just a little more effort will take you to the highest peak of the world, to freedom, where everything is in view.

Who is God?

A life lived in fear, is a life half lived.
A life without awareness, is a life half lived.
Awareness without action is half a life.
A life without Love is no life at all.

I have been asked many times in workshops to describe God. My first answer is how do you describe the indescribable? The unknowable? The unfathomable? Krishnamurti said 'There are two kinds of people, there are those who know and those who do not know.' This is what I would say about God, that when you know Him and understand Him, then it is almost impossible for the human mind to give a description of the ineffable love that is contained within His essence. The brain can only have a limited understanding of God. It could say that God is an energy that pervades all, or that God is an energy that lives in a man with a beard, or God splits Himself into many different Gods. In the end there is only one answer to all intellectual questions - love. Christ is love, Buddha is love, Krishna is love, Muhammad is love and God is love. There is only love.

When a person begins the process of clearing his astral and mental planes, that he has filled with ceaseless thinking and distorted emotions, he begins to feel the peace of his Soul. He is no longer bound by the earthly karmic laws, but becomes subject to universal laws. This is when he experiences what are known as miracles. In reality, these are natural laws that are able to work through him because of his clear space. When he becomes one with the Soul, the Soul becomes completely infused with what governs it. This is God. This fusing occurs because the Soul has balanced its passive and active principles of life through the physical form. From within himself thought ceases and he becomes emotionally detached from life, yet his whole essence is pure total love. The ego has become the passive servant and he claims nothing as his own, because every level of the Soul has become filled with an indescribable stillness and peace. He has become the witness and the observer, yet even behind the witness is a dynamic force directing the Soul. His thoughts, words and actions only occur because this directing force is bringing it about. What is this directing force? It is love. This is what is meant by true surrender; to surrender the body, emotions, mind, and Soul to love, for resistance is futile.

Our ultimate quest is to search for God. The only reason we are looking is because we have lost God or covered Him over with layers of illusion. When we have found love then our search stops. We become fulfilled. We know nothing else exists and we become free. This knowing leads us into service to help others upon their search for love and to find God. Humanity has tried to categorise God. We have placed Him in boxes, 'He does exist,' 'He does not exist,' or 'God is judgment,' etc. Whatever you portray God to be is a reflection of you. If you believe Him to be vengeful, you will have this vengeance within you. If you see Him as loving, you will have love within you. If you do not find love on the earth, you will not have love in your heaven. Your beliefs do not disappear at the point of death; they stay with you. Whatever you are here, you will be the same wherever you go, until you face yourself. It is as simple as that.

The true question is, 'What is your relationship to God?' For whatever you feel, think or believe about God is revealing you. In some religions God is to be feared. In others God is the merciful one, or does not even exist. The ultimate truth is to quest for yourself, for there are many beliefs upon the earth that will draw you in under their umbrella, but they do not have all the answers. Only you have the answers for you! It is similar to being in a sweet shop where all the sweets represent the different ways to God, but why waste your time pondering and tasting when the sweetshop owner is God Himself? We have become blinded by belief systems, when within us is the Soul waiting for us to knock at the door, so that it can move closer in and help us clear the levels of our being. Do not look outside yourself to others for answers when they themselves are stuck in beliefs. It is similar to being on a spider's web. How can another help you become free when they are also trapped? If you need an external teacher, ask the Soul to guide you there, for when the student is ready, the internal teacher will appear in human form. Who are you? What is the Self? Who is God? You are not that fearful small self. You are more than that. The self-realised man is the God-realised man.

All through this book we have seen that how we relate to others is a reflection of how we relate to God. Some people see God as something in the sky. Some see Him in statues, idols, forests, mountains or trees. One of the most important things to understand is your relationship to God. There is a saying, 'The Soul of man is a world full of beings in which the Gods are our guests, and the demons strive to possess us.' Upon this planet we have free will and it is only through our asking, that we are graced with the presence of God. There is one God, but many Gods or Demi-Gods, Archangels, Angels, Devas and so forth, so be aware, because there are many beings who will take the place as leaders. As below so it is above. In other words there are people down here on the earth who strive for power and importance. There are also beings who strive for power and importance on the spiritual planes.

It is our choice as to who or what lives within our energy field. If we want to have God living in our life, then we must ask to be graced by the presence of God. If we do not ask, then it does not necessarily happen in the way we think it does. Many people would like to believe that God is everywhere, but do they *know* God is everywhere? There are many places on this planet that are so polluted either through usage of chemicals or the thoughts of humanity, that God cannot frequent or live in these environments. The ultimate way to connect to God is to find within yourself purity of thoughts, words and actions, because if you create a pure space within you and around you, then God can enter into that purity. Would you put God in a sewer? No, but some of us create a sewer within our energy fields with our negative thoughts, words and actions. Become conscious of what you invite into your energy field and ask daily to be graced with the presence of God, so that you may share your life with God. Be it through your free will. In this way you attune your will with God's will.

Observation without Judgment

I have mentioned observation without judgment many times throughout this book. What does it really mean? When one or all of your five senses perceives something, it takes the external experience within and runs it by its belief system to see whether or not the perceived is acceptable. You then make a distorted decision and the mind justifies your decision by relating it to past experiences. For example, because of what a man has been told, he believes that all women use men. Therefore when a woman comes into his life he believes she is there to use him. He does not perceive her as she really is because his beliefs are clouding his knowing. His mind is justifying his beliefs, as it keeps reminding him of past disappointments with women. If he were to get rid of the belief system and observe the woman, then his Soul would tell him everything about her that he needed to know.

The Soul expresses itself through the physical body. Its direction and sensing basically comes through the eyes, therefore when we look at somebody without judgment, we are allowing the Soul to express love without the hindrance of the mind. If we have no belief system within us, then we can also see the truth of the person. Concepts about a person arise because we have formed a judgment and distorted this flow of love. We are no longer seeing the truth. It may be that in an observation we understand that what we were told was right, but now we have found out for ourselves. Everything that we look at in our life, be it our parents, children, friends, work, police, hospitals, is a non-truth; unless we observe it and know for ourselves, it lacks love. If you look at somebody and you see that they are a very jealous person, is that a judgment? If you look at somebody and see that they are a Soul who has come here to work on jealousy, is that a judgment? We are all here working on something. Until we accept that, then we will continue to form judgment and division around people.

Pure clairvoyance is the ability to look at something without judgment. It is this that enables you to see the truth of what you are looking at. If you have a belief system that says, 'I do not like people who have a different coloured skin from mine,' then every time you see a different coloured person you do not see them for who they are. If you take away your judgment, by not getting caught up with your mental belief programme, then you will see them for who they are. Through this act of observation, you send love into the person and love comes back. Therefore take judgment away from everything.

This same approach goes for every single thing in your life. If you observe your thoughts with just sheer observation and without any judgment, then the act of looking energetically dissolves the thought. For example, there is a war in another country and we hear about it on the television. The reporters tell us that one group is right and one group is wrong. Immediately we have a belief system. If we then observe the country through this belief system, instead of putting love into the situation, we are putting in a distorted energy. If love was pure white light, which contains all seven colours of the spectrum, then through this distortion we may only be sending purple and blue. If we remain emotionally detached and do not believe what we are told by the media, but observe the country at war, then this act of observation puts love into the situation, which will help to heal it. Sometimes it is not the persecuted who need love, but it is the persecutors. If they had love then they would no longer be persecutors. In truth, humanity does not view the world in this way. Instead, we have belief systems that separate and divide. The only thing we are dividing and separating is love.

What if two leaders from separate countries found that they were in conflict with each other, ego versus ego, pride versus pride, fear versus fear. If we took those two leaders out of their bodies and into the realm of the Soul, they could both be exactly the same…embodiments of love. If they looked at each other, they would see only themselves. It is the mind and its reactions to the emotions, that has created the division and conflict on the earth.

Exercise
Sit comfortably and visualise a person who you are having difficulty with. Now take out any judgments. In other words let go of your thoughts about this person and observe them. While you are observing them, feel any emotion that rises within you and listen to your inner self.

Quite often in that act of observation, the love that comes from you enables you to understand the distortion the person has within their energy body. You are able to see the truth. Love is powerful and active. The fact that you put this powerful acting force into something changes it. It cannot fail to change it. For love is sufficient unto love. It only knows itself and if you give love out, it will go and attach itself to other forms of love. In this process of trying to reach love, it will expose any aspects of non-love. A very loving person has the ability to expose the weaknesses in others. Their love has the power to melt and dissolve any blockages in another that are stopping love from passing freely between two Souls. Trying this exercise, a friend of mine observed his father, who he had always held in low esteem. Whilst observing without judgment, he saw the pain and suffering his father went through. Immediately there was an energy change inside him and the acceptance of his father brought about external changes.

It is sometimes said in healing circles or spiritual groups that you should not send love or healing to anyone unless they ask for it. I was once a witness to such a group. At the beginning of the meeting, rules were laid down as to when love should and should not be sent. At the end of the meeting they sent love to a war-torn area. The war torn area did not ask for love, yet it was still sent! We as human beings create so many belief systems to control the flow of love. What we fail to understand is that just looking at someone in the street without judgment will send out love. If we truly want to heal this world, then we have to really understand observation without judgment.

Forgiveness

Forgiveness allows you to fly. A grudge brings you back!

What is forgiveness? It is an exchange of love for what went on before. We accept that the energy we have received was a part of a learning experience. We then move through that experience and on to the next. Through the act of forgiveness we do not hold on to guilt or a desire for revenge, therefore we have not created karma to be played out in future lifetimes. A Soul who does not give love for what went on before will enter into another life and have to work out the dynamics of the unforgiving energy. In order to forgive, we have to first accept what has happened. Through observation without judgment, we are able to see why or how it has happened. With this comes acceptance and understanding, which is love and forgiveness.

To forgive can be painful, but not as painful as holding on to a judgment. To keep a polluted emotion held within the energy bodies makes us feel heavy, dirty and sluggish. To let it go we need to look at it so that it can be released. You may have held on to negative emotions for years. I have met many people who have told me that they have forgiven the people who had caused them pain, but when I looked into their aura I could see that, mentally they had forgiven them, but they had not faced their suppressed emotions. The issue was still there.

To forgive is to understand. We may need to understand that perhaps a person needed to do a terrible act in order to learn their lesson and experience a particular emotion. The experience might have taught them to open their heart and love their neighbour and enter into a life of service. It is possible that some people have carried out terrible atrocities because of a need to repay a karmic debt, but we still have within us the ability to forgive them. The law of karma is such that it will ensure they live out what they have done to others. As they grow older, their acts will start to torment the Soul and, at the point of death, they will see exactly what it is they have done. It is more freeing to forgive these people now, in this lifetime, whilst we already know them. This releases the desire for revenge. The saying, 'An eye for an eye and a tooth for a tooth,' is only a reality if there is no forgiveness.

Look back over your life and ask who you need to forgive. Can you observe the past experience without judgment and tell them you forgive them? Can you feel your anger, bitterness, sadness, hurt, etc? Write two letters to the person. In the first letter include all your negative thoughts and emotions, swear words included, then write a second letter which will include your words of forgiveness. Now burn the first one and let go of the energy you have held on to and decide whether to burn the second letter or whether to send it.

It is very important to forgive ourselves. We often find it easier to forgive others, yet we spend so much energy and time beating ourselves up over past situations. We all acted according to the understanding and knowledge we had available to us at the time. Yes, there are things you did in your twenties, which, now you are more mature, you would not do. This shows that you have learnt more since then and now, in your present state of knowing, you need to have compassion for yourself, forgive yourself and let it go. Some people feel that to forgive themselves admits guilt, but if forgiveness is an act of love, and love is the ultimate healer, then it is this love which removes guilt. We are here to learn to love every aspect of ourselves including the bad! So, if we do not remove the negative with love, how else will we become free? Look back over your life and ask, who do I need to ask for forgiveness? Can you observe the past experience without judgment and ask them for forgiveness? Can you observe yourself in the scenario and tell yourself you are forgiven? Write a forgiving letter to yourself. Let go of your guilt and pain, as you do not need to hold it within you anymore. Now burn the letter.

Illness is polluted energy within the body that we have stuffed into our muscles, bones, organs and skin. We hold on to it because either we feel guilty for not being loving, or we project guilt on to others for not loving us. Guilt is judgment, and judgment is belief. The whole process of healing takes a person to a point of forgiveness, which is a releasing of the belief, judgment and guilt. All *dis-ease* within the body will heal when we forgive, when we love.

Awareness

When we open ourselves up to a wider reality, we become aware of things that might have been there for a long time, but went unregistered. With this awareness comes an understanding and we can act accordingly. Unlike the physical eyes, the inner eyes of the Soul are aware of what surrounds it at all times. The Soul can see in all directions at once and it has the ability to zoom in and out on energy, therefore it is not bound by time, space and distance. When the Soul detects an energy form, it sends an impulse to the mind, which brings forth the proper response to deal with the oncoming experience through the emotions. When we shut down our awareness or when it becomes polluted by fear, we close our connection to the Soul. Our thoughts and emotions then lose the light of truth and sink into the subconscious. In other words we lose our ability to be spiritually, mentally and emotionally conscious of every impulse around us.

Exercise

Draw a large square on a piece of paper. Put a vertical line down the centre of the square and a horizontal line across the centre, so that you end up with four equal squares. In the first top square write 'conscious attitude,' then write down all that you know about your attitude to yourself and others. In the other top square write 'subconscious attitude,' now ask your partner or a very close friend, to tell you some aspects about your attitude that they are aware of, but you are not. For example, it might be that you are quick to assume, but you did not recognise that you had this trait. In the first bottom square write 'conscious physical habits,' now make a list of your physical habits. In the last bottom square write subconscious physical habits and ask your friend to tell you something you do that they are aware of, but you are not. It might be that you wave your arms about when you talk, or slurp your coffee, or constantly sigh, etc.

When you have finished, study the subconscious boxes and over a period of three days become aware of these traits. When you have become conscious of doing them, begin to look behind them for the hidden emotions and fears. For example, you go into the kitchen and find a wet patch on the floor. You quickly assume it is the dog again, so you punish it by becoming cross and putting the dog out in the garden. Later, your proud three-year-old son tells you he cleaned the dog's water bowl out on the floor! Look at how you assumed, then ask yourself, 'What made me jump to conclusions? Where did I learn this condition? Why did I punish another without finding out the truth first? Who in my past has punished me without listening to me first? Where is the blaming, punishing, non-listening parent in me? What is the emotion behind this? What is the fear?' Feel these emotions and let them go. Each time you become aware of a subconscious thought, emotion or action, bring this energy into your conscious boxes. The key is to find what fear or belief created them in the first place.

To be aware of our self is liberating. Even the realisation that sometimes we do negative things becomes transforming when we can own it, and then feel the fears and emotions behind it. Each person and situation is always revealing to us any negative hidden agendas within us. These are our shadow aspects that have fallen into our subconscious. If we can become aware of what we think, how we emotionally react and what we physically do, we take the shadow into the light. In the end our subconscious boxes will become smaller and smaller until we fully know ourselves.

This awareness begins to extend into being aware of other people's agendas. We begin to see their fears very clearly. If we use this tool with non-judgment, then the other person can hear very quickly and see what it is that they do. Not only does awareness fill you with light, but it quickens those around you, so that they too can find their shadows and enter back into the light. This is the true service of awareness.

Revealing and Clearing the Subconscious

11x22s

The subconscious is stored within our cells. To become truly aware of what is stored there it is suggested that you do an 11x22 exercise (see Bibliography for further reading). This is a very powerful technique and many who have tried it have had miraculous results! There are many powerful numbers, which when used as a healing tool, can bring about dramatic changes. The process of using numbers with repeated positive sentences actually breaks down belief patterns. On an energetic level, the positive words enter into the mind and body, pushing out distorted energy. An internal shift then occurs as the distortion is dispersed through the aura leaving it clear.

Positive Sentences
I have the right to be myself
I am perfectly acceptable as I am
I am in my power and I have abundant energy
I am well and healthy
I am fulfilling my life purpose and I have great joy and happiness
Money flows to me in a positive and abundant way right now
I am in a satisfying, fulfilling job, which I enjoy.

Sentences for Fear
I have the courage to achieve all that I desire
Life is perfect right now

Sentences for Anger
I am at peace with myself and the world
I express myself honestly in every moment

Sentence for Pride
I am equal to all life

Sentence for Illness
My……..(whichever part of the body is causing a problem) is perfect and clear.

Relationship Sentences
I have perfect relationships always
I am in a happy and fulfilling relationship

Spiritual Sentences

The Heavenly Father and I are one
The Heavenly Mother and I are one
I am one with God

Choose one of the sentences and write it on a piece of paper. You then write down everything that comes into your mind, the positive, the negative, the silly and the irrelevant. When you find a gap in the stream of thoughts that come into your mind, write the sentence you chose again, following it with the thoughts that rise in the mind. Keep this process of sentence, then thoughts, sentence, then thoughts, etc, until you have done the sentence followed by the thoughts twenty-two times. You then do the same every day for eleven days.

If at any time you write the sentence and nothing comes into your mind, then repeat the sentence to yourself. If the mind is still blank, write the words, 'no thoughts and no feelings', then carry on writing the sentence. It is possible that this may appear eight or nine times, then suddenly thoughts come back into the mind. You know when you are on top of a blockage when the mind becomes completely blank.

It does not matter if your thoughts are extremely negative or if swear words appear. This energy has to come out and be expressed on paper. The 11x22s are better when they are hand written, but as long as all your thoughts come out, typewritten or done on a computer is acceptable. You will notice the stream of thoughts from the subconscious, things you are not consciously aware of and whose context may surprise you.

Whilst you are writing the 11x22s make sure you are not disturbed, so turn off the telephone and lock the door. It is also important to do the 22 sentences all in one sitting so you may need half an hour to two hours each day, maybe even longer when you first start the process. See it as time to set aside for your healing, for your growth.

If you choose to make up your own sentence, it must only contain positive words. For example, 'I have no fear' would not work, because the word 'fear' will attract the energy of fear towards it. The idea is to remove the negative thoughts from the mind. You may find whilst writing you seem to go into what is currently called 'channelling' where a lot of information seems to come through or your thoughts seem to be using the term 'you' instead of 'I'. Whatever is happening, keep writing it down. If you have found a lot of issues have surfaced at the end of the day, then you can burn the papers or you can wait until the end of the eleven days and burn them all together. It is important that at the end of the eleven days process you rest for eleven days before starting another sentence. If you start the process but forget to do a day, then you need to start again from day one. This is because the blocked energy is moving through the energy bodies. If you stop before it is released, it begins to slide back to its original state.

I have used this technique over the last seven years. When I first tried it I used the sentence, 'I am well and healthy.' I had been suffering from an ache in the lower part of my stomach and on day eight, I suddenly got a flashback of someone trying to abuse me when I was a child. I saw myself running and hiding in a cupboard, which I locked from the inside. At the same time as the flashback I felt the ache move up through my body and disappear through my mind and be released. This proved to me that we store memories within the body because after that the ache was gone. This is a very powerful healing technique, but it does demand action when anything is revealed to you. After seeing this episode of being chased, I carried on with the next sentence. I then saw an image that appeared to be a past life memory of myself in Egypt chasing the man who chased me. In that moment there was an instant act of acceptance, forgiveness and love. The karma had been played out.

7x72s

If you find the eleven day process too long you can use exactly the same principle, but instead of writing the sentence followed by the thoughts twenty two times, you write it seventy-two times over seven days. The effect is still the same, but you may find you will need more time each day to accomplish the task.

3x75s

When you have completed the 11x22s on a few occasions, you can use the 3x75s. This is less powerful than the 11x22s and 7x72s, but quicker and still dynamic. First choose a positive sentence and then write down this sentence seventy-five times one after the other in succession. There is no need to follow the sentence with any thoughts. At the end enter into your feelings and allow any emotions to surface. If you feel the need to write down your thoughts and feelings then do so. Repeat this process again for the following two days. You must then leave a gap of three days before starting another one.

The Breath

Life begins with inhalation and ends with exhalation. Every breath is a beginning and an end!

Without air we cannot live on this planet. Without proper breathing into the abdomen area we only half live on this planet. Everything on the earth breathes, simply because we are mirrors of the inhalation and exhalation of the Godhead. Inhalation is His female principle. When you breathe into your abdomen you touch the female aspect of your self. Exhalation is His male principle. We can reach the male aspect of ourselves through proper use of the lungs. Pure balanced inhalation enters through the nose, into the abdomen and then fills the lungs. On exhalation it leaves the lungs first and then empties the abdomen. By this full breathing we are in touch with both the male and female principles, but most people shallow breathe into the lungs. This breathing into only the male aspect of ourselves reflects how we try to avoid the female energy upon this planet. This is because by breathing into the abdomen we get in touch with any emotions and issues that we have suppressed. On the earth we breathe in oxygen which contains particles of light or chi.

This light enters into the abdomen where it begins to knock loose any blockages that it encounters there. It also enters into the organs of the body and spiritually nourishes us. You can see these light particles vibrating when you look up to the sky on a cloudless sunny day. If you were to observe a tree, you would see that through the branches it collects the particles of light and sends it through the trunk and roots into the earth. The roots not only receive nutrients from the earth but also pollutants and gases, which they purify and send out as oxygen. All of nature has a purifying effect on the earth. As humans we receive earth energy through the soles of our feet into the abdomen. We then purify it through our emotions and send out high vibrating energy into the atmosphere around us. We also receive spiritual energy from the universe through the top of our heads and we take this into the abdomen. Because the abdomen is also related to the mind, we then use this energy to spiritualise our thoughts.

If we only breathe air into the lungs, we become too male in energy and as male energy is from the mental plane, our minds will be a constant stream of thoughts. If we breathe into the abdomen, but do not fully exhale all our breath, we begin to store the air in our abdomen. This creates stagnated energy. We then become too emotional or inactive, which results in being too female in energy. To be the master of our breath is a major key to balancing the male/female aspects within us and keeping the organs of the body healthy. The food we eat contains chi or energy. This chi is similar to the light in the air and the body breaks the food down to extract the chi. Different foods carry different vibrations of chi, which we can see through the varied colours of fruit and vegetables. Organic food holds more chi than food that has been chemically sprayed, which holds very little. This means that if you are breathing only into the lungs and eating treated food, hardly any light is getting into the abdomen at all. What do you think this will do to you? Humanity has polluted the air, the food, water and the earth, all because we are trying to avoid being fully integrated as physical beings.

When a pregnant woman breathes she takes the light from the air and distributes it to the growing baby. In other words she is feeding spiritual light to the physical body of the baby. If she eats organic food and breathes from the abdomen, then she is also giving the optimum light that she can allow to flow through her. If scientists decide to grow babies outside the womb then who is going to feed them spiritual light? The breath is our connection to life, and life gives to us through the breath. We inhale, we exhale, we give, we receive, we are male and we are female.

Exercise
Sit comfortably and relax the body. Begin to breathe in and take the breath into the abdomen. When the abdomen has expanded, then allow the lungs to fill. On the exhale, allow the air to come out from the lungs first, then totally empty the abdomen. Do this three times. Allow your body to find its own pattern using this process. Do not force it. For five minutes totally focus on your breath. If you get emotional allow the feelings to rise then come back to the breath. Make a point of becoming conscious of abdominal breathing when

you are alone. By mastering it in the quiet moments you are resetting a new way of being. Over time, begin to breath more fully into the abdomen when you are with other people or whilst you are shopping, etc. Try it in moments of anger, frustration, jealousy, etc. Eventually, with practice, you will find that full breathing becomes the normal way of being. Your mind will become peaceful and your emotions much clearer. You may find that whilst doing this exercise your mind becomes busy and you lose the focus on your breath. Keep bringing the mind back to the breathing. This is an aspect of what the Buddhists call mindfulness. This is not an exercise for a quick fix. This is a true process of transformation.

Cleansing of the Energy Bodies

Throughout my life I have been very lucky to be consulted by thousands of people. When I have looked into their energy fields, I have noticed that many have immense stuck energy. I have observed those on various spiritual paths, who have amazing visualisations to clear themselves, but of all the techniques I have observed, there is one that I would recommend as being the most powerful. If someone sat in front of me now and said, 'Mike, what is the greatest thing I could do to keep my energy body clear?' I would tell them they have to purify their thoughts, i.e. become thought conscious, but the most important would be to cleanse their energy body. The best way to clear the energy body is through cold showers.

This may sound extreme, but when water is cold it is in its purest form. When the cold water is poured over the body it draws out negative energy, which is then taken into the earth to be processed. If you use warm water, it causes the energy in the body to expand and push any negative energy deeper into the energy body. Therefore I would recommend that when you come home from work, have a cold shower before doing anything else. They say that eighty per cent of arguments occur at home when one partner first comes in from work. Rather than depositing the energy you have collected throughout your day onto your family and environment, have a cold shower, change your clothes and then interact with your family. Even if you live alone, your evening will be more relaxing if you cleanse yourself of the day.

Our energy body is like a sponge and we absorb energy all day from others. If you then walk into your home and hug your partner or children, you deposit collected energy onto them. If you sit in your chair, you leave this energy there. When you go to bed, you leave this energy in your bed. If you make love with your partner, you dump this energy onto your partner. But if you have a cold shower, this energy is no longer with you. When we make love we open our chakras and exchange energy. If we have a cold shower beforehand, then the experience will be more loving and purer. After making love if we have another cold shower, then this purifies our energy bodies even more. If we go out for the evening and have a cold shower when we come home, this clears the entire atmosphere we have soaked up. By taking charge of your energy in this way, you are not depositing energy that is not yours onto other people.

Each cell in our body contains water and it is the water in our bodies that absorbs memory. Therefore the water in our cells contains the memory of our thoughts, lifestyle, and who we believe we are. In order to change, we need to clear our cells of the old programming to make way for a purer way of being. Cold water has the ability to pull out stagnant energy stored within the cells of the body. This will help us clear ourselves at a faster rate. Cold showers will combat fatigue and restore energy. They also clear the energy paths or meridian lines within our bodies, which will induce sleep more easily as well as improving the quality. It has been proven by medical research that cold water improves the natural defence system by increasing the number of white blood cells. Circulation is also helped through encouraging the production of the body's natural blood-thinning enzyme. This makes it particularly effective against heart attacks, viruses, chills, influenza and colds.

Most people with such problems will avoid taking cold showers. They ask, 'Is it safe to have a cold shower?' I have worked with people who have heart problems, and daily cold showers have energetically cleared and helped to strengthen their hearts. I have heard so many arguments against having cold showers, yet each one is an excuse. Ask yourself what stops you from cleaning and clearing your energy body. If I told you that cold showers bring you peace, inner strength and a step closer to God, would you do it then? In life it is important to know ourselves. Cold showers have the ability to clear away all that is not us and leave only what is us.

When the energy body is clear, the cold water then starts to work on our internal organs by drawing out stagnant energy, which leaves them clearer and lighter. This cleansing process happens over a period of time and I have seen it dissipate emotions such as anger, jealousy and fear from people's energy fields. When you energetically clear your energy, your Soul is able to come closer and share more of its love, joy, power, wisdom, and peace with you. Try it for yourself and accelerate the speed of your Soul's growth. For that is what you are here for.

Emotional Healing

There is so much information on this topic that what I am going to tell you will probably conflict with what is already available. You do not have to have any special knowledge of chakras, types of emotions or where the emotion is within your body to heal it. When an emotion rises it does not say, 'Hi I'm coming from the third chakra, my roots are in the stomach, I got stuck when you were five and I'm the emotion of rejection!' All this is the mind separating it and controlling its release. There are two emotions, love and fear. Love expresses outwards, fear pulls inwards. The varying light vibrations that flow from love are the aspects of joy, peace, happiness, beauty etc. The varying dense vibrations that flow from fear are anger, jealousy, pride etc. These two major energies move within and around our emotional body, and according to an external or internal experience, we choose which one enters into our energetic system. If we do not let the energy flow through unhindered, then it becomes stuck within the organs and chakras of the body.

I have observed that when we choose fear we cut off the flow of energy we call love. This experience traps the emotions and thoughts that were present at the time of the cut-off point. We then store these in the chakra or organ responsible for processing the experience. Counselling and psychotherapy are techniques that people use to get in touch with these cut-off points. The only problem here is that we can get caught up in the mental picture of the experience without releasing the emotion. The mind then starts to blame others for causing the pain. At this point we are back to fear again, and we have not healed the experience that we brought forth in this life. The key to emotional healing is to enter into yourself and acknowledge what you have trapped there. Before you can start looking at your emotions, you need to understand how to use your energy as a tool for opening and clearing whatever you come across, so that healing can take place.

Our cells are made up of electrical impulses, and for these to work in harmony they need positive protons and negative electrons, which give us a pushing and pulling force like a magnet. We can see the extremes of these forces within the personality. Too much pushing force and we become aggressive, too much pulling force and we become submissive. If we were to dissect an atom we would see that the basic principle of the universe is the male positive, neutral, and female negative particles. These are in total balance with one another and they move in unison.

This understanding leaves no doubt that our cells contain male and female energy. The organs in the body also reflect this, in that the organ has a receptive force and an expressive force. For example, the liver has to receive blood to extract the toxins. It then allows the blood to move out and sends the toxins into the waste channel. The organs which govern receiving earth energy are mainly to the left of the body, i.e. the spleen, stomach, pancreas, descending colon, etc, making the left side a female pulling force. The organs which govern expressing energy are mainly in the right side of the body, i.e. liver, gall bladder, ascending colon, etc, making the right side a male pushing force. Emotional healing is about utilising these forces like a magnet, so the left side is able to pull open energy and the right side is able to extract energy.

Most healing techniques will teach you this process, along with using the right hand as the major tool for putting energy into the body. This is because the chakra in the right palm gives out more energy than it receives and the chakra in the left palm receives more energy than it gives out. In emotional healing we actually do the opposite in that the left hand is used to put energy in and the right is used to pull it out.

What most people do not realise is that whilst healing, the right hand transmits male energy. Emotional blockages are usually energy that has collected together. It has become unyielding and distorted male energy. To loosen it, female energy needs to be used, which can be given by the left hand. We also need to be aware that when you extract emotional energy from your organs using the receiving left hand, the energy re-enters the body through the arm.

When you use the right arm the emotional energy collects around the *outside* of the arm making it easy to clear using cold water. The only way you will find out this observation is to try it for yourself and feel how the energy is working through you.

The legs, genitals and abdomen areas store your early childhood experiences. Your teenage experiences are stored in the middle of the body, in the lower ribs, liver and stomach, and your adult experiences are stored in the top half of the body, in the lungs, heart and shoulders. In healing, the most important chakra or area of the body is the heart, as it is the heart energy which sits as the middle component between heaven and earth. Both of these energies are transmuted, purified and directed into the cells of the body by the heart. In order for us to clear ourselves, we are going to let the emotion rise and extract it through the heart chakra. You do not need any special skills for this other than a will to heal yourself.

A good place to begin healing is in the childhood area, as this is where a lot of our deep-rooted conditioning began. First lie down or sit comfortably, then place your left hand over your abdomen and place your right hand over your heart in the centre of your chest. The aim is to visualise your left hand gently putting white light energy into the abdomen, which will loosen your childhood emotional energy. As the energy begins to rise through the body, imagine your right hand as a pulling magnet. This will extract the suppressed energy as it reaches the heart.

There are now three possible routes you can take. The first is to choose your emotion. For example, you could focus on your anger. As you begin to feel it, let it rise and enter your heart. Your right hand may become hot, so keep taking it off the heart, gently shake it into a visualised bucket of fire and then resume. When you can feel no more anger, then move to another emotion.

The second route is to pick a memory from your childhood. Once you have the visual of it in your mind, let the visual go and begin to feel the emotion. Again your right hand may become hot, shake it and do the fire visualisation. When there is no emotion left, then choose another memory.

Use the third route if you find it difficult to enter into your emotions or memories. Visualise the emotion you want to work with as a colour and begin releasing the colour from the heart into the right hand. The stuck emotion in the body will respond and begin to move upwards. Often people first visualise the colour as a dark shade, but as they begin to feel the emotion the colour begins to change. Eventually, it will become lighter and clearer as the emotion is released. At this point you can move on to another emotion and colour.

You can also use this process by going directly into the organs. Place your left hand on the organ, your right hand over the heart and allow yourself to feel any emotion that is suppressed there. If you have difficulty on your own then work with a friend and share the journey. The beautiful thing about this process is that you do not have to tell your friend about the experience, you only have to feel it! So if you have experienced childhood abuse, but you are not ready for others to know, you can heal it in a silent and dynamic way.

The only time emotional healing through the heart is not beneficial, is when a person has heart problems. This is because the heart area is already clogged and any moving energy in the body will not be able to move up and out through the heart. A few moments a day placing your right hand on the heart and breathing white light into the heart should begin the process of clearing the stuck energy. Signs of problems in the heart also relate to relationship problems with our loved ones, so it is time to get truthful about whether the relationships we are in nurture us and bring us to a space of love. If not, question your beliefs and fears around your relationships and what stops you from fulfilling your heart's desires.

If, whilst doing emotional healing, you feel a flutter in the chest or a missed heartbeat, then you need to slow down the healing. This means the chakra is under strain in trying to rid too much in one go. This is a very powerful form of healing as it goes straight to the stuck issues within you. I have known people to release vast amounts of suppressed energy in a very short time, so you need to wash your hands in cold water at the end of each session. A cold shower would be very beneficial here! Also open the windows of the room so that the suppressed energy does not become trapped and breathed back in. Just because you cannot see emotional energy, does not mean that it is not there. Another good point is to keep a diary of your progress so you can explore your experience. Because of the power of the technique, you may find your emotional status changes very rapidly and you will become more centred and at peace with yourself.

Healing Your Thoughts

If you asked yourself what are God's thoughts, what would your answer be? Maybe you feel His thoughts are all love? Or maybe you feel He has no thoughts? Now look at the highest thought within you. What is it? Is it a thought of God? Of love? Of peace? Now ask yourself why every thought you have is not at this loftiest peak. Is it because you believe that to be constantly lofty in thought is not a living reality? Or that it is not possible? The majority of humanity is stuck between their lowest thoughts and their highest. We cannot get off the merry-go-round of this planet until we are constantly living in the thought of God. If we were let loose in the universe carrying baggage of low vibrating energy, what do you think this would do to the purified life that resides there? Our thoughts are therefore a major key to accessing the highest potential in ourselves, so how do we begin?

There are some teachings that tell us we must reach no-mind. There are others that tell us to think God in everything, but the one thing they have in common is the awareness of thought. With awareness as a tool we do not have to enter into any religion or doctrine, we just have to become aware of our thoughts from moment-to-moment. If you were to understand that how you see the world is reflecting you and that there is nothing outside of yourself, then you will begin to see how your perceptions have shaped your world. What thoughts does this sentence bring up in you? It is difficult to accept that we have light and shadow within us. We need to understand that this shadow was originally created by our low vibrating thoughts.

All the pollution, filth, death and destruction on this earth are due to the polluted thoughts of humanity. The atmosphere of our planet is densely polluted and we blame carbon dioxide, CFC gases and chemicals, yet we are using these pollutants to maintain and hold our negative thoughts. In a sense we are polluting God with our distorted beliefs. There is so much written in New Age philosophy about Spiritual Beings and Angels that visit this earth, but I can promise you that if they came in contact with such negativity it would burn them and they would be eaten alive. Until we clear our thought world and open a space for them to enter, we will continue to live a life of isolation and desolation. When we consciously take control of our thought world, clean it up and purify it, then beings of light can enter into our world.

We need to understand that wherever or whatever we think about, our energy goes to that space or place. Our thoughts can be triggered by what we hear from the TV, radio or newspapers and we get locked into collective thought forms. These are called egregores. Whilst on a trip to Egypt in October 2001, I noticed that the atmosphere was full of the word Osama Binladen. On my previous visit the most common word in the atmosphere was Allah (God). As a test, I asked those I was with and others to say the word Allah to themselves silently as often as possible. After three days I noticed that the collective word had changed. In people's thoughts Allah came back rather than Osama Binladen. What is the most popular thought that comes into your mind? Is it God, who is love? Or is it something else?

When I observe a person's thought energy, I can see that it looks like streamers moving out from the head area. Within these streamers are our thoughts. The streamers vary in colour and density according to the type of thought. I have often seen God thoughts as white and gold. This is how the halos of the prophets and teachers appeared, simply because every thought was attuned to the highest vibration. The thought energy then begins to move away from the head as it travels to where it has been directed. If we think negative thoughts about someone, this energy enters into their aura and pollutes them. It also enters into a similar vibration within the planet's atmosphere, where likewise thoughts from humanity have been collected. Whatever we send out will return, because like attracts like. After a while our polluted thoughts start to come back. When we receive them in our aura, we also receive the energetic effect that they had upon the person we directed them to as well as energy from the collective thoughts of humanity. The returned thoughts are far more polluted than the original ones that we sent out!

When I began to work on myself and clear my own thoughts, I recognised this process. I also realised that when people who were not in control of their thoughts sent me loving thoughts, some of their negativity also came. This is because whenever we think of someone we enter into their aura and an energy exchange occurs. We believe that because we are physically separate, everything we think will have no effect and therefore all our thoughts are private!

A lot of famous people will tell you that in the beginning they could not wait to be famous, to be adored. When they did reach the top of the fame ladder, they became restless. They could no longer find any privacy. This is because they are constantly being bombarded with maybe millions of people coming and going within their aura, and all the time they are exchanging energy. They cannot find peace or distinguish themselves anymore. Often drugs and alcohol take them out of this pain, but it brings with it another set of energies, which can be more personally destructive.

Whilst observing people's auras, I see images of people they know. If the person enquires about an ache, a pain, or feels unwell, I point out the image of the people I see in the aura. When the person mentally moves them out of their aura, the pain disappears. Think about who you project your energy onto, and who directs their energy towards you. If you are thinking of God or love, then your energy is with God or love and God or love is with you.

If you think of a dream house by the sea it takes form in the astral plane. The more you think about it, the more solid the energy becomes. If you were to die before it manifested in the physical, then upon the astral plane you would be able to see your house. The obstacles to bringing our dreams into reality are the emotions. This is usually due to the conflicts that we have within ourselves. Our fears block our dream from becoming a reality. Question why you cannot have your dream house right now. You may say it is because of restricted finances, but this could be worked on. There may be underlying fears that to gain your dream you have to move away from your family, and then there is also the fear of not finding work when you get there. It is these very fears which inhibit your Soul in its journey to wholeness. Can the mind be free of negative emotions?

Our childhood conditioning and beliefs affect most of our thoughts. In other words we are always comparing the past with the present. If you were to observe your thoughts you would recognise that they are either in the past or creating a future scenario. Often in our thoughts we re-live past experiences and we try to mentally change them so that we seem more worthy or superior to ourselves. Those people from the past who we still gossip about today, are the ones who made us feel worthless, and we are often trying to justify that what we said or did was right. If we observe our thoughts of the future, we will see that we are always trying to create better circumstances for ourselves, which prove we are worthy and superior. Our emotions also add to the power of our thoughts. In the past we may have felt good at being superior or maybe angry at being worthless. In the future we create emotions of satisfaction by creating scenarios of worth. All these emotions are based on one thing, which is fear. It is the fear that in the past we have not been loved, and in the future we fear not being loved again.

To know yourself, observe your thoughts. Start right now. Do not wait for tomorrow, or next week, as this is the mind putting it off through excuses. Ask yourself, what is telling you that you do not need to observe your thoughts? Or you have not got time for this exercise? It is your mind. It is your thoughts; and what fear lies behind observing your thoughts? Is it the fear of change? Of not being you? Of what others will think? Or what you will find out about you?

When you begin to observe where your thoughts are, bring your awareness to your emotions around the thought. Feel the emotion and allow it to rise. It is this emotion which was trapped at the time of the experience in the past, or what you fear feeling in the future. You do not need to force this process. In one moment you may forget to observe, then suddenly you remember again. Give yourself a mental hug, for a deeper part of you is becoming aware that you are not observing! Keep going. If the thoughts are continuous or difficult to observe, then bring your awareness to your abdomen and breathing, as proper breathing calms the mind and gives the emotions a chance to rise and heal.

Prayer

Do prayers really work? When this subject is raised in workshops, many people say they feel that their prayers go unanswered. If our energy bodies are cluttered with ceaseless thinking, imprints of other people, and suppressed emotions, then how is a prayer to God going to stretch through all the clutter and reach the higher vibrations? If it does find a way through, the light will have considerably diminished, so the higher forces can no longer decipher the message. We are not aware that our aura contains other beings who influence us. These may include discarnate family members, guides, people we think about, or people who think about us. When we send out a prayer the energy often gets picked up first by one of these beings. They then try to help, but the effect is not as powerful because it has only reached a limited space. Only when we have taken control of the mind, healed the emotions and cleared our space of these beings, can our prayers reach the higher planes.

Every prayer is therefore answered, but more often than not we do not receive what we asked for. This is because we are not clear enough for it to reach the Godhead in the pure form in which we created it. Some religions tell us that we can talk to God and he will hear us. Some tell us we are so insignificant, that in order to get our message to God, we have to go through someone else who is ordained to speak to God. What do you believe? The truth is, God, who is also known as the Beloved, yearns for contact with His true love, which is you. He can only come closer if you ask Him to enter into every corner of your life. This is a dynamic prayer for contact, because no-one else can initiate it but Him. You may then find your life starts to change. You may experience upheavals, even miracles, as God adjusts your energy to receive the answer to your prayer. The higher forces start to activate your inner teacher and you may find you begin the search for the meaning of your life. This is what is known as a spiritual awakening. Often a physical teacher comes forth to help you master your thoughts and heal your emotions.

Each small triumph you have makes space for God to move closer in as your prayers begin to reach Him directly. At the point when you become fully one with God, when your thoughts flow with His, your words speak His words and your actions follow His direction, you are then the living prayer itself, you are the Living

Word. If you want your prayers to be answered, then begin to observe what is really going on within your thoughts, emotions and beliefs, and what fears you have built your life upon. There is no other way to go but within!

Living in the Moment

When we become aware of our thoughts and realise they are either focused on the past or the future, then we begin to understand what living in the moment is all about. To live in the moment is to be spiritually, mentally, emotionally and physically focused on whatever it is we are doing. It is a total awareness from every level of our being. How many times have you put your keys down and forgotten where you have put them? How many times have you forgotten to post a letter? Our physical body is doing one thing without the full attention of the mind. This means that a portion of our energy is thinking, a portion of our energy is doing, but neither are focused on the same thing! To live in the moment is to be whole, for to be fully present on every level means that all our energy bodies are aligned. It is easy to say 'Let us live in the moment!' but it is hard to do.

When we first start to face our issues, the space we clear within ourselves allows the Soul to enter in closer and take more charge of our energy bodies. At first this creates a see-saw effect. One day we are engulfed in our emotions and the next day our thoughts are totally erratic. We may even experience old physical aches and pains resurfacing. When you give your Soul consent to start the process of healing, it sends more light into the mental, astral and etheric/physical bodies. This light begins to knock loose suppressed energy, which raises our emotions and thoughts to be cleared. At this point it is often easier to give up, as the constant observation of our thoughts and emotions takes a lot of effort. This unstable time is a sign that we have started a major journey, so keep going and do not give up.

I have read some amazing books that teach people how to live in the now. Whilst reading them you can really get taken into the moment and everything becomes clear, but the next day you are back to the same routine. What we need to understand is that to have all our energy focused in the now, we have to pull back our trapped energy from the past. We can only do this by becoming aware of where our thoughts are in every moment. It is similar to the game of twister. You cannot focus on the next move because you are back flipped over someone else. One leg is twisted on the yellow circle, the other leg resembles shaking spaghetti and your arms are double jointed on the far red circle! Until eventually you collapse from over-stretching! In life this collapse often relates to illness or a crisis situation. To be in the moment, means to re-collect yourself so that emotions from the past are not still creating your today.

Think back over today and on a piece of paper write down a list of what you have been thinking about. Going through each item, write down what emotions were behind the thoughts. Now write what you feel were the hidden fears, then take each fear and allow yourself to feel what it is you fear the most. Breathe from the abdomen and allow your emotions to surface. Each time you become aware that your thoughts are focused on past situations, creating future scenarios, blaming or attacking, then come back to your breathing and allow yourself to feel your fears and see what past events these fears and emotions are related to.

Another exercise that helps with living in the moment, is to truly listen. You can do this by concentrating on sounds around you. For example, when people are talking to you, give them your full attention without thinking about how you are going to answer them. When you walk outside, focus on the sounds of nature or the hustle and bustle of the traffic or people. If the mind tries to butt in with descriptions or judgments, then begin to focus on more distant sounds and see if you can use your ears to move in and out of sounds. This true listening skill opens your heart and allows your Soul to show you the hidden world behind the judgments of the mind. Try it with different types of music or, when you are on your own, listen to your breathing. You can even focus on the sounds your inner ear makes when all around is silent. When you listen you cannot think. When you think you cannot listen.

It is this process of mental awareness and emotional awareness that will take you more and more into living in the moment. It is very rare for a person to let go instantly of all their conditioning, pain and expectations and completely enter their true being. For the majority of us it is a gradual awakening that helps us to gain strength and trust in our Soul. When we have become fully integrated with the Soul, then our past will have been healed, our future is taken care of and our moment is filled with right thought, right words and right action. Do you live in the moment? If not, why not? Can you recognise when you are thinking in the past? Creating the future? Can you see the past memories where your emotions are still stuck? Can you allow these emotions to surface right now? Can you recognise your fears? Can you feel the emotion behind these fears? It does not matter how many books you read, or self-help courses you attend. If you do not become aware of your thoughts and master them and recognise your emotions and heal them, then you will always live in a conditioned past and in fear of the future.

The Three-Day Word Exercise

Many teachings talk about the use of mantras, but do we really know the effect that word vibrations have on the planet? Sit comfortably for a moment. Choose a negative word and repeat it to yourself ten times. Note how you feel. Now choose the highest word that is available, it might be God, Buddha, love, Krishna, Peace, etc. Repeat this word to yourself ten times. Note how you feel. What is the difference? Words have a dynamic effect on our energy bodies. Energetically we are all connected, so when we think or speak a negative word, all of life is affected from this planet right up to the Godhead. Negative words are dense and dark in colour and loving words are light and bright in colour. The words you use either add to the building of life or the destruction of life. If you were to take a plant and every day speak negatively to it, then it will become weak and dull in texture. If you were to speak lovingly to it, then it will thrive and grow strong. Even scientists have proved this exercise works, so why do we still insist on thinking, speaking and doing negative things?

Exercise
For three days take the highest word that is available and repeat it constantly to yourself. If you find yourself thinking, then bring your awareness back to the word and speed up the repetition in your mind. When you have finished the three days, answer the following questions, but do not read them before the exercise, as they may influence the outcome.

Could you maintain the thought?
If not, why not?
What does your answer to the above question reveal about you?
How did it make you feel?
Did you notice a difference each day?
How did you feel at the end of the three days?
Would you do it again?
If not, why not?

When we think and speak the highest possible, then this vibration enters into our energy bodies and begins to loosen stagnant energy. High vibrating energy is what Masters, Spiritual Teachers and Healers use to transform negative energy in the aura into light.

What is this highest vibration? It is love. Is it not amazing then, that you have access to more light from within you by attuning your thoughts to the highest form of love? Does this prove that you are able to transform yourself by directing the flow of your thoughts? This may seem like a one-off exercise, but coupled with the other healing techniques in this book, you may find that clear pure thinking is not just something available to spiritual people, but is the right of every Soul living a physical earthly life.

What Do Your Beliefs Give You?

In this book I have asked you to keep questioning your beliefs; but we also need to recognise why, even though we know what we do, we are reluctant to let go of what we receive when we enter into negative scenarios. For example, the child who pretends he is sick to receive more love and attention from his mother. The child later becomes a 'poor me' adult and uses illness as a form of attention-seeking from his family, workplace and friends. He knows inside he is deceiving those around him, but he cannot stop his need to be reassured that he is worthy of love. If he were to become himself, strong and capable, then those around him would no longer sympathise with him and give him their energy. This type of person is often draining to be around because they have forgotten how to draw in their own life-force energy, and taking light from others has become a normal way of being.

We often use our beliefs as a crutch to living our life. We become reliant on them for energy, but we find this way is a double-edged sword, because we become insatiable. We begin to demand more and more energy from those who give. Eventually our beliefs will lead us to exhaustion. This may result in major illness or a crisis situation and the only way out is to face ourself. Write a list of the things you do to get energy from others. It might be that you speak softly, dance provocatively, wear attention seeking clothes, manipulate conversations, speak loudly, complain, feign illness, exaggerate, sit quietly in the corner, put yourself down so others will defend your worth. Be really honest with yourself and look at what would happen if you stopped doing these things. Write another list for your emotional beliefs. You may say things to make people feel guilty; you may avoid making an effort, believing that success only comes to others; you may accept negative people or situations into your life because you have an 'anything will do' belief, etc. Again be honest and look at what would happen if you were to let go of these beliefs. What energy would you not receive? What is the fear?

We often join groups of people who hold similar beliefs to ours - football teams, drama clubs, religions, ashrams, workshops, etc. Write a list of all the groups you belong to and question what do you receive from being in that group? How would you feel if the group no longer existed? Question this feeling. Is it sadness, loneliness, a sense of non-belonging? Sometimes we enter into groups to gain a sense of belonging and comradeship. It is this yearning within us to be whole that often leads us into false scenarios and it also makes us become attached to the earth and its illusions. Instead of looking up to search for the loftiest, we look around us and find things to latch onto in order to keep our beliefs in place and receive an energy exchange. If we pull back from holding onto another's energy, we would find a reservoir of spiritual water to quench the thirst of our yearning from within.

There are those of us that refuse to become a part of life. We stay home sitting in front of the television and resist exercise, yoga, Tai Chi, dance, walking, running, etc. We then complain about the boredom of life. We have reached an apathetic state. There are some people who spend time going to an exercise gym, but these gyms are often in closed-up rooms where people release negative energy into the air. This is then breathed in by all those who visit. After an indoor exercise, a brisk walk in nature would be of benefit.

We should draw our life-sustaining energy from nature, the sun, the food we eat, the thoughts we think and the places we frequent. If you do not walk in nature, sit in the sun, eat healthily, think lofty thoughts and visit inspiring places, your energy field will not be at its optimum best. Therefore we should ask, from where or whom do we receive our energy?

The Inner Voice

A lot has been written about the inner voice, but very few people can tell you how to listen and what it is you are listening to. When you first decide to look at yourself, you are often instructed to go within for energy rather than relying on the external world to give to you. This is because there is nothing outside of you that can reveal the truth of you. It all has to be an inner journey. When you first start to listen to your inner voice, you may hear many different tones of your voice in the mind, clamouring for your obedience. To know which one to act upon takes time. In a sense it is a process of elimination. Often the inner voice may present itself as a gut feeling that guides you. However you get the inspiration, it is important that you act on what has been given.

Your inner voice is not going to send you around the world carrying out spiritual works. It is more concerned with your daily living and your daily life, because why would God not want to share every moment with you, if you want to share every moment with Him? Therefore, when your inner voice inspires you to buy something when you are shopping, buy it. If it tells you to prepare dinner earlier, then prepare it. If you have a feeling to ring someone, then ring them. Listen to your inner voice. Listen to your feelings and act immediately! If you put off for a moment an action, the mind will begin to question and bounce the instruction against the suppressed emotions in the body. For example, if your inner voice instructs you to tell Tom something, but you think about it and question what Tom's reaction will be, then you have stopped listening and engaged fear. It is this fear which will then stop you from acting upon your inner voice.

The principle of the inner voice is to guide you in every moment. If you have unfinished karma, then the inner voice will take you into the karma to process it and not avoid it. Often people tell me they listen to their inner voice, but when they follow the promptings the end result is not always joyous. This is because until you have faced all your karma and cleared the suppressed emotional backlog, you cannot move on to a greater space of joy. This does not mean your inner voice has guided you incorrectly. It has guided you into the karma, for only love heals karma and your inner voice is love. The inner voice is not an escape. It is a way of facing life full on.

If you are receiving spiritual messages, then really go inside and see where these messages come from. There are many forces and energies around you which can inspire but sometimes confuse your Soul. You have to learn to seek the one God and you have a choice. You can either listen to the assistants or you can listen to the boss. When you listen to the Soul, you are listening to the boss!

To communicate with the personality, the Soul uses the tools of the mind or the emotions. If a person is more female in energy, then often they will become guided by their gut feelings. If the person is more male, then the mind is used. If a person has balanced their male and female energies, then the mind and emotions work together in a very clear and precise way. There is no room for doubt! The Soul does not live in time or space. It has a three hundred and sixty degree view of every moment. It also has the ability to see instantly into every person you meet, so it knows the intent or energy of any given situation. Imagine having a best friend who could do this. You would want him to attend every business meeting, be in the family home, and be with you in every moment. You would rely on your best friend for a truthful picture which would enable you to act in the best way. In fact it would be ludicrous to do anything without consulting your friend first! Well you have this amazing friend, yet because it is not external but internal, you struggle with accepting this fact.

The Soul knows what your daily situations are going to be, so it prepares itself by getting impulses ready to send through the mind and emotions. These impulses hold information that directs you to the right way of thinking, feeling, speaking and acting. Whilst in the situation, if you choose to dismiss the Soul's impulse and do things another way, then you are acting solely from your conditioning. As most conditioning is built on fear, your choice usually brings about an effect that also has negativity attached to it. For example, you have to drive somewhere, but you have a feeling or thoughts not to go. Your conditioning tells you that you must go because you have obligations to fulfil, so you set off, only to have a car accident. The Soul was trying to tell you that energetically you did not need to be in that situation, but you ignored the impulses and followed what you have externally been taught to do by society.

The impulses that the Soul gives are only given once. If you do not follow it immediately, then you start questioning. This gives you problems because conditioned energy from the mind enters in and distorts the purity of the impulse, so you become doubtful or indecisive. Doubt is probably the most debilitating energy that there is. Its only aim is to render you incapable of movement and if you become inactive, then it allows fear to feast upon the light of your being. To be indecisive is a struggle between choosing the internal or the external, in other words to choose the Soul or your conditioning. For example, you come to a junction and your immediate feeling is to turn left, but the sign in front of you tells you that the place you are looking for is right, so you follow the external. What you did not know was that the local council put this sign up so visiting tourists would drive through the town and maybe stop to shop. You then end up on a one-way system. You arrive at your destination flustered and you suddenly realise that if you had turned left, the building was only round the corner! In each moment we are given a choice. Do we act in love or do we act in fear? If we are acting through beliefs or conditioning, then this is fear. If we are acting in love, then we are following the guidance of our Soul.

Following your conditioned patterns keeps you trapped. These patterns also appear as voices in the mind, almost like a parent! To follow the Soul is to be liberated and you become free through first listening and then acting. After a while of listening you will begin to recognise the difference between the conditioned mind and the Soul. You will notice that when you receive an impulse from the Soul, your whole being subtly responds. It is almost like a sense of knowing. If you choose the conditioned mind over the Soul, you instantly know you have made the wrong choice. These are signs that you are on the right track. There is also a sense that your beliefs and conditioning often send you 'round the houses', whereas the Soul directs you immediately to what it is you require. You could have saved yourself a lot of time and effort going all around the houses, and reached the same point the Soul originally directed you to, and been further on in your life, if you had listened to the Soul.

The most important thing to be aware of is that the Soul knows your daily needs and it directs you by communicating through your feelings and thoughts. These feelings may be a sense of dread, queasiness, uneasiness, joy, peace or something indescribable, but you just know how to act. The thoughts may come in your own voice, but they may seem above your normal thoughts, as though it is a flow that you are not in control of. Both of these forms can be finely tuned by listening. I have met very dynamic people who have both these forms active and they are constantly listening for guidance and immediately acting upon it. This communication is God whispering His daily bread to you every day. How can you be separate from Him when he is so close that he can feel you, hear you and direct you.

The one thing the Soul is not fully aware of is the questions your mind is going to form. Therefore if you are stuck with something and you ask for immediate guidance, the Soul has to send down the answer. This impulse is instantly available, but because your energy bodies are not clear enough you may find it can take a few moments to receive the information. So when you ask for guidance it is important to become still while waiting for the answer. You may even receive the answer in the external, through the words of others, through the media, a passing advert on a lorry, etc. The important thing is to listen and observe all that is around you. When you become clearer and more trusting of the guidance, the Soul moves closer in and the messages become immediate. Eventually there will be no difference between the personality and the Soul, because they will have merged as one. How do you receive your inner guidance? Look back over your life and ask what has happened when you followed your inner voice. Did you trust it? What happened when you knew what to do, but did it a different way? How can you become more open to your inner guidance? What does truly listening mean to you?

Changes

If you are living in an illusion, the inner voice leads you to reality. Quite often the world we live in is illusory. We have grown up and made our world fit around us. When you start to listen to your inner voice it will reveal to you things that you no longer need. It may tell you to change your job, to learn something new, to let go of a relationship. Your inner voice is showing you how to change. The point is to go with your feelings, rather than putting things off for another day or for someone else to do! Act as soon as the inspiration comes. The inner voice is instant. It deals with the moment. It does not deal with the future. It is telling you to get on and do what you have to do now and allow the future to take care of itself. The inner voice is an in-the-moment experience, but it does help you to clear up your past, which leads to change!

To bring about change you have to first listen within and then act. This process teaches you to trust what is being given, because by trusting you are surrendering the outcome to something which can see a bigger picture than you. It takes courage to recognise that there is a better way to live your life. You can begin by changing the small things first and when you achieve this then you can tackle the larger issues. A good place to start is by clearing out all the clutter you have accumulated over the years. Throw out any old clothes, sort out the cupboards, the shelves, under the bed, the loft, old books and photographs. Get rid of those things that no longer sing to your Soul. Keep only what you need and not what you want.

We often hold onto things because they link us to past issues where we have suppressed our emotions. We then make up excuses to keep them because we have stored not only the physical residue, but also the energetic residue. By physically clearing out your space, you open the door for an emotional and mental clear out. If you cannot bring yourself to let go fully, place some of your old things in the garage or shed. If in a year you have not looked at them, then ask if you still want them in your life? You certainly do not need them. When you have cleared out the past you will have space in your energy body. This is a good time to start something new that you have always wanted to do. Change to a healthier diet, take up walking or become creative. In a sense you are filling the space with light and joy.

When we first begin the process of changing something, often we go through setbacks and we revert back to our old ways. It is very easy to give up at this point, but these are signs that we are breaking out of our comfort zones. If we accept that we lapsed, but proceed to carry on moving forward, the ties to our old ways will become weaker until eventually we let them go. We need to understand that we have been in our comfort zones for years, so breaking out of them is a gradual process. If our commitment to a life filled with more self-love is our focus, then every time we fall down in our attempts, we get back up and persevere. It takes courage, commitment and perseverance. If you could ask God a question whose answer would dynamically change your life, what would that question be? Now listen within for the answer and then take action!

Soul Mates

I have been approached many times by people seeking their Soul mate. Each Soul has been equally created by the Godhead. What makes us unique is that each of us has travelled to the earth through different star formations. The different stars and planets we pass through add vibrations to our energy bodies. Often we travel in groups, so when we reach the earth and meet a person from our group, they are often termed our Soul mate. The Soul mate vibrates similarly to us and because of our travelling together we immediately connect and understand each other. This is why we can meet more than one Soul mate in a life. They could be our best friend, partner, child, mother or father. What we really yearn for is a relationship with the Divine and we often think it is the Soul mate who will bring this to us, but even the Soul mate's greatest gift would be to mirror our imperfections.

A relationship with a Soul mate is often very challenging. This is because we allow those who feel familiar to come closer, therefore the teaching becomes greater. When you search for your

Soul mate, what you are really saying is, 'I want someone who vibrates similarly to me on every level.' You may meet this person and at first everything is unbelievably magic. After a while you may carry on growing and altering your vibration, yet your Soul mate may stay the same, therefore you are no longer compatible and a change will occur. Soul mates are not guaranteed for life nor is the relationship certain to fulfil you. Yes, the recognition between the two Souls will be greater, but the focus to reach perfection will still be the same as in any relationship.

People have also often asked me about twin Souls. This is quite rare as the Soul usually incarnates only one aspect of itself in any given life, but if one aspect of the Soul needs special attention or if it has to accomplish something significant, then the Soul will incarnate two aspects of itself. Sometimes these twin Souls never meet, yet they work unknowingly side by side on the earth for the same goal. If the twin Souls do meet then usually they are of the opposite sex, simply because they will balance each other as creative and inspirational beings. They are very connected, in that they feel each other's emotions and pick up each other's thoughts. When they come together it is as though they have been waiting for this moment and everything else in life pales in significance. If both of them are able to let go of what surrounds them in order for the Soul to complete its task, then the effect on the world can be dynamic. The reason the Soul refrains from incarnating this way is because if one of the people cannot let go, or the fear factor is too great, then the pain this incurs can resonate through lifetimes, affecting the future incarnations of the Soul. This is because when these two people meet they merge as one. They see the potential of love on the earth and all other love relationships fail to reach this understanding of love. This knowing can affect them until they have mastered the cycle of the earth.

Enlightenment

Enlightenment is not a finished state. It is a reward upon the path of progress. To be enlightened is to have lightened the load you carry. We do this by becoming aware of our thoughts, words and actions. Many people believe that enlightenment occurs on top of a mountain where a bolt of white light hits the person and makes them an all-knowing being. This can occur if you are ready and have become the master of your way of being, but for most of us enlightenment occurs because we realise something about our self, others or a situation. It is as though the light has been turned on, which enables you to see the truth. These small flashes of light are what transform us, because once we become aware, we can act in the right way.

Life is a path of progress. Each time we face a fear, we take a step closer to God. Each step represents being filled with more light, or in other words, 'enlightening moments'. The absolute goal is to become one with the Soul and merge back into God. At the point of uniting with the Soul we may experience a larger enlightening moment and when we merge with God a total bliss of light. The point is that each time you put effort into purifying your thoughts, words and actions you are rewarded and encouraged. Nobody is ever left alone to struggle. We only believe we are.

God is all seeing, all knowing and all perfect. There is nothing that exists outside of Him. You have never been separated from Him, you only think you have. We have turned our back to Him and are now crying because we believe that if we cannot see Him, then He is not there. Upon the breath of the winds, the scents of the flowers and the joy in laughter, He is whispering, 'Take down your walls of rocks and boulders and let my love flow to you.' Your beliefs will then never feign separation from Him again.

You have searched for God in your past. He is your focus for the future. You are with Him, in Him and through Him in the now! This is your peace.

Peace Be With You.

The Breath of Love

Her breath sways the branches of all who seek her love,
The perfume of her heart sends a fragrance that shows the way.
To follow we must unload the burdens,
For her gaze reveals the truth.
Only the pure may hear her whisper,
Only the dumb may speak her name,
Only the blind may see her splendour,
For when you are all these things, you will be ready to learn.

When you are angry, you are seeking peace,
When you are jealous, you are seeking fulfilment,
When you are prideful, you are seeking worth,
When you are grieving, you are seeking permanence,
When you are fearful, you are seeking love,
When you are lost, you have already been found.

Love lies in abundance for the heart that longs to know,
When you have nothing,
You have space for love to flourish.
You call out her name,
She says be still and listen.
You hear her song
And dance the dance of love,
You touch her feet
And humility gives you power,
For to know her is to die to the moment.
To fly with her liberates your Soul,
And only then will you truly know.

References

Bibliography
(11x22) Michael Domeyko Rowland. *Absolute Happiness*. Self Communications 1993.

Courses & Workshops
Mike Robinson teaches residential courses and one-day workshops in the UK and abroad. Below is a list of currently available courses.

Spiritual Development: This is a week's course for getting in touch with the Soul. Mike teaches about the process of thought and emotional energy. He leads us beyond the veils of illusion, so that we can understand and master our way of being.

Advanced Healing Skills: A part-time course over a two-year period. It is packed with dynamic techniques that Mike has personally discovered in his twenty-five years of healing and working with others.

Additional Healing Skills: This is a week's course for those who have completed the above training. It compliments and fine-tunes the ability to work with subtle energy.

Feng Shui: Mike's understanding and vision of invisible energy makes the Feng Shui course dig deep into the unseen worlds of a person's personal space.

Chi Gong: Having been taught by a Chinese Master in Chi Gong, Mike shows his students how to utilise chi in the body and direct it into the organs, giving them vitality and strength.

Life Relationships: This course has been nicknamed, 'A Kick in the Pants!' by his latest students. It is dynamic and it covers our relationship to fear, beliefs, childhood, our parents and God. It reveals why we do what we do and who we truly are.

Partner Relationship: This weekend workshop covers our most intimate relationship. It reveals the hidden patterns of ourself and it shows us how we can heal what is not working in our relationship. This is truly looking in the mirror!

Egypt: A seven-day trip to the land of the historical Gods. Staying at the Sheraton Hotel in Luxor, the workshops will be held on feluccas sailing down the Nile, and on the Banana Island. Trips to the valley of the Queens, Karnak, Dendrah, plus so much more.

Israel: A ten-day trip to Qumran where the Essenes lived at the time of Christ. Here you will stay near the Dead Sea at the beautiful Kalia Kibbutz. There will be mountain workshops, maybe a mud bath! a sunrise on the pink mountain, a trip to Masada and so much more.

Maldives: A seven or fourteen day trip to the wonderful islands of the Maldives. Staying in a four star beach villa, your day will begin with gentle Chi Gong exercise on the beach. Also included are excursions to a deserted island with a BBQ on the beach, a local island shopping trip, a sunset cruise, workshops and a sunset meal at the edge of the Indian Ocean!

France: A seven-day stay in a luxurious villa in the South of France. The villa includes ensuite rooms, a swimming pool, library and small exercise room. There will be a Cathar Tour, a trip to Narbonne beach on the Mediterranean, wine tasting at the local Chateaux's, a workshop in the mountains, picnics and so much more...

Contact For Courses & Workshops

Mike also travels to Denmark, Australia, Canada and Singapore. If you need further details on courses available in these countries, please contact Jo Le-Rose at SOL Promotions (44) (0) 1986 785350
Email: sol.promotions@tiscali.co.uk
For all other course info and one-day workshops please contact Marillyn Gilmour (44) (0)1603 501557
Email: marillyn@onetel.net.uk

Available Audio Tapes
A Walk in the Garden – A stunning story which begins with an aspirant who observes and questions life whilst walking with Our Lord and Our lady (the male and female aspects of the self). They travel through a garden, a forest, a city, a village, etc, discovering the hidden spiritual meaning of life.

Available Video
Golden Wings Chi Gong II – A fantastic step-by-step guide into learning the gentle, yet powerful, movements of Chi Gong. Mike has utilised beautiful scenery and music with ancient art. A wonderful way to start the day!

Forthcoming Books for 2004/5
The True Dynamics of the Path – A follow on from the 'True Dynamics of Relationships'. This book is more in-depth and an absolute for the true aspirant on the path.

A Walk in the Garden – The same as the Tape Set, but with added stories and beautiful illustrations.

Plucking the Stars from Heaven – This book is a collection of the articles that Mike has written over the years. Some of these articles have been published in magazines and many have been read on the courses. An inspirational read!

Contact for Products:
For all tape, video and book requests, please contact Joan Stocking (44) (0)1902 340550

Website
www.mikerobinsonspiritualteacher.co.uk